Teaching A Psychology Of People

Resources for Gender and Sociocultural Awareness

Edited by
Phyllis Bronstein
and Kathryn Quina

American
Psychological
Association

Library of Congress Cataloging-in-Publication Data

Teaching a psychology of people.

  Bibliography: p.
  1. Psychology—Study and teaching. 2. Difference
(Psychology)—Study and teaching. 3. Minorities
—Psychology—Study and teaching. 4. Women—Psychology
—Study and teaching. I. Bronstein, Phyllis.
II. Quina, Kathryn.
BF77.T4 1988   155′.07   88-16715
ISBN 1-55798-039-X

Copies may be ordered from:
Order Department
P.O. Box 2710
Hyattsville, MD 20784

Published by the
American Psychological Association
1200 Seventeenth Street, NW
Washington, DC 20036

BF
77
.T4
1988

Printed by St. Mary's Press, Hollywood, MD
Typeset by TAPSCO, Inc., Akron, PA
Cover design by The Design Source, Inc., Washington, DC

Printed in the United States of America.

Third Printing January 1991

Teaching a Psychology of People:
Resources for Gender and Sociocultural Awareness

Dedication

This volume is dedicated to the pioneering scholars who have worked to create a psychology of all people through their teaching, writing, and participation in organizations transforming the profession of psychology. In particular, we would like to honor the memory of six extraordinary people who, as innovators, scholars, and mentors, permanently changed and enriched psychology and helped create an indisputable place for new voices within the field:

Jeanne Humphrey Block

Nancy Datan

Marcia Guttentag

Clara Mayo

Carolyn Wood Sherif

Barbara Strudler Wallston

We consider this volume to be an extension of their work and a part of the continuing fulfillment of their dream. Thus, any profits will be given to APA Divisions 9 (Society for the Psychological Study of Social Issues) and 35 (Psychology of Women) in their honor.

Contents

Foreword

Teaching a Psychology of People: Resources for Gender and Sociocultural Awareness fills an important and much needed place in raising the consciousness of psychologists who teach undergraduates. Psychology does not have an admirable record in educating students about the importance of social–environmental factors (particularly the role of gender, race, and ethnic forces) in behavior. The history of prejudice, long part of the teaching by psychologists, is cause for shame and repentance. It is past time that psychology courses undo the damage that has been done.

Recently, I have been reviewing the literature on the almost unbelievable prejudices held by leaders of society—beliefs that psychologists also held during the early years of our discipline. Galton's (1869) *Hereditary Genius*, and subsequent inheritors of his biased arguments, emphasized the "scientific" evidence that social class was genetically determined; and furthermore, that women could not be expected to produce works of genius because of their constitutional defects. Cecil Rhodes, for whom Rhodesia (now Zimbabwe) was named, proposed that 4,000 Nordic gentlemen be educated to rule the world. (Not surprisingly, neither women nor Blacks were allowed to be named Rhodes Scholars for most of that honor's history.) Social Darwinism was popularized in England by Herbert Spencer and was presented in American universities where the upper class educated their sons.

Psychology often reflected blatant racism and sexism. G. Stanley Hall thought women were unsuitable for graduate and professional education because of intellectual deficiencies (although he sponsored several successful women graduate students). Eugenics and Social Darwinism were popular with psychologists; several APA presidents believed that various non-White groups had inferior intelligence and opposed the immigration of the "brunette races" to the United States. Henry Garrett published racist tracts, and Robert Yerkes endorsed the racist and ethnocentric test findings from World War I that indicated that Nordics were superior to other races. Only when "radical" anthropologists such as Franz Boas, Ruth Benedict, and Margaret Mead joined forces with intellectual European immigrants did cracks begin to appear in this belief system.

There were *some* environmentalists among the early psychologists. John B. Watson's (1925) oft-quoted statement, although written in language now considered sexist, was a clear exposition of the relative importance of environment:

> Give me a dozen healthy infants, well formed, and my own specified world to bring them up in, and I'll guarantee to take any one at random and train him to become any type of specialist I might select— doctor, lawyer, artist, merchant chief, and, yes, even beggar-man and thief, regardless of his talents, penchants, tendencies, abilities, vocations, and race of his ancestors. (p. 82)

vii

I read the chapters in *Teaching a Psychology of People* with pleasure and gratitude to the writers. I have been an environmentalist for a long time without being fully conscious of it. My doctoral dissertation, 40 years ago, examined sex, age, class, and racial differences in the delusions of schizophrenics. I was convinced, even then, that social forces were the major influence in the development of psychopathology, that schizophrenia did not simply unfold from predetermined templates caused by faulty genes.

This book raises a question for me about social influence: Is the written word sufficient to effect significant change in psychology? Clearly, written information is important, for knowledge is empowering. But my experience in the profession of psychology has taught me that sometimes change comes only through confrontation and social activism. To illustrate this thesis, let me reminisce about the exciting and changing times that psychology went through in the late 1960s and early 1970s.

For years, the American Psychological Association (APA) drifted along with the rest of society as a relatively sexist, racist, and homophobic organization. Jobs were filled by the old-boy system, and it was assumed that academic positions were for men. Textbooks and journals talked about "men and girls." Validations of interest tests in which similar profiles suggested that men become doctors and women become nurses were published. Sexist language was the standard style for APA publications. In its early form, the APA "Ethical Standards of Psychologists," otherwise a model of scientific probity, began with a statement, "*He* [the psychologist, italics added] is committed to increasing man's understanding of *himself* [italics added] and others. . . ." (1963, p. 56).

The APA Council meeting of 1967 was relatively silent about the role of women and minorities in the APA. Leona Tyler's report on APA policy in public affairs was adopted. It recommended that public statements and public actions by APA be direct and forceful when scientific interests are affected or threatened; that a somewhat less active stance be taken about professional issues; and that the greatest caution be exercised in public policy issues where psychology has relatively little direct evidence based on research.

In 1968, Bill McKeachie, APA Secretary, predicted that the Council would spend a majority of its time at the APA Convention in San Francisco debating issues concerning accreditation of graduate programs. He had not foreseen, as had few others, that the violent beating of students and other war protestors that accompanied the Democratic Convention in Chicago would appear on television during our meeting. The APA Council responded to this "police riot" with an intensity that matched the reactions of many others throughout the country. The Council debated the wisdom of holding its next meeting in Chicago as scheduled and decided that it would seek an opportunity to meet elsewhere. Black psychologists, who had recently formed the Black Psychological Association, proposed that APA hold its meeting in Watts, a section of Los Angeles which had been the scene of earlier racial demonstrations. Although this suggestion was considered only briefly because of the logistical difficulties, the fact that it was considered *at all* reflected the growing politicization of the academic community and the increasing concern with racial justice and related social issues.

Toward the end of the 1968 Convention, Charles W. Thomas, an officer in the Black Psychological Association, presented a statement of concerns to the APA

Council. During the meeting of the APA Board of Directors on the last day of the Convention, the board room was visited by the entire Board of Directors of the Association of Black Psychologists, who argued forcefully about the problems of underrepresentation of Blacks and other minorities in the halls of power of APA and the lack of opportunity for graduate study by Black students.

At the next regular meeting of the APA Council in Washington, DC, further formal demands were made by the Association of Black Psychologists, and a militant group of Black students demanded that APA make provisions for increased enrollment of Black graduate students. A report by a special committee on Black involvement in psychology, chaired by Lauren Wispe, revealed the shameful and shocking underrepresentation of Blacks in doctoral programs. Of the 10 universities with the most prestigious PhD programs, which had graduated several thousand PhDs over a period of 46 years, only eight PhDs had been awarded to Black students.

A conference on recruitment of Black and other minority students into psychology was commissioned by the APA Board of Directors. This special meeting was chaired by me and reported in the *American Psychologist* (Albee, 1969). Representatives of the Association of Black Psychologists were invited to Washington, DC, to meet with representatives of the APA Board. They declined and instead invited representatives of the APA Board to meet with them in Watts. George Miller (APA President, 1968) and I (President-Elect) flew to Los Angeles and spent several days meeting with members of the Board of the Association of Black Psychologists and the Black student group. These negotiations resulted in subsequent changes in APA bylaws that allowed for a third of the membership of major APA boards and committees to be filled by Blacks. A Black Student Psychological Association office with space to be available in the APA Central Office in Washington, DC, was proposed and a noninterest-bearing seed loan was provided.

Another major group of psychologists, underrepresented in APA, formed their own organization in a hotel room at the 1969 Convention—the Association for Women in Psychology. They came to the 1969 Council of Representatives with a series of demands, which expressed their unhappiness with accreditation policies that permitted discrimination against qualified women applicants, sexist language in APA journals and textbooks, and many other sexist policies and procedures long existent in male-dominated psychology. (Although women comprised nearly a third of the APA membership, the registration form at APA conventions still asked for "Member's name" and "Wife's name.") Another important concern was that female psychologists were paid significantly less than their male counterparts for the same positions.

By the 1970 APA Convention, the Association for Women in Psychology was well organized, articulate in its demands, and prepared to demonstrate and disrupt if their demands were not taken seriously. The APA Board appointed a Task Force on the Status of Women in Psychology. A series of changes to sexist and racist APA policies were examined, and new policies were made to implement real change.

Kenneth B. Clark was elected APA President-Elect in 1970. In early 1970, Clark offered to write a paper on psychology and social justice for consideration at a special meeting of the Board of Directors in December 1970. This paper, which was accepted and distributed widely by the Board, called for the establishment of a Board of Social and Ethical Responsibility for Psychology (BSERP), thus putting in place a structure for the continuous monitoring of issues involving social justice.

The changes in the structure of APA's Central Office continued with the establishment of the Office of Women's Affairs, a Committee on Women that reported to BSERP, and, subsequently, committees and task forces concerned with justice for other groups (Gay and Lesbian Concerns, Psychology and the Handicapped, Children, Youth and Families). A Board of Ethnic Minority Affairs was created and new Divisions concerned with issues affecting women, gays and lesbians, and minorities were established. An Open Forum, where members may bring their concerns to the attention of the Board of Directors, has become a feature of the annual convention.

Overall, it seems quite clear that changes in the public social values of American psychology occurred at a time when similar changes were occurring in the broader American society. In retrospect, it is important to realize that the most dramatic changes occurred when the civil rights movement was in full swing and the Vietnam War was increasingly unpopular on college and university campuses. Very large numbers of psychologists were increasingly supportive of these trends.

It also seems clear that the changes in each of these contexts occurred because of strong articulation of the need for change from oppressed and underrepresented groups. Today, we are being asked to look again at the need for change. At this writing, a group of minority and Third World students are on a hunger strike sit-in in the president's office at the University of Vermont. They have wrung more concessions from the administration in a few days than were achieved in several years of friendly dialogue. We are reminded that the issues raised in the 1960s are not resolved, that there is much more to do, and that we do not change easily without external pressure to do so.

I come back to the power of the written word. Information is the first step toward consciousness raising. Enriching psychology courses with the material and approaches contained in this book can be a beginning. But, let us also make public commitment to social change and social justice. We need to teach and to model support for the oppressed and the exploited. This volume is an excellent place to start.

George W. Albee

References

Albee, G. W. (1969). A conference on recruitment of Blacks and other minority students and faculty. *American Psychologist, 24,* 720–723.

American Psychological Association. (1963). Ethical standards of psychologists. *American Psychologist, 18,* 56–60.

Galton, F. (1869). *Hereditary genius.* London: MacMillan.

Watson, J. B. (1925). *Behaviorism.* New York: W. W. Norton.

Preface

Our original interests in the integration of diversity into the psychology curriculum developed along converging paths. As new teachers of psychology, we both discovered that our widely-used textbooks contained little or no scholarship on women or gender, ethnicity, race, or sociocultural issues. We also recognized the isolation and institutional fragility of the single psychology of women course at each of our respective institutions. In spite of this, we also found many students eager to learn about these topics and extremely supportive of us as teachers and of our efforts to bring this information to them in the classroom.

At the same time, some students were concerned that perhaps what they had learned wasn't real psychology, because it was different from what they had learned in other classes. When we discussed this problem with colleagues, we found that many seemed willing—some even eager—to include new scholarship in their classes but were busy just trying to keep up with their own fields. Clearly, a better exchange of resources and ideas was needed.

In 1980, the New England Association for Women in Psychology was encouraging the formation of interest groups in different areas of feminist psychology. Joined by Mary Kanarian, Mary Roth Walsh, and Bernice Lott, we formed a group focusing on our concerns about the way psychology was being taught outside of psychology of women courses. With the theme "one Psychology of Women course is not enough," we offered symposia on integrating the new scholarship on women into mainstream psychology courses at the 1980 meeting of the Association for Women in Psychology and the 1981 Annual Convention of the American Psychological Association, with Nancy Henley serving ably as discussant. In the years following, we were pleased to see an increasing number of symposia offered on related instructional issues at national conferences, including curriculum integration of racial and cultural minorities, gays, lesbians, the disabled, and the elderly.

The positive responses to these presentations were evidence that it was time to share this exciting body of information with the rest of psychology. We decided to bring the new theories and data together into a resource work that could serve the needs expressed by a growing number of colleagues: a work that would be stimulating and straightforward, with easy-to-use ideas and references. We invited some of the participants from the various symposia on curriculum diversity, along with other instructors known for their classroom effectiveness in addressing minority and gender issues, to develop their scholarship and teaching practices into the format of this volume.

When we saw the extraordinary work these psychologists were submitting, we realized that a wealth of material existed. Our original plan of covering a few areas in depth would not do justice to that richness. Thus, we decided to try to include as many areas as possible, from a wide range of contributors, even if it meant that some of the areas could only be covered briefly.

It proved to be a challenging task for all of us, as contributors and editors, to condense years of work developing bibliographies and creative exercises into a few pages per chapter. The materials left out were sometimes as exciting as those included, and we have urged several contributors to publish them as separate papers. Moreover, from the beginning we have been deeply impressed not only with the quality of the contributors' work and their willingness to adjust to our space requirements, but also by the individuals themselves. We have come to know some exceptional people who have been pioneers—often at great personal cost—in the effort to diversify traditional psychology. Our gratitude goes to them, and our hope of a stronger future psychology goes to those whom they teach.

No volume of this sort can be created by two people alone. We have many to thank for a range of contributions: Mary Roth Walsh and Bernice Lott, who offered encouragement and helpful input right from the inception of the project; Sharon Golub, who led an important task force on integrating the psychology of women into the curriculum for APA Division 35; the Wellesley Center for Research on Women, which provided space and resources for Kat Quina to pursue a curriculum integration project as a Mellon Scholar in 1984–1985; Daniel Perlman, who encouraged us to seek APA publication; Gary R. VandenBos, Brenda K. Bryant, Julia Frank-McNeil, and Stephanie Selice of the APA Publications Office, who carried out an enormous editorial and production task with great patience; Jacqueline Goodchilds and others who reviewed and supported the project and who helped shape the final product; and Jennifer Marcotte and Anne Marie Famiglietti, who shouldered much of the typing burden. We also thank our students, who have often been challenged and excited by the new information we have introduced, and who in turn have challenged us both to refine and expand our thinking about the issues involved and to hone our skills as communicators of controversial material.

We also want to thank those people in our lives who provided personal support and who helped make it possible on a daily basis for us to carry on our tasks as editors. From Phyllis, special appreciation goes to Robert Rossel, Elise Burrows, Joanna Burrows, Martha Fitzgerald, Lynda Myles, and Paula Fives-Taylor. For Kat, those special people who deserve appreciation are David Miller, Patricia Gallagher, Mary Kanarian, Janet Kulberg, and MaryAnn Paxson.

Phyllis Bronstein
Kathryn Quina

Contributors

Alexis Deanne Abernethy, PhD
School of Medicine and Dentistry
University of Rochester

George W. Albee, PhD
Department of Psychology
University of Vermont

Rosita Daskal Albert, PhD
Department of Psychology
University of Minnesota

Adrienne Asch, MS
Department of Counseling, Social, and
Organizational Psychology
Teachers College
Columbia University

Augustine Barón, Jr., PsyD
Counseling and Psychological
Services Center
University of Texas, Austin

Lynne A. Bond, PhD
Department of Psychology
University of Vermont

Phyllis Bronstein, PhD
Department of Psychology
University of Vermont

Alice Brown-Collins, PhD
Black Studies Department
Wellesley College

Felipe G. Castro, PhD
Department of Psychology
University of California, Los Angeles

Philip A. Cowan, PhD
Department of Psychology
University of California, Berkeley

Halford H. Fairchild, PhD
Consulting Psychologist
Los Angeles

Roberto Gurza, MA
Department of Psychology
University of California, Berkeley

Karen Huei-chung Huang, PhD
Department of Psychology
San Francisco State University

Mary A. Kanarian, PhD
Submarine Signal Division
Raytheon Company
Portsmouth, RI

Mary Ann Yael Kim, PhD
Wright Institute
Berkeley

Neal King, PhD
California State University,
Sonoma

Janet M. Kulberg, PhD
Department of Psychology
University of Rhode Island

Hope Landrine, PhD
Department of Psychology
California State University, San
Bernardino

Albert J. Lott, PhD
Department of Psychology
University of Rhode Island

Bernice Lott, PhD
Department of Psychology
University of Rhode Island

B. Jeannie Lum, MA
Philosophy of Education
University of California, Berkeley

Delia Magaña
Department of Psychology
University of California, Los Angeles

Vickie M. Mays, PhD
Department of Psychology
University of California, Los Angeles

Michele Paludi, PhD
Department of Psychology
Hunter College

Kathryn Quina, PhD
Department of Psychology
University of Rhode Island

Marylyn Rands, PhD
Department of Psychology
Wheaton College

Dan Romero, PhD
Career Planning and Placement Center
University of California, Berkeley

Elizabeth Scarborough, PhD
Department of Psychology and
    Office of the President
State University of New York, Fredonia

Mavis Tsai, PhD
Clinical Psychologist
Seattle

Anne Uemura, PhD
Counseling Center
University of California, Berkeley

Rhoda Kessler Unger, PhD
Department of Psychology
Montclair State College

Melba J. T. Vasquez, PhD
Counseling and
    Mental Health Center
University of Texas, Austin

Trudy Ann Villars, PhD
Department of Psychology
Wheaton College

Toward a Psychology of People: Rationale for a Balanced Curriculum

1

Phyllis Bronstein and Kathryn Quina

Perspectives on Gender Balance and Cultural Diversity in the Teaching of Psychology

Over the past 25 years, important movements calling for recognition of the rights and needs of minorities and women have surfaced in this country. The women's movement and the civil rights movement have brought about social change on a nationwide level; smaller advocacy groups such as those for lesbian and gay rights, for the elderly, and for disabled persons are becoming more visible and more determined to effect change. These movements have stimulated psychologists—particularly ones who are members of those groups—to reexamine the existing body of psychological theory and research and to question to what degree it is relevant to their own life experiences and concerns.

This questioning has formed the basis for new areas of scholarly work, focusing on populations who previously had been omitted both from the subject pools of psychological research and from the theoretical concerns of mainstream psychology. Journals such as *Psychology of Women Quarterly, Sex Roles*, the *Hispanic Journal of Behavioral Science*, and the *Journal of Black Psychology*, as well as special issues of more established journals such as the *Journal of Social Issues* (Levinger, 1987; Marsh, Colten, & Tucker, 1982; Smith & Stewart, 1983; Stewart & Platt, 1982), the *Journal of Marriage and the Family* (Peters, 1978), and *Professional Psychology* (Sobel & Russo, 1981) attest to the fact that there is a growing body of psychological research focusing on women and gender and on racial and ethnic minorities. As further evidence, Walsh (1986) counted more than 13,000 citations of articles on women in the psychology literature, and Mays (in press) has compiled a bibliography of over 2,000 references concerning Black women. As evidenced by recent publications in journals such as *American Psychologist*, there is an increasing interest in identifiable subgroups such as disabled persons, the elderly, gays, and lesbians as subjects of study.

At the same time that this new scholarship has been developing, the number of females and minorities within academia—in undergraduate and graduate student bodies, in faculties, and in professional organizations—has increased. Women comprise over 65% of undergraduate and graduate students in psychology and earn about half the doctorates (U.S. Department of Education, 1987). While minorities continue to be underrepresented, 8% of the baccalaureate degrees awarded in 1981 were earned by Blacks, 4.4% by Hispanics, and 2% by Asian Americans—a substantial increase for each group over 1976 figures. In 1984,

Blacks earned 4.1% of the psychology doctorates; Hispanics earned 2.8%; Asian Americans earned 1.5%; and American Indians earned less than 1% (Howard et al., 1986). Although these numbers continue to seriously underrepresent the population at large, the academic advancement of minorities over the past decade is important. These numbers, however, are only part of the story. Professional organizations such as the Association for Women in Psychology, the Association of Black Psychologists, the Association of Gay and Lesbian Psychologists, and the American Psychological Association's (APA) Divisions 35 (Psychology of Women) and 44 (Society for the Psychological Study of Lesbian and Gay Issues) have served to bring together individuals with common concerns. Task forces of the American Psychological Association on concerns of various populations have publicly called attention to those groups' underrepresentation in psychology and have proposed ways to increase their inclusion.

The Current Curriculum: Where are the Women and Minorities?

The teaching of psychology, which should reflect this broadened representation and perspective, has not kept up with changes in scholarship and in the population of psychologists. Most undergraduate and graduate psychology curricula, whether in Ivy League institutions or 2-year community colleges, large coed universities or small single-sex schools, urban or rural settings, do not include much of the new scholarship on women and minorities. Walsh (1986) reported that less than one quarter of 4-year colleges polled in two separate surveys offered a course on the female life experience. Courses on ethnic minorities are scarcer; a 1982 survey of 100 undergraduate department chairs found that only six departments offered such a course (American Psychological Association, 1983). And while some schools offer single courses such as the Psychology of Women, Black Psychology, or Cross-Cultural Counseling, very few institutions have made any systematic effort to incorporate these areas into the psychology curriculum. Thus, the enormous body of psychological theory and research that is taught in this country's academic institutions remains primarily by and about White males.

When a course focusing on cultural or minority issues is offered, it is generally because there is a minority faculty member there to teach it. However, the total number of minority psychologists is less than 10% (Howard et al., 1986); still fewer hold academic positions. If a department were to attempt to integrate minority and cultural issues more broadly into the general curriculum, the faculty would find that existing texts on both the introductory and advanced levels are generally inadequate to the task. There is very little consideration of sociocultural factors in the study of human psychology. Thus departments, as well as individuals, who wish to integrate cultural and minority issues into their teaching have no easily available resources.

In the area of gender, the picture is a little different. Women constitute about one third of the membership of APA (Walsh, 1985), and a sizable number of them are interested in research on women and gender. There are several journals, a range of textbooks, and widely available teaching resources such as videotapes, films, and course syllabi devoted to the psychology of women and gender. The omission of gender-related theory and research from mainstream psychology courses is therefore all the more striking. Like cultural and ethnic issues, gender issues tend to be confined to one token course and are only sparsely represented in basic and advanced texts in all other areas of psychology.

Rationale for Change

As individual teachers, we have an intellectual and ethical responsibility to provide our students with the most current and accurate information possible, a responsibility underscored in Principle 1.e of the "Ethical Principles of Psychologists" (APA, 1981):

> As teachers, psychologists recognize their primary obligation to help others acquire knowledge and skill. They maintain high standards of scholarship by presenting psychological information objectively, fully, and accurately. (p. 633)

This responsibility also extends to departmental and college leaders, who are in the strongest position to support and promote a revised curriculum. Historically, colleges and universities have served as leaders in the formulation and implementation of social change. They have a unique opportunity once again to demonstrate their leadership, showing society at large the benefits of helping women and minorities achieve full representation and respect.

Effects on Students

A more inclusive psychology will have a number of important effects on students. It will expand their worldview by exposing them to the life experiences of people very different from themselves. It will make them cognizant of culture, ethnicity, and gender as important psychological variables in their everyday life and help them to be more aware of the part that such factors have played in their own development and the limitations that they may have imposed. It will make students aware of the extent to which traditional psychological theory has been developed by and about White majority-culture men, taking little account of women and minorities or regarding them as deviant or deficient. A more inclusive psychology will provide them with the skills to recognize and evaluate such biases. It will also sensitize students to similar omissions and prejudices within the society at large and enable them more readily to recognize and counteract discrimination when they encounter it. In addition, it will enable students to understand the degree to which scientific inquiry and the interpretation of findings may be influenced by personal or political ideology. Finally, it will introduce students to research from a sociocultural and cross-cultural perspective and to the new directions of research on sex differences and gender issues, thus challenging students to begin formulating questions, theories, and research problems of their own.

In a more general sense, however, we believe students will benefit from an increased appreciation of diversity in any of their future roles, as parents, teachers, community leaders, co-workers, employers, and voters. At one level, their exposure to diversity from a positive perspective can help them in their later interactions with co-workers and colleagues from different social or cultural backgrounds. Most importantly, however, we believe that the opportunity to learn about people from backgrounds different from their own is a meaningful and enriching life experience.

Effects on the Discipline

We can also expect revisions in our curriculum to have a positive effect on psychology as a discipline. The discussions generated within classes will stimulate new research ideas, as the experiences of several of the authors in this volume and of Psychology of Women instructors interviewed by Walsh (1986) attested. As these new research ideas are published and become part of the mainstream psychological literature, they will reshape the questions future psychologists seek to answer. For example, feminist research on women's balancing of work and family roles has led to new questions about the role of the father in children's development (e.g., Bronstein & Cowan, 1988)—questions that were hardly given notice two decades ago.

With this new and exciting scholarship, we may be more successful in attracting a more diverse set of people to psychology. In particular, a racially and culturally relevant discipline may entice larger numbers of talented minority women and men into pursuing a career in psychology and create an enduring diversity within the profession.

A revised curriculum should also promote cultural, social, and gender awareness in the mental health system. Problems are well documented in the delivery of mental health services to ethnic minorities (Sue, 1977), women (Brodsky et al., 1975), disabled persons (Asch & Rousso, 1985), lesbians (Boston Lesbian Psychologies Collective, 1987) and gays (Morin & Charles, 1983). These people, who together make up the clear majority of all clients, will benefit enormously from revised curricula for clinical training.

Effects on Ourselves

Finally, revising the curriculum toward gender balance and sociocultural diversity will have important effects on ourselves. By continuing to think and teach within the well-delineated structure of traditional psychology, we participate in and perpetuate the limits and biases that currently exist. Revising the curriculum, on the other hand, creates an educational process that affects our own lives as well as those of our students. It allows us to experience more actively that we are part of a multicultural community and moves us toward becoming more aware, connected citizens of the world. This in turn enhances our teaching, informs our scholarship, and enriches our own lives.

Instituting Change: Problems and Solutions

There are two general debates that bear on the approaches we have chosen to adopt in this volume. One is whether material about women and minorities is best served by integrating it into the mainstream curriculum or by maintaining separate, in-depth courses. The second concerns the potential positive and negative effects of exploring differences among populations.

Integration or Separate Courses?

Is it best to integrate information about women and minority groups into traditional psychology courses to achieve cultural and gender balance in the psychology curriculum? Or is it best to treat each population separately in special courses? Each approach has its advantages and its drawbacks. The integration approach depends on the willingness and ability of all instructors to deal with diversity in a positive manner. Ideally, diversity can be appreciated with different cultural values and practices accorded validity and respect. However, an instructor who treats special populations as marginal groups could in effect eliminate them from serious consideration for psychological research (Kahn & Jean, 1983).

Separate courses allow more in-depth knowledge about a particular population. The existing special courses and programs that focus on underrepresented groups (e.g., the psychology of women, cross-cultural counseling, Chicano psychology) have proven to be very well received by students and are highly rated not only for scholarly importance but also for personal impact. Their popularity also has given them a new economic role, which is likely to be even more important in the future as colleges and universities look to minorities and women to increase enrollment.

However, these special courses remain the exceptions in most psychology curricula outside the academic mainstream. The instructors, who are frequently women or minority group members, risk isolation by taking on the task of teaching them. At the same time, majority-group instructors of other psychology courses do not feel the need to include material on minorities or women, as it is being covered in the special course. Even when several of these courses are taught in the same department, they are often isolated from each other; for example, many psychology of women courses have not dealt with minority women (Brown, Goodwin, Hall, & Jackson-Lowman, 1985). Thus, a richer and more meaningful exploration of diversity, made possible through an integrated inclusion of a variety of people, cannot be provided. Finally, students are usually limited in the number of topical courses they can take, and those courses are usually included only in the undergraduate curriculum.

We believe that such special courses are valuable, but they cannot provide the sole source of information about cultural diversity for the majority of students. We propose instead a two-pronged approach: special courses and an integration of cultural diversity into the academic mainstream. This book rejects the "either/or" approach that has worried scholars in these areas and argues that there are valuable roles for each format.

Diversity Versus Difference

The second problem arises from a legitimate concern that by grouping together individuals along a single, labeled dimension—lesbian, disabled person, or White male—we will promote stereotyping and unidimensional views of individual members of those groups (Asch, 1984; Krauss, Krauss, Wright, & Cole, 1984). The potential for this error is increased when we treat statistical group differences as categorical or when we place groups in opposition (e.g., Blacks versus Whites) for purposes of comparison.

A number of social scientists have recognized this problem (Allport, 1958; Cronbach, 1975; Lott, 1981; Krauss et al., 1984; Sue & Zane, 1987), and we have drawn on their ideas for our approach. We have attempted to recast the perspective away from group differences and insidious comparisons, toward themes and variations among and within races, genders, cultures, sexual orientations, and life circumstances such as disability or poverty. The instructor can adopt this perspective in several ways.

First, we must help students appreciate that the variability among individuals within an ethnic, gender, or social group is always greater than variability among groups. One way is to have students examine research results that have found group differences and to contrast these with data demonstrating variations within each of those groups (e.g., Lott, 1987). Another approach, offered by several authors in this volume, is to focus on individual lives and experiences through interviews, autobiographies, or novels, not as representatives of *all* Black women or *all* gays, but as illustrations of the real impact of race, gender, sexual orientation, or other circumstances on individual lives.

Second, we must help all students recognize the similarities among the issues raised by a person's ethnic background, gender, race, or social status and draw on common themes wherever possible. One way is to focus on the relations between group membership and social structures, such as the relations between gender and power or race and economic stratification, rather than to focus on specific groups. In Chapter 22 of this book, Unger discusses the ways students' awareness of the larger political and power issues underlying social stratification can be substantially raised through academic course work. Another approach is to help students relate personally to a member of one minority group and then generalize aspects of that experience. For example, disability is included in this volume as a social minority status with civil rights issues similar to those of other minorities (Kahn, 1984). Nondisabled students may have a family member or close friend with a disability, or students can at least come to recognize that a disability could happen to them during their lifetime. Thus, they can appreciate the disabled individual's experiences in a very personal way (Asch, Chapter 19). In a third approach, A. Lott (Chapter 6) demonstrates how biographical and autobiographical portrayals of men and issues of masculinity can be useful as tools for learning about the impact of gender on all our lives.

Objectives and Plan of the Book

This volume brings together the viewpoints, research, and experiences of scholars from a wide range of areas within psychology and from a variety of cultural and ethnic backgrounds to provide information for integrating issues of human diversity into the psychology curriculum. Its four main objectives are to:

1. Reveal the serious deficiencies in psychological theory and research relevant to cultural, ethnic, and gender issues, and thereby heighten psychology teachers' awareness of them;

2. Present information about underrepresented populations, to enable psychology teachers to become more knowledgeable about recent theory and research, and to better understand the importance of integrating these areas into the curriculum;

3. Provide approaches to teaching about these underrepresented areas, including suggestions for course organization, readings, projects and assignments, and supplementary exercises and materials; and

4. Discuss problems and obstacles that may be encountered and how to deal with them, as well as ways to evaluate the effectiveness of a given course or program in increasing students' awareness of sociocultural issues in the study of psychology.

We have, for the most part, tried to describe a process rather than present a packaged product; our goal has been to spark ideas as much as it has been to provide information. We have not attempted to present a complete set of materials for teaching any given course; rather, we have provided resources, perspectives, and techniques to guide and support instructors in developing approaches suitable for their own courses, students, and teaching styles. There are many other topics that could have been covered, and particular readings or ideas presented may soon seem outdated. However, we believe that the teaching approaches presented here will endure as meaningful educational models, which can be used to change the face of psychology.

The book is divided into four sections. Section I presents an overall rationale for teaching a *true* psychology of people. In addition to the points raised in this chapter, Albert (Chapter 2) discusses the importance of adopting a broader cultural perspective.

Section II takes the integrative approach with introductory-level courses in the basic areas of psychology. As these courses represent the only contact many students will have with psychological theory and data, a culture- and gender-balanced approach is especially important. Each chapter offers resources and techniques for achieving gender and sociocultural balance in a different introductory-level course. For example, Landrine (Chapter 4) provides a rich historical perspective on the biases that pervade abnormal psychology; Bond (Chapter 5) describes projects in developmental psychology that increase writing skills; Bronstein (Chapter 7) describes experiential exercises designed to help students learn the importance of sociocultural factors in their own personality development; and Brown-Collins (Chapter 12) provides an extensive resource list on Third World women to broaden the focus of the psychology of women course. The chapters by Quina and Kulberg (8) and Villars (9) challenge both traditional research methods and course contents.

Section III includes chapters on more specialized courses designed to heighten the awareness of cultural, ethnic, and gender issues related to specific populations. Some of these chapters focus on a broad range of ethnic psychology and some focus on specific groups such as Asian Americans, African American women, disabled persons, or gays and lesbians. Each, however, can be used as a resource for teaching either a course on a particular topic or for introducing diversity into a more general psychology course.

Section IV presents models that have been developed and implemented for systematically integrating gender and sociocultural issues into the curriculum on a program- or department-wide basis. Rands (Chapter 23) describes one department's successful efforts to develop a gender-balanced introductory psychology course. Quina and Kanarian (Chapter 24) consider ways to provide courses that are meaningful for adult learners, and Mays (Chapter 25) presents one department's model for a graduate clinical program that includes training in ethnic and sociocultural issues as part of its core curriculum.

In the final chapter, we have offered personal and anecdotal information about the various contributors' experiences in teaching the courses about which they write. We describe successes and setbacks, problems and solutions, and some of the things the contributors learned along the way. We present their data from formal course evaluations as well as the more informal responses of students, guest lecturers, and colleagues. Of all the chapters, this one perhaps most vividly reveals the effects of teaching a true psychology of people.

References

Allport, G. (1958). *The nature of prejudice.* Garden City, NY: Doubleday.

American Psychological Association. (1981). Ethical principles of psychologists. *American Psychologist, 36,* 633–638.

American Psychological Association Educational Affairs Office. (1983, February). *Results: Phase I survey of undergraduate department chairs.* Washington, DC: Author.

Asch, A. (1984). The experience of disability: A challenge for psychology. *American Psychologist, 39,* 529–536.

Asch, A., & Rousso, H. (1985). Therapists with disabilities: Theoretical and clinical issues. *Psychiatry, 48*(1), 1–12.

Boston Lesbian Psychologies Collective. (1987). *Lesbian psychologies: Explorations and challenges.* Champaign: University of Illinois Press.

Brodsky, A., Holroyd, J., Payton, C., Rubinstein, E., Rosenkrantz, P., Sherman, J., & Zell, F. (1975). Report of the task force on sex bias and sex-role stereotyping in psychotherapeutic practice. *American Psychologist, 30,* 1169.

Bronstein, P., & Cowan, C. P. (Eds.). (1988). *Fatherhood today: Men's changing role in the family.* New York: Wiley.

Brown, A., Goodwin, B. J., Hall, B. A., & Jackson-Lowman, H. A. (1985). Review of psychology of women textbooks: Focus on the Afro-American woman. *Psychology of Women Quarterly, 9*(1), 29–38.

Chronbach, L. (1975). Beyond the two disciplines of scientific psychology. *American Psychologist, 30,* 116–127.

Howard, A., Pion, G. M., Gottfredson, G. D., Flattau, P. E., Oskamp, S., Pfafflin, S. M., Bray, D. W., & Burstein, A. G. (1986). The changing face of American psychology: A report from the Committee on Employment and Human Resources. *American Psychologist, 41,* 1311–1327.

Kahn, A. S. (1984). Perspectives on persons with disabilities. *American Psychologist, 39,* 516–517.

Kahn, A. S., & Jean, P. J. (1983). Integration and elimination or separation and isolation: The future of the psychology of women. *Signs: Journal of Women in Culture and Society, 8,* 659–671.

Krauss, B. J., Krauss, H. H., Wright, B., & Cole, O. J. (1983, August). *Initiatives in intergroup understanding: Addressing minority issues in psychology curricula.* Symposium presented at the annual convention of the American Psychological Association, Anaheim, CA.

Levinger, G. (1987). Black employment opportunities: Macro and micro perspectives [Entire issue]. *Journal of Social Issues, 43*(1).

Lott, B. (1981). A feminist critique of androgyny: Toward the elimination of gender attributions for learned behavior. In C. Mayo & N. Henley, *Gender and nonverbal behavior* (pp. 171–180). New York: Springer-Verlag.

Lott, B. (1987). Women's lives: Themes and variations in gender learning. Belmont, CA: Brooks-Cole.

Marsh, J. C., Colten, M. E., & Tucker, M. B. (Eds.). (1982). Women's use of drugs and alcohol: New perspectives [Entire issue]. *Journal of Social Issues, 38*(2).

Mays, V. M. (in press). *The Black woman: Bibliographic guide to research materials on Black women in the social sciences and mental health.* New York: Praeger.

Morin, S. F., & Charles, K. (1983). Heterosexual bias in psychotherapy. In J. Murray & P. R. Abramson (Eds.), *Bias in psychotherapy* (pp. 309–338). New York: Praeger.

Peters, M. F. (1978). Black families [Special issue]. *Journal of Marriage and Family, 40*(4).

Smith, A., & Stewart, A. J. (1983). Racism and sexism in Black women's lives [Entire issue]. *Journal of Social Issues, 39*(3).

Sobel, S. B., & Russo, N. F. (1981). Sex roles, equality, and mental health [Special issue]. *Professional Psychology, 12*(1).

Stewart, A. J., & Platt, M. B. (1982). Studying women in a changing world [Entire issue]. *Journal of Social Issues, 38*(1).

Sue, S. (1977). Community mental health services to minority groups: Some optimism, some pessimism. *American Psychologist, 32,* 616–624.

Sue, S., & Zane, N. (1987). The role of culture and cultural techniques in psychotherapy: A critique and reformulation. *American Psychologist, 42,* 37–45.

U.S. Department of Education, Center for Statistics. (1987, July 15). Earned degrees conferred in 1984–85 by U.S. colleges and universities. *Chronicle of Higher Education,* p. 34.

Walsh, M. R. (1985). Academic professional women organizing for change: The struggle in psychology. *Journal of Social Issues, 41*(4), 17–28.

Walsh, M. R. (1986). The Psychology of Women course: A continuing catalyst for change. *Teaching of Psychology, 12*(4), 198–203.

2

Rosita Daskal Albert

The Place of Culture in Modern Psychology

A number of psychologists, recognizing the importance of a cultural perspective in psychology, have pointed to the overreliance on the individual as our explanatory unit and have made a persuasive case for the need to examine sociocultural or contextual factors (e.g., Maehr, 1974; Moscovici, 1972; Tajfel, 1972). Campbell (1975) exhorted psychologists to attend

> not only to the biological sources of behavioral tendencies, and not only to the person's own past history of reinforcement, but also to the culturally inherited baggage of dispositions, transmitted by example, indoctrination and culturally provided limitations on perspectives and opportunities. (p. 1105)

Pepitone (1976) and Triandis (1975) suggested that lack of a cross-cultural orientation may have been a critical reason for the so-called crisis in social psychology in the 1970s, in which some researchers began to question the scientific status of the field (Gergen, 1973) and others saw a paradigmatic crisis (Berkowitz, quoted in Smith, 1972) or a crisis of confidence (Elms, 1975).

Historical Perspective

Interest in cultural variables has fluctuated during psychology's history, varying with the political and social climate of the times. From the 1930s to the 1950s, psychology was strongly interpersonal in orientation, perhaps because of the European influence of Kurt Lewin, Fritz Heider, and Solomon Asch. A number of societal concerns such as the emergence of fascistic, authoritarian governments, social conformity, and intergroup relations were reflected in American psychology. The study of groups became important, and the field of group dynamics emerged (see Cartwright & Zander, 1968). Interpersonally oriented theories such as Heider's balance theory were developed, and researchers became interested in the study of "national character" (Inkeles & Levinson, 1969) and in the relation between personality and social structure (see, for example, the work on the "authoritarian personality," Adorno, Frenkel-Brunswik, Levinson, & Sanford, 1950).

In the ensuing decades, however, Americans turned politically and socially inward, and psychologists correspondingly turned to intra-individual processes such as cognitive dissonance, attitude change, and attributions. Laboratory experiments flourished, and there was a narrowing of substantive content as well as of methodological approaches.

In the late 1960s and early 1970s, our society had to cope with national discontent over an unpopular war, governmental corruption, and a diminution of American influence and power in the world. It was a time of increasing social awareness, evidenced by the antiwar movement, the civil rights movement, and the women's movement. A parallel discontent arose in psychology, with many psychologists arguing that the field had become too narrow and its approaches methodologically sophisticated but stale.

This period of upheaval has led to a renewed expansion of psychology both methodologically and substantively. Interest in field studies and in real-world settings—educational, medical, or community—has flourished. As our society continues to change, there is a need for psychology to address new concerns. For example, within the next decade, Hispanics, a group both linguistically and culturally different from the majority, are expected to constitute our largest minority (U.S. Bureau of the Census, 1987). Such a change underscores the need for an increased awareness of the importance of culture in the study of psychology.

Cross-Cultural Studies and the Neglect of Cultural Variables

Cross-cultural researchers (Brislin, Lonner, & Thorndike, 1973; Strodtbeck, 1964; Triandis, 1972, 1980) have pointed out the following special advantages of cross-cultural studies:

• Information can be obtained that is not easily available or obtainable in one's own culture. For example, cross-cultural investigations (Ramirez & Castaneda, 1974; Witkin, 1967; Witkin & Berry, 1975) have shown that in some cultures (e.g., Mexican American) people tend to be more field sensitive than in American culture, thus suggesting the need for revision in the notion that all persons move from field dependence to independence.

• Information can be obtained about the incidence of a particular phenomenon in a different cultural environment. An example of this is Durkheim's (1951/[1897]) classic work on the rate of suicide in different countries, which enabled him to demonstrate that suicide followed certain social and cultural prescriptions.

• Values or behavior patterns that are characteristic of a particular cultural group can be investigated. For example, research on Hispanic and Anglo perceptions and interpretations of behavior (Albert, 1983a, 1986a) has demonstrated that Hispanics saw shame as a very important explanation for the behavior and feelings of Hispanics.

• The generality of certain laws of behavior can be tested by looking at data from several cultures. This is an important function of cross-cultural studies. An example of this is research on Piaget's stages of development in a variety of cultures to see if the proposed stages are indeed universal (Dasen, 1977a, 1977b).

Factors Leading to the Neglect of Cultural Variables

Despite the general desirability of research that takes cultural variables into account, a number of powerful factors have led to the neglect of cultural variables. These include psychology's focus on the behavior of individuals rather than on normative patterns (Pepitone, 1976), the difficulty of obtaining funds for this kind of enterprise (Holtzman, Diaz-Guerrero, & Schwartz, 1975), and the methodological difficulties involved in many cross-cultural studies (Brislin et al., 1973; Cole & Scribner, 1974; Triandis, 1972). However, certain social and psychological factors may play an even greater role in the neglect of cultural variables. In the remainder of this chapter, I shall identify these factors, discuss the ways in which they limit the perspective of the field, and point out what can be gained in each area by including cultural variables in the study of psychological phenomena.

Cultural variables have been neglected because of our relative lack of direct experience with other cultures. Because a culture consists, in part, of unstated assumptions, shared values, and characteristic ways of perceiving the world that are normally taken for granted by its members, people do not ordinarily become aware of the cultural basis for many of their own behaviors. Often it is only when they have direct contact with persons from a different culture that they begin to realize that there are some culturally based differences in patterns of behavior. Thus, the inclusion of cultural variables will be helpful in broadening the perspective of individuals as well as the field.

The need to simplify events may have contributed to lack of attention to cultural variables. As a number of social psychologists (e.g., Heider, 1958) have shown, we seek to understand the world and render it predictable. This motivation to find and create order leads us to simplify events and seek immediate causes for them. Given the important cognitive function these mechanisms serve, it is not surprising that we find them at work in the attempts of psychologists, as well as those of the lay public, to understand and explain behavior.

For both psychologists and the lay public, simplification may take two forms. One is a reductionistic tendency to focus on the individual rather than on the larger sociocultural context; the other is a tendency to ignore cultural variability and assume cultural universality or at least similarity. Deliberate attention to cultural issues can help counter the tendency to simplify psychological phenomena.

Cultural variability has been overlooked because of fears of creating or reinforcing stereotypes. A stereotype, according to Allport (1958), is "an exaggerated belief associated with a category. Its function is to justify (rationalize) our conduct in relation to the category" (p. 187). He argued that we can only distinguish between a stereotype and a valid generalization concerning a particular group *if we have data concerning true group differences.*

Psychologists, who historically have sought to identify stereotypes in order to contribute to their eradication, do not want to foster new ones. Thus, it is important to follow Allport's injunction about obtaining data on true group differences while at the same time devising strategies for the use of such data for overcoming stereotypic conceptions. For example, in reports of my own work (Albert, 1983a, 1983b, 1986a, 1986b), I have attempted to do this by stressing the variability of behavior within any group, pointing out that the distributions of behavior for different cultural groups often overlap and emphasizing the complexity of human behavior. In any particular situation, behavior is dependent on complex interactions of individual, sociocultural, and situational factors.

Cultural variables have been ignored because findings of between-group differences have been used in the past to discriminate against members of some cultural groups. For example, differences in measures of intelligence for different cultural groups have been used to support claims of racial inferiority (see Kamin, 1974); one result of this has been that being culturally different has acquired a connotation of inferiority in the minds of many. Though the neglect of cultural variables has in one sense prevented further misuse of such findings, it is important that we continue to learn as much as possible about different cultural groups so that ill-founded assumptions and negative stereotypes can be dispelled.

A focus on cultural differences may be seen as incongruent with our society's equalitarian ideology. The American political system is predicated on the value of equality—equality under the law and equality of opportunity. To many individuals, a concern with cultural difference seems to pose a threat to this basic American value. For example, as part of a multiyear research program on cross-cultural differences in attributions and on the development of cross-cultural sensitization materials (Albert, 1983a, 1983b, 1986a, 1986b; Albert & Adamopoulos, 1976; Albert & Triandis, 1979), American teachers and Hispanic pupils were interviewed regarding their interactions with each other. The teachers often voiced the opinion that "All children are the same," and "Children are children," ignoring the possibility that in some instances Hispanic children might behave differently than Anglo American children—for example, using touch more frequently than Anglo American children do. (For a discussion of the differences in perceptions and attributions found between Hispanics and Anglo Americans, see Albert, 1983a, 1986a.)

It is important that we come to understand that true cultural variability does not undermine the value of equality. In fact, such understanding can serve to reaffirm another cherished American value: the value of diversity (Albert & Triandis, 1985).

The exploration of cultural differences can be perceived as being contrary to the historic American goal of assimilation. As a society, we have subscribed until recently to the melting pot theory of assimilation. In line with this, our educational system has attempted to Americanize children in the process of educating them.

To members of minority groups, however, awareness of ethnic or cultural differences can be an essential aspect of self-definition; for example, McGuire, McGuire, Child, and Fujioka (1978) found that minority high school students used ethnic group identification in their self-descriptions more frequently than did nonminority students and that the use of ethnic descriptors tended to increase as the population became more heterogeneous. Thus, as minority populations continue to grow in this country, we need to become more appreciative of the importance of cultural factors in shaping the identity and self-concept of minority individuals.

The dominant political and economic position of the United States may account for our relative lack of interest in cultural factors. Because of the economic and political power this nation has historically wielded, it has not been necessary for us to move beyond our traditional independent and somewhat isolationist stance. At present, however, the nations of the world are becoming more interdependent, and our influence seems to be decreasing. It is likely that we will become even more interdependent and that the volume of our cross-cultural interactions in many spheres will increase. Greater awareness of cultural issues and of cultural differences can do much to improve our relations with other countries in the world.

Our ethnocentric tendencies may constitute a more fundamental source of resistance to the investigation of cultural variables. Ethnocentric tendencies have been manifested in two ways: (a) Many of our citizens believe that our ways of behaving are the best; and (b) psychologists have tended to assume that our patterns of behavior, or at least many of the processes that have been found to govern our patterns of behavior, are universal. The investigation of cultural differences raises the possibility that some of these patterns and processes might not be universal—there might be other (and for some purposes, perhaps better) ways of being and behaving. This is likely to challenge in a fundamental way the concepts held by the American public and American psychologists. As the strong response to Gergen's (1973) arguments that social psychology may not be a true science have shown, the notion that our patterns of behavior may not be universal is unsettling to many of our colleagues.

For most of its history, psychology has been a science based to a large extent on research conducted by American investigators with middle-class American subjects. European (Jahoda, 1979; Moscovici, 1972; Tajfel, 1972), Latin American (Diaz-Guerrero, 1975, 1977; Leite, 1976), and American colleagues (Maehr, 1974; Pepitone, 1976; Price-Williams, 1985; Ramirez, 1983; Smith, 1978; Triandis, 1975) have challenged psychologists to take culture more seriously. We should meet that challenge and use the investigation of cultural differences as a means of developing a more accurate science of human behavior.

Recent Trends

Some changes are already evident. In the last few years, there has been a burgeoning of cross-cultural research in psychology and scientific exchanges that facilitate this type of research. This can be seen in the publication of six volumes of the *Handbook of Cross-Cultural Research* (Triandis & Berry, 1980; Triandis & Brislin, 1980; Triandis & Draguns, 1981; Triandis & Heron, 1981; Triandis & Lambert, 1980; Triandis & Lonner, 1980) and a number of other significant books in addition to those cited previously (see, e.g., Brislin, 1981; Landis & Brislin, 1983; Segall, 1979). In addition, there are three journals—the *International Journal of Intercultural Relations*, the *Journal of Cross-Cultural Psychology*, and the *Hispanic Journal of Behavior Sciences*—and several societies devoted to reports of cross-cultural investigations.

In the coming years, as intercultural contact increases around the world, as the Hispanic population in the United States increases, as more international students enter our universities, and as our colleagues in other nations help us forge our future directions, an expanded role for culture in psychology will be essential. A concern with culture will aid us in the development of new theories, challenge us in the methodological realm, and invite us to deal with important societal problems. At the same time, it may offer an opportunity for psychology to replenish itself by going back to some of its intellectual roots.

References

Adorno, T. W., Frenkel-Brunswik, E., Levinson, D. J., & Sanford, R. W. (1950). *The authoritarian personality.* New York: Harper & Row.

Albert, R. D. (1983a). Mexican-American children in educational settings: Research on children's and teacher's perceptions and interpretations of behavior. In E. E. Garcia (Ed.), *The Mexican American child: Language, cognition and social development* (pp. 183–194). Tempe: Arizona State University Press.

Albert, R. D. (1983b). The intercultural sensitizer or culture assimilator: A cognitive approach. In D. Landis & R. W. Brislin (Eds.), *Handbook of intercultural training: Vol. 2. Issues in training methodology* (pp. 186–217). New York: Pergamon Press.

Albert, R. D. (1986a). Communication and attributional differences between Hispanics and Anglo Americans. *International and Intercultural Communication Annual, 10,* 42–59.

Albert, R. D. (1986b). Conceptual framework for the development and evaluation of cross-cultural orientation programs. *International Journal of Intercultural Relations, 10,* 197–213.

Albert, R. D., & Adamopoulos, J. (1976). An attributional approach to culture learning: The culture assimilator. *Topics in Culture Learning, 4,* 53–60.

Albert, R. D., & Triandis, H. C. (1979). Cross-cultural training: A theoretical framework and some observations. In H. Trueba & C. Barnett-Mizrahi (Eds.), *Bilingual multicultural education and the professional: From theory to practice* (pp. 181–194). Rowley, MA: Newbury House.

Albert, R. D., & Triandis, H. C. (1985). Intercultural education for multicultural societies: Critical issues. *International Journal of Intercultural Relations, 9,* 319–337.

Allport, G. W. (1958). *The nature of prejudice.* New York: Doubleday.

Brislin, R. (1981). *Cross-cultural encounters.* New York: Pergamon Press.

Brislin, R., Lonner, W., & Thorndike, R. (1973). *Cross-cultural research methods.* New York: Wiley.

Campbell, D. T. (1975). On the conflicts between biological and social evolution and between psychology and moral tradition. *American Psychologist, 30,* 1103–1126.

Cartwright, D., & Zander, A. (1968). Origins of group dynamics. In D. Cartwright & A. Zander (Eds.), *Group dynamics* (3rd ed., pp. 3–21). New York: Harper & Row.

Cole, M., & Scribner, S. (1974). *Culture and thought.* New York: Wiley.

Dasen, P. R. (Ed.). (1977a). *Piagetian psychology: Cross-cultural contributions.* New York: Gardner.

Dasen, P. R. (1977b). Are cognitive processes universal? A contribution to cross-cultural Piagetian psychology. In N. Warren (Ed.), *Studies in cross-cultural psychology* (pp. 155–201). London: Academic Press.

Diaz-Guerrero, R. (1975). *Psychology of the Mexican.* Austin: University of Texas Press.

Diaz-Guerrero, R. (1977). Mexican psychology. *American Psychologist, 32,* 939–944.

Durkheim, E. (1951). *Suicide.* Glencoe, IL: Free Press. (Original work published 1897)

Elms, A. C. (1975). The crisis of confidence in social psychology. *American Psychologist, 30,* 967–976.

Gergen, K. J. (1973). Social psychology as history. *Journal of Personality and Social Psychology, 26,* 309–320.

Heider, F. (1958). *The psychology of interpersonal relations.* New York: Wiley.

Holtzman, W. H., Diaz-Guerrero, R., & Swartz, J. D. (1975). *Personality development in two cultures.* Austin: University of Texas Press.

Inkeles, A., & Levinson, D. J. (1969). National character: The study of modal personality and sociocultural systems. In G. Lindzey & E. Aronson (Eds.), *The handbook of social psychology* (2nd ed., Vol. 4, pp. 418–506). Reading, MA: Addison-Wesley.

Jahoda, G. (1979). A cross-cultural perspective on experimental social psychology. *Personality and Social Psychology Bulletin, 5,* 142–148.

Kamin, L. J. (1974). *The science and politics of IQ*. Potomac, MD: Erlbaum.

Landis, D., & Brislin, R. (1983). *Handbook of intercultural training*. New York: Pergamon Press.

Leite, D. M. (1976). *O carater nacional brasileiro* [The Brazilian national character] (3rd ed.). Sao Paulo, Brazil: Pioneira.

Maehr, M. L. (1974). Culture and achievement motivation. *American Psychologist, 29*, 887–896.

McGuire, W. J., McGuire, C. V., Child, P., & Fujioka, T. (1978). Salience of ethnicity in the spontaneous self-concept as a function of one's ethnic distinctiveness in the social environment. *Journal of Personality and Social Psychology, 36*, 511–520.

Moscovici, S. (1972). Society and theory in social psychology. In J. Israel & H. Tajfel (Eds.), *The context of social psychology: A critical assessment* (pp. 17–68). London: Academic Press.

Pepitone, A. (1976). Toward a normative and comparative biocultural social psychology. *Journal of Personality and Social Psychology, 34*, 641–653.

Price-Williams, D. R. (1985). Cultural psychology. In G. Lindzey & E. Aronson (Eds.), *The handbook of social psychology. Vol. 2: Special fields and applications* (3rd ed., pp. 993–1042). New York: Random House.

Ramirez, M. (1983). *Psychology of the Americas*. New York: Pergamon Press.

Ramirez, M., & Castaneda, A. (1974). *Cultural democracy, bicognitive development and education*. New York: Academic Press.

Segall, M. H. (1979). *Cross-cultural psychology*. Monterey, CA: Brooks/Cole.

Smith, M. B. (1972). Is experimental social psychology advancing? *Journal of Experimental Social Psychology, 8*, 86–96.

Smith, R. J. (1978). The future of an illusion: American social psychology. *Personality and Social Psychology Bulletin, 4*, 173–176.

Strodtbeck, F. L. (1964). Considerations of meta-method in cross-cultural studies. *American Anthropologist, 66*, 223–229.

Tajfel, H. (1972). Experiments in a vacuum. In J. Israel & H. Tajfel (Eds.), *The context of social psychology: A critical assessment* (pp. 69–119). London: Academic Press.

Triandis, H. C. (1972). *The analysis of subjective culture*. New York: Wiley.

Triandis, H. C. (1975). Social psychology and cultural analysis. *Journal for the Theory of Social Behavior, 5*, 81–106.

Triandis, H. C. (1980). Introduction to handbook of cross-cultural psychology. In H. C. Triandis & W. W. Lambert (Eds.), *Handbook of cross-cultural psychology: Vol. 1. Perspectives* (pp. 1–14). Boston: Allyn & Bacon.

Triandis, H. C., & Berry, J. W. (Eds.). (1980). *Handbook of cross-cultural psychology: Vol. 2. Methodology*. Boston: Allyn & Bacon.

Triandis, H. C., & Brislin, R. W. (Eds.). (1980). *Handbook of cross-cultural psychology: Vol. 5. Social psychology*. Boston: Allyn & Bacon.

Triandis, H. C., & Draguns, J. G. (Eds.). (1981). *Handbook of cross-cultural psychology: Vol. 6. Psychopathology*. Boston: Allyn & Bacon.

Triandis, H. C., & Heron, A. (Eds.). (1981). *Handbook of cross-cultural psychology: Vol. 4. Developmental psychology*. Boston: Allyn & Bacon.

Triandis, H. C., & Lambert, W. W. (Eds.). (1980). *Handbook of cross-cultural psychology: Vol. 1. Perspectives*. Boston: Allyn & Bacon.

Triandis, H. C., & Lonner, W. J. (Eds.). (1980). *Handbook of cross-cultural psychology: Vol. 3. Basic processes*. Boston: Allyn & Bacon.

U.S. Bureau of the Census. (1987). *Population profile of the United States, 1984–85* (Current Population Reports, Special studies series P-23, Number 150). Washington, DC: U.S. Government Printing Office.

Witkin, H. A. (1967). A cognitive style approach to cross-cultural research. *International Journal of Psychology, 2*(4), 233–250.

Witkin, H. A., & Berry, J. W. (1975). Psychological differentiation in cross-cultural perspective. *Journal of Cross-Cultural Psychology, 6*, 4–87.

Section II

Integrating Diversity Into General Psychology Courses

3 ⸻

Phyllis Bronstein and Michele Paludi

The Introductory Psychology Course From a Broader Human Perspective

The introductory psychology course is usually students' first exposure to the field of psychology. For many it is the only exposure they will have, beyond what they may pick up from the media or from involvement with the mental health system. The questions, issues, facts, and possible biases that students encounter in the introductory course can have lasting effects on their perceptions of both human nature and the field of psychology, as well as on their expectations as consumers of psychological services. The course may enhance their understanding of their own motivations, affect their social perceptions and attributions, shape their beliefs about mental illness, and inform their future behavior as parents. Thus, it is important that it cover not only a sufficient range of topics but also a sufficient diversity of human experience by including issues and information about sociocultural factors, ethnicity, and gender in its content.

It is apparent from the contents of current introductory texts that the typical introduction to psychology course does not do this. The texts show some improvement over the last 7 years (cf. Bronstein-Burrows, 1981); for example, all 13 of the current texts reviewed for this chapter contain discussions of heredity and environment in relation to IQ, with critiques of Jensen's (1969) argument, and 10 of the 13 include at least some consideration of gender-role socialization. With a few notable exceptions (e.g., Davidoff, 1987; Feldman, 1987; Simons, Irwin, & Drinnin, 1987; Wade & Tavris, 1987), most go no further in including sociocultural factors. To remedy this deficiency, the instructor can provide supplemental lectures, readings, exercises, and projects. In addition, a traditional text in the hands of an aware instructor can be an effective tool for heightening students' awareness of sociocultural biases in mainstream psychology.

Overview of the Field

Many instructors begin the course with an overview of the field. This is an appropriate time to have students consider whether the topics that are emphasized in

We thank Toby Silverman-Dresner for sharing her knowledge and resources with us, which facilitated the writing of this chapter and enriched its content.

their textbook represent what is most important for us to know about human nature and behavior. For example, feminist theorists have advanced the argument that psychological theory has been developed mainly by and about majority-culture males and that the field reflects predominantly male experiences, perspectives, and values (Belenky, Clinchy, Goldberger, & Tarule, 1986; Denmark, 1983; Gilligan, 1982; Sherman & Beck, 1979). As illustration, in almost all introductory texts there are separate major sections devoted to different cognitive processes such as perception, memory, thinking, and learning, whereas emotional processes, which have traditionally been regarded as relevant more to female than to male experience, are covered in only one section—usually along with motivation or stress. No major sections are devoted to such important aspects of human functioning as family or friendship, and those topics are not discussed at all in about half of the texts. Aggression appears in every index, with an average of seven subheadings; in fact, one of the most widely used texts (Zimbardo, 1985) has 20 subheadings for aggression, 6 for violence, and 4 for conflict. Altruism and intimacy, on the other hand, which relate more to the perspective and experiences of women (Belenky et al., 1986; Gilligan, 1982; Miller, 1976), are frequently not listed in the index at all. And although aggression is such an extensively discussed topic, we found only two texts (Davidoff, 1987; Feldman, 1987) presented a meaningful consideration of rape.

There are other indications that majority-culture and male perspectives predominate in the introductory texts. Fewer than half of the texts reviewed include a discussion of racism, sexism, or prejudice. They generally emphasize isolated aspects of individual functioning rather than the individual as a complex whole, interconnected with other individuals and affected by social context. In addition, they tend to emphasize problem behaviors and psychopathology rather than cooperation, intimacy, and mental health.

It is also important for instructors to point out to beginning students that the cultural values of objectivity and abstract reasoning over social context, interpersonal connectedness, and feelings have led to an overemphasis in psychology on research methods that have been adopted from the physical sciences (Wallston & Grady, 1985). This has, in turn, fostered an emphasis on examining those questions that can most easily be answered in the laboratory or through the use of "objective" questionnaires, which most easily lend themselves to statistical analyses. Though surveys and experimental paradigms are important tools for psychologists, it is useful for students to consider how much they can actually reveal about the experience of growing up Black or Asian American in this culture or the effects of sexism on women's life choices. For a discussion of the ways that various components of the scientific process can be used to produce biased findings in psychology research, see Messing (1983), Paludi (1987), and Chapter 8 by Quina and Kulberg in this volume.

In addition to making students aware of biases and limitations within the field, a course that offers a broader perspective can introduce students to recent theories and findings about groups that have traditionally been under- or unrepresented within mainstream psychology. For example, feminist scholars have been developing new paradigms that focus on women's life experiences and development within the larger social context (Baruch, Barnett, & Rivers, 1983; Belenky et al., 1986; Gilligan, 1982; Miller, 1976). Similarly, as described in other chapters in this volume, there are growing areas of scholarship that reflect a new perspective on various ethnic groups, gays and lesbians, disabled persons, and the elderly, as well as cross-cultural research in a number of different areas of psychology. This new scholarship, which includes a range of research methodologies, can also be used to introduce students to more contextual and less controlled approaches to data collection such as clinical observation, behavioral coding, and open-ended interviews and questionnaires.

Theory and research on underrepresented areas can be included in the introductory psychology course as separate topics, or they can be integrated into the traditional topic areas throughout the semester. We have taken a mixed approach, for example, interweaving theory and research about ethnicity, socioeconomic factors, and gender into sections on human development, social psychology, and personality, while also presenting a separate section on gender. Because all the chapters in this book can serve as resources for the introductory psychology course, we do not attempt to provide comprehensive coverage here. Rather, we focus on areas of psychology in which gender and minority issues are particularly relevant and suggest theoretical concerns that might be raised, teaching exercises, student projects, and additional resources.

Human Development

A central debate in the study of the human experience is over the roles played by biological versus social factors. This debate is especially relevant in the study of how humans develop, particularly in understanding how those factors may contribute to human diversity. In the following areas, an exploration of social and cultural factors can challenge stereotypes that students are likely to hold and give them the tools to question explanations for diversity that are mainly biological.

Gender Role Socialization

One important aspect of gender role socialization that is not included in most texts involves parents' interactions with children, beginning in infancy. As might be predicted from Rubin, Provenzano, and Luria's (1974) well-known study of parents' perceptions of newborns and Paludi and Gullo's (1986) study of adults' expectations of infants' development, parents begin to treat girls and boys differently in the first few months of life. In addition, right from the beginning, parents are modeling different gender role behaviors for their children; for example, mothers spend a greater proportion of their interaction time with infants in caretaking activities, whereas fathers spend a greater proportion in playful and sociable activities and engage in more physically active and stimulating interaction with infants and young children (particularly sons) than mothers do. Reviews of the research on parent–child interaction in relation to gender role socialization have been completed by Block (1983), Bronstein (1988), and Paludi (1985).

Cross-cultural literature on child rearing can further enrich students' understanding of gender role socialization. Barry, Bacon, and Child (1957), studying ethnographic reports from 110 nonliterate societies, found that in most instances girls more than boys were pressured to be nurturant, obedient, and responsible, whereas boys were pressured more toward achievement and self-reliance. As a likely reflection of those kinds of socialization pressures, Whiting and Whiting (1975), in their observational study of children's social behavior in six cultures, found that girls were more likely to be nurturant (i.e., offering help, offering support), whereas boys were more likely to act dominant or seek attention.

Moral Development

Along with the traditional presentation of Kohlberg's theory of moral development, most of the texts reviewed mention Gilligan's (1982) critique of the theory's gender bias, and some briefly describe her alternative model for female moral development. It is useful for students also to consider cultural biases that may be embedded in Kohlberg's theory. Snarey (1985), in his review of research on moral development in 27 countries, concluded that processes of moral reasoning are to some degree culture specific and that Kohlberg's scoring system does not recognize higher-stage reasoning in certain cultural groups. Snarey argued that such reasoning does occur, but that it may, for example, reflect values related to communal equity and collective happiness (Israel), the unity and sacredness of all life forms (India), filial piety and collective utility (Taiwan), or the relation of the individual to the community (New Guinea), rather than a concern for individual rights and abstract principles of justice. Examples such as these can help students become more aware of human development as a variable process, whose stages—as well as what are perceived to be desired outcomes—are very much shaped by the values, belief systems, and traditional roles and structures within each culture.

Intelligence, Learning, and Academic Performance

Race and IQ

All the texts include some discussion of the role of heredity in IQ, with at least a brief critique of Jensen's argument that genetic factors account for racial differences in IQ test performance. A more thorough examination of the issues and a persuasive antiheredity argument can be found in Lewontin, Rose, and Kamin (1984); also, see Chapter 9 by Villars in this volume for further references in this area. Interestingly, the environmental explanations given for IQ differences generally focus on demographic factors such as family income and parents' level of education. The instructor may also wish to make students aware of the likely impact of the educational setting on children's developing intellectual competencies—not only in terms of the differences that have commonly existed between schools in low-income, predominantly Black urban neighborhoods and those in middle-class White suburbs, but in terms of the quality of teacher–student interaction. For example, there is research evidence that teachers may give more negative academic and behavioral feedback to Black than to White students and that White teachers may have more negative attitudes and beliefs about Black children than about White children (Irvine, 1985).

Gender and Intelligence

The issue of gender differences in intellectual functioning takes a different form from that of the racial issue, since IQ tests were specifically constructed so as *not* to distinguish between the sexes. However, gender differences have emerged in scores on the College Board's Scholastic Aptitude Tests (SATs), both for college applicants and for seventh- to eighth-grade children who took the test as part of a program to identify gifted youngsters (Benbow & Stanley, 1983), with male scores being substantially higher, particularly on the section intended to measure mathematical aptitude. Benbow and her colleagues discount environmental explanations for differences within the latter group (Benbow & Stanley, 1983; Raymond & Benbow, 1986); refutations of their conclusions have been made by Bleier (1984), Eccles and Jacobs (1986), Fausto-Sterling (1985), and Fennema and Peterson (1985). An important point to note about gender differences in college applicants' SAT scores is that the differences do not correspond to the levels of academic performance found once students enter college. The SAT is intended to be a means for colleges to predict applicants' academic performance. In fact, however, SAT scores underpredict women's academic performance and overpredict men's, suggesting that there are biases in the design of the test that favor men (Rosser, 1987; Selkow, 1984).

Another important issue in the consideration of gender differences in intellectual functioning is that of men's alleged superior aptitude for spatial tasks. Researchers are currently debating whether brain lateralization, sex hormones, or life experience is the main factor accounting for differences that have been found, and questions about definition, measurement, degree of difference, and methods of data analysis have also been raised. Reviews of the research and the various arguments have been reported by Caplan, MacPherson, and Tobin (1985), Chipman, Brush, and Wilson (1985), Fausto-Sterling (1985), Halpern (1986), and Linn and Peterson (1986). Also of interest is an article by Kimura (1985) that considered sex differences in brain organization in relation to hormonal fluctuations and life experience and research in progress that indicates that with training, girls' spatial ability can equal or surpass that of boys (Phelps & Damon, cited in *Murray Research Center News*, 1987).

All of the reviews of the debates on gender differences in math and spatial abilities mention environmental factors. The instructor may wish to present specific findings about differences between the female and male classroom experience—in particular, teacher behaviors to female and male students that seem likely to contribute to the differential development of abilities in those areas. For reports on recent studies and reviews of the research, see Irvine (1985), Sadker and Sadker (1985), and Wilkinson and Marrett (1985).

Personality

Psychoanalytic Theory

Although all of the texts reviewed include psychoanalytic theory, only a few effectively critique Freud's theories about female personality development (Simons et al., 1987; Wade & Tavris, 1987; Wortman & Loftus, 1985), with most texts not considering them at all. Feminist critiques of Freud's views on women can be found in most psychology of women textbooks (e.g., Hyde, 1985; Matlin, 1987; Tavris & Wade, 1984; Williams, 1983), and have been offered by Duley, Sinclair, and Edwards (1986), Garner, Kahane, and Sprengnether (1985), Lerman (1986), Lewis (1986), and Mead (1979). The instructor may wish to have students consider the applicability of traditional personality theories to women and, in the process, to expose students to theories developed specifically about women by women (e.g., Bernay & Cantor, 1986; Chodorow, 1978; Dinnerstein, 1976; Gilligan, 1982; Miller, 1976; Weskott, 1986). Brief discussions of contemporary feminist personality theories can also be found in most psychology of women textbooks.

Culture and Personality

An introductory course offering a broader human perspective should also include information about the effects of culture on personality development. Anthropological sources can be very useful in this area by providing descriptions of child rearing and culturally sanctioned behaviors within different societies (e.g., Briggs, 1970; LeVine, 1974; Mead, 1935) as well as a model defining the links among ecological factors, child rearing, personality development, and cultural belief systems (Whiting, 1961). Novels and autobiographies can be rich sources of information about the effects on personality development of growing up as a member of a particular subculture within the United States; see Chapters 6, 12, 15, 20, 21, and 25 in this volume for suggestions.

Social Psychology

Methodology and Manipulation

Social psychology, the study of humans in social context, has perhaps suffered more than any other area within psychology from the overuse of laboratory research focusing on the manipulated behavior of college undergraduates. Lykes and Stewart (1986) found that of the articles published in the field's most prestigious journal between 1963 and 1983, approximately two thirds used traditional experimental methods and two thirds used college students as research subjects. In critiquing social psychology research, feminist scholars have argued that male-constructed models of science stress separation, compartmentalization, and linear causality as opposed to interaction, interdependence, and process and that the vocabulary of scientific experimentation (e.g., control, dependent variable, experimental manipulation) show a preoccupation with power, dominance, and an adversarial stance toward nature (Lott, 1985; Wallston & Grady, 1985).

These characteristics can be seen in the choices of topics to be studied as well as in the approaches to studying them. For example, two classic social psychology studies that appear in almost every introductory psychology text are Milgram's obedience experiments (1974) and Zimbardo's prison study (Zimbardo, Haney, &

Banks, 1973). In both studies, participants were subjected to extreme coercion and were induced to behave destructively toward other human beings. This is not to say that topics such as aggression, coercion, and obedience should not be studied. However, it may be useful to ask students to consider ways of studying these phenomena as they actually occur in life (such as looking at coercion and obedience in the military or control and aggression in actual prisons) rather than constructing laboratory analogues that attempt to control and manipulate behavior. A comparative research example that may be useful here is Wener, Frazier, and Farbstein's (1987) work on the relation between environment and violence in prisons. In addition, A. Lott in Chapter 6 of this volume suggests materials that help students understand aggression, authoritarianism, and obedience in a social and historical context and examines the effects of violence and oppression on individuals rather than mainly attempting to evoke the dark side of human nature in the laboratory. Lott further provides a model of social psychology teaching that includes a focus on intimacy, commitment, and interpersonal responsibility.

Prejudice and Racism

Fewer than half the reviewed texts include an examination of prejudice or racism. Resources are provided in other chapters in this volume, such as readings on the psychology of poverty offered by B. Lott (Chapter 21), readings and media presentations on discrimination against Asian Americans offered by Tsai and Uemura (Chapter 15), readings on the racism experienced by Black Americans offered by Fairchild (Chapter 16) and Mays (Chapter 17), and readings on the racism experienced by Third World women offered by Brown-Collins (Chapter 12). In addition, students can be introduced to the use of experimental methods in a field setting, where human reactions to prejudice-evoking stimuli are observed rather than manipulated or coerced. Some of the studies by Bickman and his colleagues (Bickman, 1971; Gaertner & Bickman, 1971) provide good models—such as the effects of the experimental confederate's race or apparent social status on people's willingness to return a dime left in a phone booth or to make a phone call on behalf of a stranded motorist.

Abnormal Psychology

Most of the introductory texts reviewed do not consider psychopathology in relation to culture, race, socioeconomic factors, or gender. The instructor can begin with a discussion of cultural variations (and similarities) in the definition of normalcy and abnormalcy, providing examples from anthropology and cross-cultural clinical studies (Al-Issa & Dennis, 1970; LeVine, 1974; Murphy, 1976; Murphy & Leighton, 1965) and studies of clinical work with ethnic minorities in the United States (Abad & Boyce, 1979; Jones & Korchin, 1982; Korchin, 1980; Marsella & White, 1982; Mays & Cochran, 1987); also, see Landrine's discussion of normalcy in Chapter 4 of this volume. Another important question for students to consider from a sociocultural perspective is why certain distressed patterns of behavior occur with greater frequency among men (e.g., antisocial personality, paranoia, substance abuse) or among women (e.g., depression, agoraphobia, eating disorders). Franks and Rothblum (1983) provided a useful resource for considering the effects of sexism on women's mental health; in a similar vein, the well-known study by Broverman, Broverman, Clarkson, Rosenkrantz, and Vogel (1970) offered telling evidence that mental health professionals' views of optimal female functioning tend to be shaped by sexist stereotyping. In addition, epidemiological information can be used to provide socioeconomic explanations of mental illness (Albee, 1982; Dohrenwend & Dohrenwend, 1974; Landrine [Chapter 4 of this volume]; Lewontin et al., 1984), which can be contrasted with biogenetic explanations.

Emotion

Introductory psychology texts tend to present a limited view of emotional processes. Not only are they allotted few pages relative to physiological and cognitive processes, but the central focus tends to be on the debate over whether emotions have any inherent meaning or are simply labels that we apply to general states of physiological arousal (Cannon, 1927; James, 1890; Schachter & Singer, 1962). This latter view was popularized by the Schachter and Singer study, which attempted to manipulate participants into giving up their own perceptions and emotional reactions and accepting the experimenters' definitions of what was going on. Though the study's findings are highly questionable (Burrows, 1975), the theory has influenced many areas of current social psychology research (such as self-perception, attribution, and interpersonal attraction), in a way that reflects this culture's masculine gender role stereotype of feelings as something to be denied, controlled, or reasoned away.

The instructor may wish to provide supplementary information about innate emotional processes, the importance of emotional expression in our daily lives, and the ways that gender role socialization affects how we experience and express our emotions. Evidence for innate emotional processes can be found in the work of Ekman and his colleagues (Ekman, Levenson, & Friesen, 1983; Ekman, Sorenson, & Friesen, 1969), Izard (1977), Tompkins (1962, 1963), and in the infancy literature (Sroufe, 1979). Bronstein (1984) reviewed the evidence for the importance of emotional expression for healthy physical as well as psychological functioning, and Nichols and Zax (1977) discussed the role of catharsis in clinical work. Jourard (1971) presented a compelling argument that denial and suppression of feelings in men shorten their life span. Research revealing differential perceptions of and reactions to emotions in girls and boys is reviewed by Bronstein (1984).

Gender Roles

In addition to integrating information about gender into many aspects of the course, the instructor may include a discussion of what it means to be female or male. Readings that can work well (or which can be used elsewhere in the course) are Gould's (1972) wonderful tale of nonsexist child rearing and descriptions of gender-role behaviors by Miller (1976), Doyle (1983), Pleck (1981), Pleck and Brannon (1978), and Pleck and Sawyer (1974). It can also be useful to provide readings and discussions on role changes that women and men are currently experiencing. Baruch et al.'s (1983) in-depth study of women's work and family lives is a good resource as are first-person accounts of women's struggles to develop career identities (Chicago, 1977; Ruddick & Daniels, 1977). Current perspectives on men's changing role in the family are offered by Bronstein and Cowan (1988). The instructor may also wish to consider the meaning and measurement of the constructs masculinity, femininity, and androgyny (Bem, 1976; Lott, 1981; Moraw-ski, 1987; Spence, Helmreich, & Stapp, 1975), since these constructs have become a popular focus of personality and social psychology research. In addition, the class can explore how differences in verbal and nonverbal behaviors relate to societal roles (Thorne & Henley, 1975; LaFrance & Carmen, 1980; Mayo & Henley, 1981; Quina, Wingard, & Bates, 1987).

Projects and Exercises

Suggestions for gender-relevant discussion topics, projects, and exercises that can be used in teaching the introductory psychology course can be found in Golub and Freedman (1987) and in Russo and Malovich (1980). In addition, suggestions for gender- and culture-related experiential learning can be found in many of the chapters in this volume and in texts by Paludi (in press) and Benjamin and Lowman (1981). Sample projects and exercises are provided below.

Projects

We have found that small research projects can enhance students' awareness of the impact of gender-role socialization while giving them a hands-on introduction to the research process. Students can be instructed to unobtrusively observe parent–child interaction in public places such as supermarkets, bowling alleys, shoe stores, restaurants, and museums and to code frequencies of particular behaviors that parents may show to girls versus boys or of child behaviors that may reveal gender differences. For example, a student in one of our classes who observed parents and children at a McDonald's found that parents more often kept girls with them and ordered for them, whereas boys were more often allowed to wander off and to order for themselves. Another type of research that is easy for students to do yet also very informative is a content analysis that focuses on gender-relevant variables in some product of the culture such as children's books, magazine ads, comic strips, television commercials, talk shows, and pop song lyrics. Other projects have included gender-relevant naturalistic observations of peers (in bars, in class, on sports teams, in line at the movies) and questionnaires administered to peers to tap differences in attitudes, self-perceptions, or feelings. One student created "projective" collages out of magazine pictures to investigate gender differences in responses to images of power, violence, and intimacy. Some of the above projects can be adapted to illustrate cultural differences, stereotyping, and prejudice; for example, students can observe and compare social behaviors in different ethnic neighborhoods or analyze portrayals of ethnic minorities or the elderly on television shows or commercials.

Careful instructions and supervision are necessary for students to carry out such projects in a meaningful and ethical way. First, it is important for the instructor to educate students about observer bias, experimenter effects (Rosenthal, 1966), and ethics in research and to emphasize that finding no gender differences can be just as meaningful (and earn just as high a grade) as finding differences. Otherwise, it is not uncommon to have beginning students' results and interpretations turn out strongly in the direction that they think the instructor would prefer. Second, procedures involving the active participation of subjects (even if it is only the roommates and friends of the student) will usually necessitate obtaining their informed consent. And third, any instrument or procedure to be used with subjects must be carefully scrutinized by the instructor in advance, not only for potential effectiveness but for elements that may be inappropriate or distressing. Thus, to ensure that the research experience is a fruitful one, it is best to have students submit detailed proposals (including any instruments) in advance for the instructor's approval.

Exercises

Class exercises can also give students a sense of the research process by providing the experience of being researcher and subject simultaneously while also highlighting gender- or culture-related topics in psychology. The following are some examples of exercises that will usually elicit differences in attitudes and perceptions related to sociocultural factors.

Stereotyping and prejudice. As an introduction to studying stereotyping and prejudice (and if possible, before students have been exposed to readings or lectures on these topics), students can be asked to respond to anecdotes such as the following one. They are done anonymously in class, with no explanation provided in advance, and collected and tabulated by the instructor immediately afterwards.

> On August 4, 1983, Claire Owens, 28, of Cedardale, Iowa, reported to the local police that she had seen an unidentified flying object. She told Sgt. Harold Feakes that she had been walking home from a neighbor's about 2 hours after sunset, when suddenly there had been a flash of light beyond the clump of woods that borders on the back of her property. She reported that a "warm eerie glow" seemed to bathe the whole wooded area, then there was a rushing sound, as a gush of air swirled around her, and then, just as suddenly, darkness and silence. After a while, she said, she heard strange noises: "Almost like voices, but not like any human voices I've ever heard. I'm sure there was something out there—I know it!" she told Sgt. Feakes. Investigation by the police, however, has thus far failed to turn up evidence of any environmental disturbance.
> Which do you think is most likely?
> Claire Owens _____ may have seen a UFO
>   _____ probably saw some unusual natural phenomenon but not a UFO

_____ probably imagined or fantasized the experience
_____ probably made it up, to get some attention
or notoriety

One third of the class is given the above version. Another third is given the same version, except that the subject's age has been changed to 68. In the version given to the final third, no age is given in the first sentence, and the second sentence begins, "She told Sgt. Harold Feakes that she had been sitting on her back porch in her wheelchair, about 2 hours after sunset, when suddenly. . . ." The 28-year-old Claire Owens will generally be viewed as more credible than either the 68-year-old or the disabled one, providing students with an immediate demonstration of their own stereotypes about the elderly and the disabled. Obviously, character-istics such as gender and ethnicity can also be varied depending on the point the instructor wishes to illustrate. Other anecdotes that have worked well have de-scribed a person attempting to return a faulty final-sale article of clothing to a store or going on a job interview, with different versions varying the ethnicity or social class of the protagonist (by changing the name or the description of clothes and appearance) or the gender. Students are given a range of choices requiring them to judge whether the saleperson should accept the returned article of cloth-ing and whether the interviewer should hire the applicant.

Effects of sexism. Today's undergraduates will often in class discussion ex-press the view that although sexism was a problem of the previous generation, it has not impacted on their lives, and that women of their generation have the same opportunities and expectations as men. To shake the foundation of these beliefs and promote lively discussion, students can be asked (before any discussion of sexism takes place) to list all the reasons they can think of for why they might want to be the opposite sex and, when they are finished, to list all the reasons they can think of for wanting to be the sex they are. The exercise is done anonymously, with students indicating only whether they are male or female. When they are finished with the second list, they are then asked to count the number of items on each list and write this total at the bottom of the respective page. The instructor then collects the lists, writes the student totals on the board under each of the four possibilities—males being female, females being male, males being male, and females being female—and computes a mean for each list (if it is a large class, the instructor can simply examine only a third or half of the responses). Females will generally be able to think of more reasons to want to be male than males will be able to think of reasons to want to be female, and the difference (if any) in the number of reasons for wanting to be one's own gender will also provide provoca-tive material for discussion. Samples of the lists' content can also be shared with the class at that time, or the instructor may wish to take time between classes to summarize the contents before presenting them for additional discussion.

Gender and emotion. To illustrate the effects of gender-role socialization on the experiencing and expression of emotion, students can be asked to keep a daily log over the period of a week of the following:

1.   How often they feel sad or hurt, how often they cry, whether they cry alone or with another person present, whether that other person is female or male, and how that person reacts to their crying; and

2.   How often they feel angry, how often they express that anger at or in the presence of another person, whether that other person is female or male, and how that person reacts to their anger.

The exercise can provide enhanced self-awareness of students' own emotional processes and meaningful small-group or whole-class discussion of gender and emotion, especially if the instructor gives students a summary of the self-reports compiled according to gender.

Conclusion

At present, we believe that there is no model Introduction to Psychology course. Many of the theories and much of the research literature of traditional psychology are being challenged and amended by scholars who have recognized that the field has had a narrow focus on a small segment of human society (e.g., Denmark, 1983). Now must come a time of exploration, openness, and creativity, when no topics are taken entirely for granted as static major areas in the field and new approaches and questions are not dismissed as being unworthy of consideration or "not psychology." Social issues, historical events, anthropological reports, literature, and individual experience all can inform the study of psychology and be integrated into the introductory course. Such integration can help students learn that human behavior exists not in a vacuum but within a social and cultural context and that individuals and cultures interact and continue to shape one another. With these ideas as guiding principles, the introductory psychology course can play an important role in helping students to understand themselves and others, to welcome diversity into their lives, and to become more socially aware and active participants in a changing world.

References

Abad, V., & Boyce, E. (1979). Issues in psychiatric evaluations of Puerto Ricans: A sociocultural perspective. *Journal of Operational Psychiatry, 10*(1), 28–39.

Albee, G. W. (1982). Preventing psychopathology and promoting human potential. *American Psychologist, 37,* 1043–1050.

Al-Issa, I., & Dennis, W. (Eds.). (1970). *Cross-cultural studies of behavior.* New York: Holt, Rinehart & Winston.

Barry, H., Bacon, M. K., & Child, I. L. (1957). A cross-cultural survey of some sex differences in socialization. *Journal of Abnormal & Social Psychology, 55,* 327–332.

Baruch, G., Barnett, R., & Rivers, C. (1983). *Lifeprints: New patterns of love and work for today's women.* New York: McGraw-Hill.

Belenky, M. F., Clinchy, B. M., Goldberger, N. R., & Tarule, J. M. (1986). *Women's way of knowing: The development of self, voice, and mind.* New York: Basic Books.

Bem, S. L. (1976). Beyond androgyny: Some presumptuous prescriptions for a liberated sexual identity. In J. Sherman & F. Denmark (Eds.), *Psychology of women: Future directions of research* (pp. 1–23). New York: Psychological Dimensions.

Benbow, C. P., & Stanley, J. C. (1983). Sex differences in mathematical reasoning: More facts. *Science, 222,* 1029–1031.

Benjamin, L. T., & Lowman, K. D. (Eds.). (1981). *Activities handbook for the teaching of psychology.* Washington DC: American Psychological Association.

Bernay, T., & Cantor, D. W. (Eds.). (1986). *The psychology of today's women: New psychoanalytic visions.* Hillsdale, NJ: Analytic Press.

Bickman, L. (1971). The effect of social status on the honesty of others. In L. Bickman & T. Henchy (Eds.), *Beyond the laboratory: Field research in social psychology* (pp. 102–104). New York: McGraw-Hill.

Bleier, R. (1984). *Sex and gender: A critique of biology and its theories on women.* New York: Pergamon Press.

Block, J. H. (1983). Differential premises arising from differential socialization of the sexes: Some conjectures. *Child Development, 54,* 1335–1354.

Briggs, J. L. (1970). *Never in anger.* Cambridge, MA: Harvard University Press.

Bronstein-Burrows, P. (1981, August). *Introductory psychology: A course in the psychology of both sexes.* Presented at the annual meeting of the American Psychological Association, Los Angeles.

Bronstein, P. (1984). Promoting healthy emotional development in children. *Journal of Primary Prevention, 5*(2), 92–110.

Bronstein, P. (1988). Father–child interaction: Implications for gender role socialization. In P. Bronstein & C. P. Cowan (Eds.), *Fatherhood today: Men's changing role in the family* (pp. 107–124). New York: Wiley.

Bronstein, P., & Cowan, C. (Eds.). (1988). *Fatherhood today: Men's changing role in the family.* New York: Wiley.

Broverman, I. K., Broverman, D. M., Clarkson, F. E., Rosenkrantz, P. S., & Vogel, S. R. (1970). Sex-role stereotypes and clinical judgments of mental health. *Journal of Consulting and Clinical Psychology, 34*(1), 1–7.

Burrows, P. (1975). A critical analysis of Schachter and Singer's "Cognitive, social, and physiological determinants of emotional state." Unpublished manuscript, Harvard University.

Cannon, W. B. (1927). *Bodily changes in pain, hunger, fear, and rage* (rev. ed.) New York: Appleton-Century.

Caplan, P. J., MacPherson, G. M., & Tobin, P. (1985). Do sex-related differences in spatial abilities exist? A multilevel critique with new data. *American Psychologist, 40,* 786–799.

Chicago, J. (1977). *Through the flower: My struggle as a woman artist.* Garden City, NY: Anchor Books.

Chipman, S. F., Brush, L. R., & Wilson, D. M. (Eds.). (1985). *Women and mathematics: Balancing the equation.* Hillsdale, NJ: Erlbaum.

Chodorow, N. J. (1978). *The reproduction of mothering: Psychoanalysis and the sociology of gender.* Berkeley, CA: University of California Press.

Davidoff, L. L. (1987). *Introduction to psychology* (3rd ed.). New York: McGraw-Hill.

Denmark, F. L. (1983). Integrating the psychology of women into introductory psychology. In C. J. Scherere & A. R. Rogers (Eds.), *The G. Stanley Hall Lecture Series* (Vol. 3, pp. 37–71). Washington, DC: American Psychological Association.

Dinnerstein, D. (1976). *The mermaid and the minotaur: Sexual arrangements and human malaise.* New York: Harper & Row.

Dohrenwend, B. P., & Dohrenwend, B. S. (1974). Social and cultural influences on psychopathology. *Annual Review of Psychology, 25,* 417–452.

Doyle, J. A. (1983). *The male experience.* Dubuque, IA: William C. Brown.

Duley, M. I., Sinclair, K., & Edwards, M. I. (1986). Biology versus culture. In M. I. Duley & M. I. Edwards (Eds.), *The cross-cultural study of women: A comprehensive guide* (pp. 3–25). New York: Feminist Press.

Eccles, J. S., & Jacobs, J. E. (1986). Social forces shape math attitudes and performance. *Signs: Journal of Women in Culture and Society, 11*(21), 367–389.

Ekman, P., Levenson, R. W., & Frieson, W. V. (1983). Autonomic nervous system activity distinguishes among emotions. *Science, 221,* 1208–1210.

Ekman, P., Sorenson, E. R., & Friesen, W. V. (1969). Pan-cultural elements in facial displays of emotion. *Science, 164,* 86–88.

Fausto-Sterling, A. (1985). *Myths of gender: Biological theories about women and men.* New York: Basic Books.

Feldman, R. J. (1987). *Understanding psychology*. New York: McGraw-Hill.

Fennema, E., & Peterson, P. (1985). Autonomous learning behavior: A possible explanation of gender-related differences in mathematics. In L. C. Wilkinson & C. B. Marrett (Eds.), *Gender influences in classroom interaction* (pp. 1–14). Orlando, FL: Academic Press.

Franks, V., & Rothblum, E. (Eds.). (1983). *The stereotyping of women: Its effects on mental health*. New York: Springer.

Gaertner, S., & Bickman, L. (1971). A nonreactive indicator of racial discrimination: The wrong number technique. In L. Bickman & T. Henchy (Eds.), *Beyond the laboratory: Field research in social psychology* (pp. 162–169). New York: McGraw-Hill.

Garner, S. N., Kahane, C., & Sprengnether, M. (Eds.). (1985). The *(m)other tongue: Essays in feminist psychoanalytic interpretation*. Ithaca, NY: Cornell University Press.

Gilligan, C. (1982). *In a different voice: Psychological theory and women's development*. Cambridge, MA: Harvard University Press.

Golub, S., & Freedman, R. J. (1987). *Psychology of women: Resources for a core curriculum*. New York: Garland.

Gould, L. (1972). X: A fabulous child's story. *Ms., 1* (6), pp. 74–76, 105–106.

Halpern, D. (1986). *Sex differences in cognitive abilities*. Hillsdale, NJ: Erlbaum.

Hyde, J. S. (1985). *Half the human experience*. Lexington, MA: Heath.

Irvine, J. J. (1985). Teacher communication patterns as related to the race and sex of the student. *Journal of Educational Research, 78*(6), 338–345.

Izard, C. E. (1977). *Human emotions*. New York: Plenum Press.

James, W. (1890). *Principles of psychology*. New York: Henry Holt.

Jensen, A. R. (1969). How much can we boost IQ and scholastic achievement? *Harvard Educational Review, 39*, 1–123.

Jones, E. E., & Korchin, S. J. (1982). *Minority mental health*. New York: Praeger.

Jourard, S. M. (1971). *The transparent self*. New York: Van Nostrand.

Kimura, D. (1985, November). Male brain, female brain: The hidden difference. *Psychology Today*, pp. 50–58.

Korchin, S. J. (1980). Clinical psychology and minority problems. *American Psychologist, 35*(3), 262–269.

LaFrance, M., & Carmen, B. (1980). The nonverbal display of psychological androgyny. *Journal of Personality and Social Psychology, 38*, 36–49.

Lerman, H. (1986). *A mote in Freud's eye: From psychoanalysis to the psychology of women*. New York: Springer.

LeVine, R. A. (1974). *Culture and personality: Contemporary readings*. New York: Aldine.

Lewis, H. B. (1986). Is Freud an enemy of women's liberation? Some historical considerations. In T. Bernay & D. W. Cantor (Eds.), *The psychology of today's woman: New psychoanalytic visions* (pp. 7–35). Hillsdale, NJ: Analytic Press.

Lewontin, R. C., Rose, S., & Kamin, L. J. (1984). *Not in our genes: Biology, ideology, and human nature*. New York: Pantheon.

Linn, M. C., & Petersen, A. C. (1986). A meta-analysis of gender differences in spatial ability: Implications for mathematics and science achievement. In J. S. Hyde & M. C. Linn (Eds.). *The psychology of gender: Advances through meta-analysis* (pp. 67–101). Baltimore, MD: The Johns Hopkins University Press.

Lott, B. (1981). A feminist critique of androgyny: Toward the elimination of gender attributions for learned behavior. In C. Mayo & N. M. Henley (Eds.), *Gender and nonverbal behavior* (pp. 171–180). New York: Springer-Verlag.

Lott, B. (1985). The potential enrichment of social/personality psychology through feminist research and vice versa. *American Psychologist, 40*, 155–164.

Lykes, M. B., & Stewart, A. J. (1986). Evaluating the feminist challenge to research in personality and social psychology: 1963–1983. *Psychology of Women Quarterly, 10*(4), 393–411.

Marsella, A. J., & White, G. M. (1982). *Cultural conceptions of mental health and therapy*. London: Reidel.

Matlin, M. (1987). *The psychology of women*. New York: Holt, Rinehart & Winston.

Mayo, C., & Henley, N. M. (Eds.). (1981). *Gender and nonverbal behavior*. New York: Springer-Verlag.

Mays, V. M., & Cochran, S. D. (1987, March). *Mental health concerns of Black lesbians.* Presented at the annual meeting of the Association for Women in Psychology, Denver.

Mead, M. (1979). On Freud's views of female psychology. In J. Williams (Ed.), *Psychology of women: Selected readings* (pp. 53–61). New York: Norton.

Mead, M. (1935). *Sex and temperament in three primitive societies.* New York: William Morrow.

Messing, K. (1983). The scientific mystique: Can a white lab coat guarantee purity in the search for knowledge about the nature of women? In M. Lowe & R. Hubbard (Eds.), *Women's nature: Rationalizations of inequality* (pp. 75–88). New York: Pergamon Press.

Milgram, S. (1974). *Obedience to authority.* New York: Harper & Row.

Miller, J. B. (1976). *Toward a new psychology of women.* Boston: Beacon Press.

Morawski, J. G. (1987). The troubled quest for masculinity, femininity, and androgyny. In P. Shaver & C. Hendrick (Eds.), *Sex and gender: Review of personality and social psychology* (Vol. 7). Newbury Park, CA: Sage.

Murphy, J. M. (1976). Psychiatric labeling in cross-cultural perspective. *Science, 191,* 1019–1028.

Murphy, J. M., & Leighton, A. H. (1965). Native conceptions of psychiatric disorder. In J. M. Murphy, & A. H. Leighton (Eds.), *Approaches to cross-cultural psychiatry* (pp. 3–20). Ithaca, NY: Cornell University Press.

Murray Research Center News (1987, Fall). Cambridge, MA: The Henry A. Murray Research Center of Radcliffe College.

Nichols, M. P., & Zax, M. (1977). *Catharsis in psychotherapy.* New York: Gardner.

Paludi, M. A. (1985). Sex and gender similarities and differences and the young child. In C. McLoughlin & D. F. Gullo (Eds.), *Young children in context.* Springfield, IL: Charles C. Thomas.

Paludi, M. A. (1987, August). *Teaching psychological statistics: A feminist restructuring of the curriculum.* Presented at the annual meeting of the American Psychological Association, New York.

Paludi, M. A. (in press). *Teaching the psychology of women: A manual of resources.* Albany: State University of New York Press.

Paludi, M. A., & Gullo, D. F. (1986). The effect of sex labels on adults' knowledge of infant development. *Sex Roles, 16,* 19–30.

Pleck, J. H. (1981). *The myth of masculinity.* Cambridge, MA: MIT Press.

Pleck, J. H., & Brannon, R. (Eds.). (1978). Male roles and the male experience [Special issue]. *Journal of Social Issues, 34*(1).

Pleck, J. H., & Sawyer, J. (Eds.). (1974). *Men and masculinity.* Englewood Cliffs, NJ: Prentice-Hall.

Quina, K., Wingard, J. A., & Bates, H. G. (1987). Language style and gender stereotypes in person perception. *Psychology of Women Quarterly, 11*(1), 111–122.

Raymond, C. L., & Benbow, C. P. (1986). Gender differences in mathematics: A function of parental support and student sex typing? *Developmental Psychology, 22*(6), 808–819.

Rosenthal, R. (1966). *Experimenter effects in behavioral research.* New York: Appleton-Century-Crofts.

Rosser, P. (1987). *Sex bias in college admissions tests: Why women lose out.* National Center For Fair and Open Testing, Cambridge, MA.

Rubin, J. Z., Provenzano, F. J., & Luria, Z. (1974). The eye of the beholder: Parents' views on sex of newborns. *American Journal of Orthopsychiatry, 44*(4), 512–519.

Ruddick, S., & Daniels, P. (Eds.). (1977). *Working it out: 23 women writers, artists, scientists, and scholars talk about their lives and work.* New York: Pantheon Books.

Russo, N. F., & Malovich, N. J. (1980). Assessing the introductory psychology course. In J. M. Gappa & J. Pearce (Eds.), *Sex and gender in the social sciences: Reassessing the introductory course.* Washington, DC: American Psychological Association.

Sadker, M., & Sadker, D. (1985, March). Sexism in the schoolroom of the 80s. *Psychology Today,* pp. 54–57.

Schachter, S., & Singer, J. E. (1962). Cognitive, social, and physiological determinants of emotional state. *Psychological Review, 69,* 379–399.

Selkow, P. (1984). *Assessing sex bias in testing: A review of the issues and evaluations of 74 psychological and educational tests.* Westport, CT: Greenwood.

Sherman, J., & Beck, E. (Eds.). (1979). *The prism of sex.* Madison: University of Wisconsin Press.

Simons, J. A., Irwin, D. B., & Drinnin, B. A. (1987). *Psychology: The search for understanding.* St. Paul, MN: West.

Snarey, J. (1985). Cross-cultural universality of social-moral development: A critical review of Kohlbergian research. *Psychological Bulletin, 97,* 202–232.

Spence, J. T., Helmreich, R., & Stapp, J. (1975). Ratings of self and peers on sex-role attributes and their relation to self-esteem and conceptions of masculinity and femininity. *Journal of Personality and Social Psychology, 32,* 29–39.

Sroufe, A. L. (1979). Socioemotional development. In J. D. Osofsky (Ed.), *Handbook of infant development* (pp. 462–516). New York: Wiley.

Tavris, C., & Wade, C. (1984). *The longest war: Sex differences in perspective* (2nd ed.). New York: Harcourt Brace Jovanovich.

Thorne, B., & Henley, N. (Eds.). (1975). *Language and sex: Difference and dominance.* Rowley, MA: Newbury House.

Tompkins, S. S. (1962). *Affect/imagery/consciousness: Vol. 1. The positive affects.* New York: Springer.

Tompkins, S. S. (1963). *Affect/imagery/consciousness: Vol 2. The negative affects.* New York: Springer.

Wade, C., & Tavris, C. (1987). *Psychology.* New York: Harper & Row.

Wallston, B. S., & Grady, K. E. (1985). Integrating the feminist critique and the crisis in social psychology: Another look at research methods. In V. E. O'Leary, R. K. Unger, & B. S. Wallston (Eds.), *Women, gender, and social psychology* (pp. 7–33). Hillsdale, NJ: Erlbaum.

Wener, R., Frazier, W., & Farbstein, J. (1987, June). Building better jails. *Psychology Today,* pp. 40–44.

Weskott, M. (1986). *The feminist legacy of Karen Horney.* New Haven, CT: Yale University Press.

Whiting, J. W. M. (1961). Socialization process and personality. In F. L. K. Hsu (Ed.), *Psychological anthropology: Approaches to culture and personality* (pp. 355–380). Homewood, IL: Dorsey Press.

Whiting, B. B., & Whiting, J. W. M. (1975). *Children of six cultures: A psychocultural analysis.* Cambridge, MA: Harvard University Press.

Wilkinson, L. C., & Marrett, C. B. (1985). *Gender influences in classroom interaction.* Orlando, FL: Academic Press.

Williams, J. (1983). *Psychology of women: Behavior in a biosocial context* (2nd ed.). New York: Norton.

Wortman, C. B., & Loftus, E. F. (1985). *Psychology* (2nd ed.). New York: Knopf.

Zimbardo, P. G. (1985). *Psychology and life* (11th ed.). Glenview, IL: Scott, Foresman.

Zimbardo, P. G., Haney, C., & Banks, W. C. (1973, April 8). A Pirandellian prison. *The New York Times Magazine,* pp. 38–60.

4 ——

Hope Landrine

Revising the Framework
of Abnormal Psychology

In teaching abnormal psychology, clinical psychologists generally approach the subject matter with an implicit framework that determines what will and will not be taught in the course. This framework, which is perpetuated by our abnormal psychology textbooks, has traditionally viewed ethnicity, gender, and social class as largely peripheral to concepts of psychopathology and has virtually ignored the historical and contemporary context of power relations in which such concepts are constructed. Although new texts with broader and more accurate social, historical, and cultural accounts of psychopathology are needed, we can restructure our courses to compensate for some of the existing deficiencies. This chapter provides information and resources to compensate for two significant deficiencies in our texts: the role of misogyny and racism in the development of concepts of psychopathology and the relevance of social and cultural variables to contemporary concepts of normalcy and abnormalcy.

Historical Perspective

Two important events—the persecution of witches and slavery— provide the historical bases upon which current clinical frameworks regarding women and Blacks, respectively, have been built.

Witches and Women

In their sections on the history of psychopathology, all major abnormal psychology texts include a discussion of witches. Although the texts vary, all of them say something like this: In the Middle Ages a relatively small number of women (and a few men) told the Inquisition that they had relationships with and were possessed by the Devil. Inquisitors accepted these confessions at face value and responded to the assertions of demonic possession with torture and execution. Early psychiatry offered the "insight" that these women were not possessed by the Devil, but were possessed by psychopathology. Their statements were delusions or hallucinations, the products of hysterical or psychotic conditions. These were severely disturbed women who had needed treatment, not torture.

This presentation of witches in abnormal and in many introductory psychology texts is one that I read as an undergraduate and that students still read today. However, it is inconsistent with historical scholarship. Many historians argue that the women who were tortured and burned as witches were in fact members of an ancient and widespread matriarchal religion (Murray, 1921) that celebrated women and practiced medicine. They used herbs to cure disease, acted as midwives, performed abortions, gave counsel, used their organic potions to relieve pain (Ehrenreich & English, 1973; Forbes, 1966), and advised people against eating sugar, at a time when the Catholic Church had a major financial investment in it and was advocating its use (Dufty, 1975). As such, they were knowledgeable, respected, and feared women whose effective therapeutic interventions cast aspersions on and undermined the authority of the Church (Dufty, 1975; Szasz, 1970). For these and similar reasons related to power, women hating, and economics, the Church led an assault on witches and their followers. Under torture many confessed to hearing, seeing, and having intercourse with the Devil, and an estimated 9 million women in 7 countries were burned at the stake as heretics (Dworkin, 1974; Szasz, 1970).

Contemporary clinicians perpetuate the fabrication that the women burned as witches were mad and use confessions removed from their context of torture as evidence for that madness (Szasz, 1970). Zilboorg and Henry's (1941) history of medical psychology proclaimed that the witches were hysterics and psychotics. Alexander and Selesnick's (1966) classic history of psychopathology text informed us that a witch's confessions (e.g., "I have intercourse with the devil") were admissions of her sexual fantasies and were given publicly to an audience of men so that she could achieve sexual gratification yet simultaneously relieve her guilt about those fantasies. When our students read in their abnormal psychology texts that an epidemic of madness once mysteriously overcame millions of women, they may interpret this misinformation as historical evidence for the inherent madness of women.

Instructors can correct this erroneous impression by presenting an accurate historical summary and by assigning Szasz's (1970) paperback along with the main text to the course. Szasz gave a detailed account of the persecution of the witches and the clinical construction of them as mad, although he presented their persecution as almost entirely religious and failed to grasp the misogynist intents of the Inquisitors. In addition, Szasz discussed the psychiatric persecution of gays; the racist and bizarre theories of Benjamin Rush, father of the medical model; and the social consequences of receiving a psychiatric diagnosis. Thus, the book touches on social issues that are either ignored or mentioned only in passing in abnormal psychology texts. Additional discussions can lead students to raise questions about the role of social and political factors in contemporary diagnoses of psychopathology in women, categories such as hysteria, dependent personality, and agoraphobia typically labeled as female.

Slaves and Blacks

Abnormal psychology texts as well as the histories of psychopathology upon which they depend generally include no clinical theories regarding Blacks or slavery. Interestingly, slaves stood in the spotlight of clinical attention at one time and had a substantial amount of clinical theory focused on them. In the early 1800s, Samuel Cartwright, a prominent physician, theorized that there were two forms of psychopathology that were frequent among the slaves, *drapetomania* and *dysathesia aethiopica*, both nerve disorders. Drapetomania consisted of a single symptom, that the slave ran away. Dysathesia aethiopica, on the other hand, consisted of a constellation of symptoms, including destroying plantation property, talking back, fighting with or attacking masters, and procrastinating or refusing to work. Dysathesia aethiopica was also known as "rascality" (Stampp, 1956). In the clinical framework, sanity for a slave was synonymous with submission, and protest and seeking freedom were the equivalent of psychopathology. Although these categories were never added to the existing clinical taxonomy, the ideological framework persisted into this century.

The sixth U.S. census in 1840 reported that Blacks in the northern states had far higher rates of psychopathology than Blacks in the slave states. The clinicians of the day interpreted these data to mean that the care, supervision, and control provided by slavery were essential to the mental health of Blacks. Slavery was defended as good for Blacks in the name of mental health (Deutsch, 1944). Even though Jarvis (cited in Deutsch, 1944) later demonstrated that the census data were fabricated, the data remained uncorrected. For the next few decades, clinicians continued to advance the theory that freedom was the etiology of psychopathology among Blacks and supported their theory with data known to be fraudulent (Thomas & Sillen, 1972). Meanwhile, many clinicians refused to admit Blacks to mental hospitals, and with few exceptions Blacks who actually were disturbed were simply jailed (Dain, 1964).

After emancipation and through the early 1900s, clinicians advanced theories whose sole and unambiguous intent was to justify segregation on mental health grounds. For example, mainstream theoretical giants such as William Alanson White, G. Stanley Hall, William McDougall, and Eugene Bleuler theorized the following: Blacks had failed to reach the evolutionary stage of Whites; they existed at a psychosocial level not easily distinguishable from dementia praecox and were thereby prone to schizophrenia, if not intrinsically schizophrenic; and being innately happy-go-lucky and emotionally simple, they were immune to depression (Morais, 1967; Thomas & Sillen, 1972). Jung added to this view his belief that the effect on Whites of living with what he regarded as a sexualized, lower race was to pull Whites in that direction; that the presence of Blacks endangered White American mental health and made sexual repression a necessity; and that segregation was thereby necessary for maintaining the mental health of White Americans (Thomas & Sillen, 1972).

Contemporary clinicians, using a different language, appear to have maintained these racist concepts. They have argued that Blacks are lacking in ego strength and are culturally deprived, nonverbal, concrete, hostile, unmotivated, religious, and paranoid while at the same time essentially immune to depression (Sabshin, Diesenhaus, & Wilkerson, 1970). This immunity is no longer attributed to their innate happy-go-lucky nature but to their having nothing to lose—no jobs, property, or esteem (Prange & Vitols, 1962). Thus, clinicians continue to misdiagnose depressed Blacks as schizophrenic (Simon & Fleiss, 1973). When Wilson and Lantz (1957) theorized that a successful civil rights movement would create madness in Blacks (because of the loss of a "well-defined status"), they echoed the notion that freedom seeking and protest are synonymous with psychopathology for Blacks. The etiology was now no longer dysathesia aethiopica. A 1967 article on the role of brain disease in urban riots, published in the *Journal of the American Medical Association,* pointed to a modern neurological disorder, *temporal lobe dysfunction,* for which recommended treatment, for Blacks, was psychosurgery (Mark, Sweet, & Ervin, 1967).

Inclusion of this information in psychology courses will give students a more complete picture of the sociopolitical context, particularly the role of racism, in concepts of psychopathology. In addition to the resources cited in this summary, Chapters 1 and 10 of Thomas and Sillen (1972) are especially useful. Further information on the impact of ethnicity and race on psychopathology and psychotherapy, and curriculum guidelines for integrating this information into existing courses, can be found in texts by Chunn, Dunston, and Ross-Sheriff (1983) and Jones and Korchin (1982).

Contemporary Perspective

Contemporary concepts of normalcy and psychopathology perpetuate the construction of the behavior of minorities and women as pathological along with the view that culture is peripheral to psychopathology. Thus, another important responsibility is to help students understand the sociocultural foundations of our concepts of normalcy and psychopathology.

Normalcy

The term *normal* suggests, among other things, an individual who exhibits abstract and logical thinking, emotional control, independence, delay of gratification, happiness, a concern with developing one's own potential to the fullest, and a sense of the self as an autonomous individual who exerts personal control over self and environment (Jourard, 1974; Offer & Sabshin, 1966). It is crucial that students understand that this concept is irrelevant to many people in this country and, indeed, in the world. For example, the sense of the self described above—from which many of the other characteristics derive—is not how the poor experience the self (Sennett & Cobb, 1972), how Blacks experience the self (Nobles, 1980), how Asian Americans experience the self (Marsella, DeVos, & Hsu, 1985; see also Chapter 15 by Tsai and Uemura in this volume), how women experience the self (Gilligan, 1977), or how most people throughout the world experience the self (Shweder & Bourne, 1982). This concept of normalcy, held by the U.S. lay public and professionals alike, is a cultural one, which is largely synonymous with the characteristics of upper income White men in this country (Marsella & White, 1982) and is firmly rooted in the social meanings shared by middle-class White Americans (Chapman & Chapman, 1967; Marsella & White, 1982; Townsend, 1978).

To help students understand these assertions regarding normalcy, the instructor might begin the course by repeating a recent experiment of mine (Landrine, 1987b). I gave case descriptions, which were actually stereotypes of a variety of social groups (but without gender, cultural, or ethnic details specified), to a sample of PhD and MD clinicians and asked them to provide diagnoses. Although the clinicians labeled the stereotype of upper-class White American men as prototypically normal, *none* of them considered the stereotype of any other group to be normal. Stereotypes of women were diagnosed as hysterical, dependent personality, or neurotic depression; stereotypic lower-class speech patterns were labeled schizophrenic; and stereotypic young lower-class men were labeled antisocial. Having students judge the normalcy of several stereotypes will help them understand that our concept of normalcy is culturally based; that women, minorities, and the poor can easily be judged pathological; and that gender, ethnicity, and social class are inherent in definitions of normalcy and psychopathology.

Psychopathology

Abnormal psychology textbooks make little or no reference to the epidemiology of the disorders that they describe. Those that mention epidemiology do not present the theories that attempt to account for epidemiological patterns or the empirical tests of those theories. As a result, students receive the impression that psychological disorders are essentially randomly distributed when in fact they are reliably predicted by gender, ethnicity, and socioeconomic status.

There are numerous reliable epidemiological patterns. Hysterical, dependent, and borderline personalities (Kaplan, 1983); depressives (Rothblum, 1983); and phobics (Brehony, 1983; Marks, 1969) are usually women. On the other hand, substance abusers (Chesler, 1972; Gove, 1980) and antisocial, narcissistic, paranoid, and compulsive personalities (Kass, Spitzer, & Williams, 1983) are usually men. In addition, schizophrenics are usually lower-income and are more likely to be Black or female (Taube, 1971; Warheit, Holzer, & Arey, 1975), and the overall rate of psychopathology in women is higher than that of men. These findings, however, must be viewed in light of the data on marital status: Single, divorced, and widowed women generally have lower rates of psychopathology than their male counterparts. In contrast, married women generally have a rate of disorder that far exceeds that of married men, and they account for the overall higher female rate of psychopathology (Gove, 1972).

Introducing these epidemiological data will raise questions for students regarding the social and political meanings of psychopathology. The rates for many different types of psychopathology by sex and marital status, for example, raise sociohistorical questions because they preclude genetic explanations based on individual deficiencies or on gender per se as a biological determinant of psychopathology. Using these data, the instructor can help students generate social and political hypotheses aimed at understanding abnormality in its context of gender, race, and class. Hypotheses generated by students will invariably include those that have already been suggested (e.g., Gove, 1972; Kaplan, 1983; Phillips & Segal, 1969) and rejected on empirical grounds (e.g., Abramowitz & Dockeci, 1977; Gove, 1980; Kass et al., 1983; Stricker, 1977).

Once these ideas have been considered, the instructor might then present alternative hypotheses—those that discuss the relation between specific disorders and the roles or cultures of the groups that tend to exhibit those disorders (Landrine, 1987b). Another exercise can help students understand these alternative hypotheses (Landrine, 1987a; 1987b): Students are given verbatim descriptions of disorders from the *Diagnostic and Statistical Manual of Mental Disorders*, third edition revised (DSM-III-R) (American Psychiatric Association, 1987) and asked to predict the sociocultural characteristics of the persons described therein. The instructor is likely to find, as I did in two studies, that the students reproduce epidemiological data; for example, they will judge the histrionic prototype to be young, White, single, and female, and will judge the antisocial prototype to be young, Black, male, and lower-class. Such data may be interpreted to mean that certain diagnostic categories are in fact manifestations of the stereotypes of the groups that tend to receive the diagnoses most often. This can lead the class into a discussion of the controversies over some of the disorders included in the *DSM-III-R*, perhaps supplemented by the videotape "Diagnosis Today: Ms. Diagnosis?" (Intelligence in Media, 123 West 44th Street, New York, NY 10036).

Conclusion

There are many ways the approaches suggested in this chapter can be incorporated into an abnormal psychology course. For an eye-opener, to sensitize students early on to the issues that will be raised, it is useful to run the diagnostic exercises at the very beginning of the course. Historical and contemporary sociocultural information can be presented as background or introduced when relevant to the topic being covered. The epidemiology of each disorder can be addressed and epidemiological theories included in theories of the etiology of each disorder. Finally, if a paper is required, it could address cross-cultural, historical, or gender role issues in psychopathology.

In this chapter, I have deliberately not given a sketchy catalogue of gender and cultural differences that instructors could present alongside the text to the course. If we present the topic in that manner—whether diligently or perfunctorily—we inevitably communicate that race, culture, and gender are peripheral to the essence of psychopathology. As long as students do not understand that the tacit standard for normalcy in our society is based on the culturally acquired characteristics of upper income White males, the behaviors of women and minorities will continue to be viewed in ways that reinforce that hidden standard. Furthermore, because our traditional way of talking and thinking about behavior is one that abstracts it from its context, a cookbook approach to gender and culture that does not address these more fundamental issues will simply further the problem it seeks to solve. Before examining gender and cultural differences, then, we must make it possible for our students to understand the history, the context, and the politics of our concepts and categories in abnormal psychology.

References

Abramowitz, C. V., & Dockeci, P. R. (1977). The politics of clinical judgment: Early empirical returns. *Psychological Bulletin, 84*(3), 460–476.

Alexander, F. G., & Selesnick, S. T. (1966). *The history of psychiatry.* New York: Harper & Row.

American Psychiatric Association. (1987). *Diagnostic and Statistical Manual of Mental Disorders (3rd edition—revised).* Washington, DC: Author.

Brehony, K. A. (1983). Women and agoraphobia: A case for the etiological significance of the feminine sex-role stereotype. In V. Franks & E. D. Rothblum (Eds.), *The stereotyping of women: Its effect on mental health* (pp. 112–128). New York: Springer.

Chapman, L., & Chapman, J. (1967). Genesis of popular but erroneous psychodiagnostic observations. *Journal of Abnormal Psychology, 72,* 193–204.

Chesler, P. (1972). *Women and madness.* New York: Avon Books.

Chunn, J. C., Dunston, P. J., & Ross-Sheriff, F. (1983). *Mental health and people of color: Curriculum development and change.* Washington, DC: Howard University Press.

Dain, N. (1964). *Concepts of insanity in the United States, 1789–1865.* New Brunswick, NJ: Rutgers University Press.

Deutsch, A. (1944). The first U.S. census of the insane (1840) and its use as pro-slavery propaganda. *Bulletin of the History of Medicine, 15,* 469–482.

Dufty, W. (1975). *Sugar blues.* New York: Warner Books.

Dworkin, A. (1974). *Woman hating.* New York: E. P. Dutton.

Ehrenreich, B., & English, D. (1973). *Witches, midwives, and nurses: A history of women healers.* New York: Feminist Press.

Forbes, T. R. (1966). *The midwife and the witch.* New York: Yale University Press.

Gilligan, C. (1977). In a different voice: Women's conception of the self and of morality. *Harvard Educational Review, 47*(4), 481–517.

Gove, W. R. (1972). The relationship between sex-roles, marital status, and mental illness. *Social Forces, 51,* 34–44.

Gove, W. R. (1980). Labelling and mental illness: A critique. In W. R. Gove (Ed.), *Labelling deviant behavior* (pp. 53–99). Beverly Hills, CA: Sage.

Jones, E. E., & Korchin, S. J. (1982). *Minority mental health.* New York: Praeger.

Jourard, S. M. (1974). *Healthy personality: An approach from the viewpoint of humanistic psychology.* New York: Macmillan.

Kaplan, M. (1983). A woman's view of the DSM-III. *American Psychologist, 38*(7), 786–792.

Kass, F., Spitzer, R. L., & Williams, J. B. (1983). An empirical study of the issue of sex bias in the diagnostic criteria of DSM-III Axis II personality disorders. *American Psychologist, 38*(7), 799–801.

Landrine, H. (1987a). On the politics of madness: A preliminary analysis of the relationship between social roles and psychopathology. *Genetic, Social and General Psychology Monographs, 113,* 341–406.

Landrine, H. (1987b, March). *The politics of personality disorder.* Paper presented at the annual convention of the Association for Women in Psychology, Denver.

Mark, V. H., Sweet, W. H., & Ervin, F. R. (1967). Role of brain disease in riots and urban violence. *Journal of the American Medical Association, 201,* 895.

Marks, I. M. (1969). *Fears and phobias.* New York: Academic Press.

Marsella, A. J., DeVos, G., & Hsu, F. (1985). *Culture and self: Asian and Western perspectives.* New York: Travistock.

Marsella, A. J., & White, G. M. (1982). *Cultural conceptions of mental health and therapy.* London: Reidel.

Morais, H. M. (1967). *The history of the Negro in medicine.* New York: Publishers Co.

Murray, M. (1921). *The witch cult in Western Europe.* London: Oxford University Press.

Nobles, W. W. (1980). Extended self: Rethinking the so-called Negro self concept. In R. L. Jones (Ed.), *Black psychology* (pp. 99–105). New York: Harper & Row.

Offer, D., & Sabshin, M. (1966). *Normality: Theoretical and clinical concepts of mental health.* New York: Basic Books.

Phillips, D., & Segal, B. (1969). Sexual status and psychiatric symptoms. *American Sociological Review, 34,* 58–72.

Prange, A. J., & Vitols, M. M. (1962). Cultural aspects of the relatively low incidence of depression in southern Negroes. *International Journal of Social Psychiatry, 8,* 104–112.

Rothblum, E. D. (1983). Sex-role stereotypes and depression in women. In V. Franks & E. D. Rothblum (Eds.), *The stereotyping of women: Its effect on mental health* (pp. 83–111). New York: Springer.

Sabshin, M., Diesenhaus, H., & Wilkerson, R. (1970). Dimensions of institutional racism in psychiatry. *American Journal of Psychiatry, 127,* 786–793.

Sennett, R., & Cobb, J. (1972). *The hidden injuries of class.* Englewood Cliffs, NJ: Prentice-Hall.

Shweder, R. A., & Bourne, E. J. (1982). Does the concept of the person vary cross-culturally? In A. J. Marsella & G. M. White (Eds.), *Cultural conceptions of mental health and therapy* (pp. 97–137). London: Reidel.

Simon, R., & Fleiss, J. (1973). Depression and schizophrenia in hospitalized patients. *Archives of General Psychiatry, 28,* 509–512.

Stampp, K. M. (1956). *The peculiar institution: Slavery in the antebellum South.* New York: Knopf.

Stricker, G. (1977). Implications of research for psychotherapeutic treatment of women. *American Psychologist, 32*(1), 14–22.

Szasz, T. (1970). *The manufacture of madness: A comparative study of the inquisition and the mental health movement.* New York: Dell.

Taube, C. (1971). *Admission rates to state and county mental hospitals by age, sex and color, United States, 1969.* Washington, DC: Department of Health, Education, and Welfare, Biometry Branch.

Thomas, A., & Sillen, S. (1972). *Racism and psychiatry.* Secaucus, NJ: Citadel.

Townsend, J. M. (1978). *Cultural conceptions of mental illness: A comparison of Germany and America.* Chicago: University of Chicago Press.

Warheit, G. J., Holzer, C. E., & Arey, S. A. (1975). Race and mental illness: An epidemiological update. *Journal of Health and Social Behavior, 16,* 243–256.

Wilson, D. C., & Lantz, E. M. (1957). The effect of cultural change on the Negro race in Virginia as indicated by a study of state hospital admissions. *American Journal of Psychiatry, 114,* 24–32.

Zilboorg, G., & Henry, G. (1941). *A history of medical psychology.* New York: Norton.

5

Lynne A. Bond

Teaching Developmental Psychology

Whether the course is titled Developmental Psychology, Human Development, Life Span Development, Child Psychology, or Adolescence, it is a course about people. However, if we followed the edict of truth in advertising, we would probably have to rename many such courses The Development of White Male Middle Class Citizens of the United States with Mention of Variations From the "Norm." Of course, it would be impossible to cover all ages, all peoples, and all aspects of development, both typical and atypical, in such a course; therefore, boundaries must be drawn when teaching this course, as when teaching any.

The problem with most developmental psychology courses is not simply that the instructor imposes limits upon the breadth of coverage. Rather, it is that a narrowly construed model of development is presented, and alternative patterns of influence, outcome, and interactions are seen as the variations from the norm. What makes this dangerous is the suggestion that such research has somehow objectively identified a norm of development. If we look carefully at the research upon which most texts and lectures are based, we find that it is not representative of the development of even the spectrum of persons who live in the United States.

Increasingly, scholars are recognizing that models of development have often emerged from research on select or so-called privileged populations. For example, gender bias has been noted in long-accepted models of achievement motivation (see Parsons & Goff, 1978) and moral development (see Gilligan, 1982), which had been based solely on data from males. Similarly, the race bias in perspectives on language development has been documented (e.g., Labov, 1973; Laosa, 1981). Ageist stereotypes of the phases of human development are also coming under scrutiny—for example, middle age as a static period of equilibrium and old age as a return to a state of helplessness and inactivity.

However, this growing intellectual awareness reflects only the tip of the iceberg in terms of teaching about the development of people. Our personal biases and those of society continue to creep into our discussions and portrayals of development in subtle yet powerful ways. For example, we continue to speak of deviations from the norm and their impact upon development. We might talk of the effect of working mothers upon a child's development but would rarely present the discussion in terms of the effect of non-employed mothers on child development—despite the fact that more than half of the mothers of children under 18 years in the United States are employed outside the home (Masnick & Bane, 1980). Although fewer than 16% of families in the United States are comprised of a breadwinning husband, a homemaking wife, and at least one child (Masnick & Bane,

1980), this remains the norm with which other family constellations are compared.

On a related theme, there are serious problems with certain basic labels and concepts that we use when discussing human development. For example, "deprived background," "disadvantaged," and "lack of stimulation" are among a number of phrases that are used loosely in conjunction with certain populations and family environments without careful consideration or specification of their precise referents. Upon closer examination, many of those environments are quite stimulating and have distinct advantages as well as disadvantages. At the same time, discussions of the effects of poverty on development frequently equate minority membership with the poor. Although it is important to acknowledge the disproportionate representation of certain ethnic and racial groups at the lower socioeconomic levels and the significance of such environments to these groups' development, this oversimplified equation of minority status with poverty perpetuates stereotypes and obscures the factors that contribute to this relationship. It is critical for students to recognize that ethnicity or race and low socioeconomic status are not one and the same; there is variation among racial and ethnic minority members as well as between racial and ethnic groups.

In order to guide our teaching of the development of people, I feel we must focus on a twofold theme. On the one hand, we need to emphasize the uniqueness of all individuals as well as subpopulations of persons. Categories such as the lesbian parent, the American Indian, or the adolescent male do not refer to homogeneous groups of individuals; development is far too complex to think in such generalities. Each group includes persons with varied and distinct experiences and perspectives. On the other hand, we need to underscore the universality of much of human experience. Despite the uniqueness of our individual experience, common factors are enmeshed in all of our lives—friends and families, societal norms and institutions, and physiological structures are but a few examples.

Course Content

Although we often think of demographics as necessarily dry and uninteresting, I have found that they comprise some of the most striking data and generate some of the most memorable discussions in a developmental psychology course. In addition to public census data, two excellent sources of demographic information are a study from the Children's Defense Fund (1985) and a report by the Joint Center for Urban Studies of MIT and Harvard University (Masnick and Bane, 1980). With a broader perspective on the great variation in individual and family demographics, the fallacy of our stereotypic norms become immediately apparent (e.g., only 7% of households are comprised of an employed husband, a homemaking wife, and two children). The diversity of adult roles for which children need to be prepared also becomes more clear; consider the rise in female-headed households, childless marriages, and adults living alone (Masnick & Bane, 1980).

In a developmental psychology course, there needs to be explicit and extended discussion of the fact that a child's development is not solely, or perhaps even primarily, a product of the mother's direct influence. The important roles of fathers, siblings, and peers (as well as teachers, extended family, and other children and adults in the community) must be more thoroughly considered in understanding the diversity of developmental experiences. Moreover, the effects of societal structures and organizations (e.g., educational, political, and economic) need to be highlighted. For example, consider the multiple factors that contribute to the development of low self-esteem and helplessness in some developmentally disabled persons—such as the restrictions created by our educational and recreational facilities, stereotypes of attractiveness, and financial demands of providing support services (see Asch, Chapter 19 this volume).

Cross-cultural analyses of development can be instrumental in illustrating the diversity of norms which, in fact, exist. For example, Stevenson's (1986) text, *Child development and education in Japan,* provides a framework for considering development from a cross-cultural perspective, which can also be used to consider development within subcultures of the United States (e.g., Laosa, 1981; Rogoff, Gauvain, & Ellis, 1984). Historical comparisons of the treatment of specific age or ethnic groups or of sexuality and child-rearing strategies provide another sort of cross-cultural comparison that highlights the diversity of human experience in the context of development (e.g., excerpts from child-rearing books of the early 20th century such as Watson (1928) provide a striking example of this variation).

Any effective course on developmental psychology must address gender role development. A consideration of biochemical and physiological factors, socializing agents (e.g., parents, peers, siblings, teachers, media), and processes of gender role acquisition (e.g., observational learning, gender self-categorization, gender labeling) are central to this understanding (e.g., Ruble, 1984). At the same time, although an individual's experience of his or her environment is inextricably tied to gender, students need to learn that similarities across gender far outweigh dissimilarities, and there is considerably more variation within than between gender groups (Maccoby & Jacklin, 1974; Ruble, 1984).

Ethnic and racial diversity of experience in our society call for discussion of:

• the disproportionate representation of many of these groups within the lower socioeconomic levels and the common effects of this experience (e.g., both Laosa, 1981, and Zill, 1985, reported that variations in family relations are more strongly tied to social class than to ethnicity or race);

• the recurring patterns throughout history of discriminatory treatment of racial and ethnic groups (see Kamin, 1974, for a discussion of the use of intelligence testing); and

• the variation within any particular ethnic or racial group in personal characteristics, values, and family and community structure (e.g., McQueen, 1979, documented variations among poor urban Blacks who were more versus those who were less successful at coping with societal and family demands).

Moreover, the particular strengths of family and community structures that characterize racial and ethnic minority groups merit greater attention (for examples pertaining to the contribution of Black kinship bonds and networks, see Hill, 1971; Kellam, Ensminger, & Turner, 1977; McAdoo, 1978).

Classroom Techniques

I believe that a learning process that actively engages the student is far more powerful than one in which the student is merely a listener. I have found the following student and classroom activities to be both productive and engaging. Although these were developed in the context of teaching developmental psychology, I have used each in other courses as well with only slight modifications.

Journals

With a renewed interest in the use of writing to promote thinking, there has been an evolving focus on writing-across-the-curriculum. The increasing use of student journals is one outgrowth of this movement. The specific form and content of the journal may vary from instructor to instructor and from student to student. But what they share is an emphasis on informal writing as a vehicle for both stimulating and capturing student insights. Students are asked to make entries in their journals several times a week or even daily. They are to write in an uncensored manner, ignoring considerations of spelling, grammar, and punctuation. When they feel that they have nothing to say, they are to push themselves to continue writing whatever comes to mind; often this leads to some of the most insightful thinking. Students are to use their journals as personal tools for asking questions and constructing ideas rather than simply recording conclusions (see Fulwiler, 1986).

Journal entries may be in any form—lists, outlines, informal notes, prose, doodles, cartoons—and can be used to accomplish a variety of tasks:

• to respond to specific questions assigned by the instructor (e.g., "Write about the major sources of stress you experienced in high school");

• to react to class lectures and readings. As one of my students wrote,

> Boy, I can't believe how the text described life with divorced parents. They made it sound like we [children of divorce] are culturally deprived or something. That really gets me mad. I can see how Puerto Ricans feel when everybody just assumes things about their life without really knowing. . . .

• to record and respond to daily observations—at the school cafeteria, shopping mall, or wherever. One student wrote,

> I can't believe it—after all our class talk about even nursery teachers treating girls and boys differently (which I never really believed) I actually saw it. I was just walking by the playground . . . and this teacher only paid attention to the girls when they were close up. . . .

• To raise questions and to speculate. One student began an entry in the following way:

> I wonder if some older people seem helpless just because they think they're supposed to be helpless. I mean, if you grew up in a culture where everyone said that the older you get, the more strong,

smart, and independent you get, I bet that might actually come true. I mean, how much do our assumptions really shape who we become?

- To draw connections between different aspects of life and experience, for example, "That cross-cultural comparison of parenting reminded me of something my history teacher said about colonial times . . ." or "I saw a segment on '60 Minutes' tonight that reminded me of the article we read on. . . ."

Journals have proven extraordinarily useful for helping students to reflect on factors that have been important in shaping their own lives and the lives of others. Much to their own surprise, students find themselves writing about persons, pressures, and experiences that they had not consciously considered important. These discoveries can be fostered by having the class share journal entries. I sometimes ask students to volunteer to read specific entries to the class, to respond to other students' entries in journal entries of their own, or to compare and integrate the various perspectives they have heard (rather than to judge their appropriateness or validity). Class members are usually more willing to tackle this task by writing in their journals rather than by speaking aloud (particularly in large lecture classes).

In another activity, I read aloud students' entries on a particular issue; then the class speculates on the gender, race, religion, and socioeconomic status of the author. By first writing individual reactions and then engaging in class discussion, students both explore their own assumptions and stereotypes and also come to appreciate the differences among people's experiences.

Interviews

The simple activity of interviewing or being interviewed by classmates or roommates helps students gain insight into significant influences in their own and others' lives. This is a powerful technique for promoting an awareness of both the individuality and the commonality of experiences, as well as for self-reflection. Once the class has agreed on the interview questions, I ask students to describe briefly, in writing, the responses that they expect to emerge. We also discuss the importance of anonymity and informed consent, and how a violation of ethical standards can hurt an individual respondent. Students subsequently report surprise not only at what others have to say but also at the ways in which they find themselves responding to particular questions. Small groups of students review responses to individual items on the interviews. Class analyses of interview data allow an opportunity to investigate assumptions regarding similarity and diversity among members of particular groups (e.g., by age, gender, SES).

Student interviews with members of diverse community groups can be particularly revealing. Although this task might seem to require complicated planning, it is surprisingly simple to arrange. In fact, most people are flattered that their words are important enough to record. The instructor can usually make arrangements with schools or agencies, and the interviews can be conducted during a class outing or at individually arranged times.

If it is not feasible for students to make direct contact with members of diverse populations, transcripts of interviews from other sources can be obtained. Anonymous interview data from one's own or others' research projects may be available. These may include data gathered for purposes far removed from those of one's course but relevant to age groups, sociocultural factors, and populations covered by the course. Instructors may also arrange to swap interviews (or journal entries) across varied educational or community settings. For example, an exchange can be arranged between students at a southern, predominantly Black, public agricultural college and those at a small, predominantly White, New England private college.

Pilot Research

Engaging in pilot research is perhaps most important because it enables students to learn more about the process of data collection and interpretation. In so doing, students become more aware of the potential of research that is well designed and well executed, as well as the limitations of that which is not. Furthermore, the student comes to recognize the tremendous variability and intricacy of data that are so often masked by summary statements of findings. Because institutional review of research involving human subjects is often required, advance planning for a pilot study is important.

Pilot research can be designed to highlight the limitations of present (and likely future) research. For example, when conducting a class project or small-group projects, each student (or group of students) collects and interprets data from only one select sample of subjects (defined narrowly by age, SES, academic class, gender, etc.). Once students' reports are written (a written report appears to add commitment to thinking), the class data are combined and students are asked to reconsider their findings and interpretation. These results are generally substantially different from the first findings, even when the class has not had access to a particularly heterogeneous subject population. This helps students discover the ways in which selected samples bias data and the models that those data generate. The activity can be followed by presentations of published and widely publicized research that has subsequently been demonstrated to have precisely these sorts of biases. As mentioned earlier in the chapter, these include models of achievement motivation, moral development, and language development, among others (see Parsons & Goff, 1978; Gilligan, 1982; Labov, 1973; Laosa, 1981). Students can then speculate on additional topics covered in the course that may suffer from similar but as yet undocumented limitations (an issue that is frequently considered in subsequent journal entries).

Using a related approach, each student can be asked to construct a model of development using only the information from her or his own journal entries. If students restrict their considerations to the written contents of the journal without regard to background information or knowledge of circumstances that led to specific entries, they become frustrated with the ways in which they are forced to misrepresent who they really are, based upon their restricted data. This presents a useful analog of the development of certain models of human development.

What If?

The What If? exercise is a class favorite. It is a fairly simple activity I use to encourage students to think more carefully about the potential applicability, biases, and implications of developmental theories or models. In small group discussions (or individually in writing), students are asked to assume that a particular model or theory is true and then to generate the implications of that position for a specified diversity of developmental conditions designated by the instructor. For example, I ask students, "What if Freud's theory of gender role development is accurate? What would you then expect to find in the development of (a) a boy who is raised in a single mother-headed household from the time he is a year old? (b) a girl whose parents divorce when she is three, and whose father single-handedly raises her to adolescence? (c) a girl raised from birth by two lesbian parents? What if the cognitive-developmental perspective is correct? What would you then expect. . . ?" In developing their responses to these questions, students also create a framework from which to consider the validity and limitations of these theories and models in dealing with the diversity of developmental conditions in our society, including some in which they themselves have lived (e.g., divorce).

Conclusion

I have presented—albeit quite briefly—examples of content and structure that I believe can help integrate diversity into a course on developmental psychology. Many additional topics (such as ageism and the developmental tasks of the physically and mentally handicapped) and class activities (such as role play, class field experiences, and guest lectures by members of underrepresented populations, community organizations, and policy-making groups) can also be included in a course on the development of people. But as I mentioned at the outset, every instructor must impose limits on the breadth of a course, and many of us will never feel that we have had sufficient class time to give a fair representation of the diversity and complexity of human experience. However, although we cannot teach all the essential facts, we can try to convey those central principles that will guide students to be more sensitive to and aware of the diversity of human experience. An appreciation of the individuality and simultaneous universality of such experience can be central to achieving this goal.

References

Children's Defense Fund. (1985). *Black and white children in America: Key facts.* Washington, DC: Author.

Fulwiler, T. (1986). The journal. In L. A. Bond & A. S. Magistrale (Eds.), *Writer's guide: Psychology* (pp. 19–32). Lexington, MA: Heath.

Hill, R. B. (1971). *Strengths of black families.* New York: Emerson Hall.

Kamin, L. J. (1974). *The science and politics of IQ.* Hillsdale, NJ: Erlbaum.

Kellam, S. G., Ensminger, M. A., & Turner, J. T. (1977). Family structure and the mental health of children. *Archives of General Psychiatry, 34,* 1012–1022.

Gilligan, C. (1982). *In a different voice: Psychological theory and women's development.* Cambridge, MA: Harvard University Press.

Labov, W. (1973). *Language in the inner city: Studies in the Black English vernacular.* Philadelphia: University of Pennsylvania Press.

Laosa, L. M. (1981). Maternal behavior: Socio-cultural diversity in modes of family interaction. In R. W. Henderson (Ed.), *Parent-child interaction* (pp. 125–167). New York: Academic Press.

Maccoby, E. E., & Jacklin, C. N. (1974). *The psychology of sex differences*. Stanford, CA: Stanford University Press.

Masnick, G., & Bane, M. J. (1980). *The nation's families: 1960–1990*. Boston: Auburn House.

McAdoo, H. (1978). Factors related to stability in upwardly mobile black families. *Journal of Marriage and the Family, 40*, 761–776.

McQueen, A. J. (1979). The adaptation of urban black families: Trends, problems and issues. In D. Reiss & H. A. Hoffman (Eds.), *The American family: Dying or developing* (pp. 273–295). New York: Plenum.

Parsons, J. E., & Goff, S. B. (1978). Achievement motivation and values: An alternative perspective. In L. J. Fyans, Jr. (Ed.), *Achievement motivation: Recent trends in theory and research* (pp. 349–373). New York: Plenum.

Rogoff, B., Gauvain, M., & Ellis, S. (1984). Development viewed in its cultural context. In M. H. Bornstein & M. E. Lamb (Eds.), *Developmental psychology: An advanced textbook* (pp. 533–571). Hillsdale, NJ: Erlbaum.

Ruble, D. N. (1984). Sex-role development. In M. H. Bornstein & M. E. Lamb (Eds.), *Developmental psychology: An advanced textbook* (pp. 325–371). Hillsdale, NJ: Erlbaum.

Stevenson, H. (Ed.). (1986). *Child development and education in Japan*. New York: Freeman.

Watson, J. B. (1928). *Psychological care of infant and child*. New York: Norton.

Zill, N. (1985). *Happy, healthy and insecure*. New York: Doubleday.

6

Albert J. Lott

Cultural Diversity
in the Undergraduate
Social Psychology Course

Social psychology might seem like the area least in need of special efforts to introduce information on cultural diversity; however, analysis of the field indicates that this is not true.

Jones (1983) surveyed articles reporting studies of African American and other ethnic groups in mainstream social psychology journals between 1968 and 1980 and found that the number of journal articles related to racial ethnicity, racism, culture, cross-culture, discrimination, and prejudice dropped off sharply after 1973. Further, he found that pre-1960 social psychology textbooks gave attention to broadly viewed culture and the cultural context of people's behavior, while after 1960 the narrower topics of prejudice and discrimination took the place of culture. He concluded that in recent years social psychology contributed little to the understanding of non-White subcultures or to theories of intercultural relations. Jones' findings for journals and textbooks are mirrored in a study of social psychologists' presentations at APA conventions (Pedersen & Inouye, 1984).

This decline in social psychologists' attention to ethnic groups, cultural diversity, and underrepresented populations increases our need to consider them in social psychology courses. Consideration of human diversity not only broadens and enriches the students' understanding of social behaviors, but also provides new data and perspectives for other areas of psychology.

The Social Psychology Course: An Alternative Model

In this chapter, I suggest how the undergraduate social psychology course can be improved by including information on cultural minorities such as African Americans, lesbians, gays, and Vietnam veterans. These groups are examples of special populations that can be included in a social psychology course to make it more a psychology of people.

Research Methods in Social Psychology

Following McGuire's (1973) exhortation that social psychology expand its methodological horizons and ways of generating research hypotheses, there has been an increased interest in using a wide variety of research techniques. Morin (1977) detailed the limitations and implicit biases in most work on homosexuality; issues regarding sampling and generalizations have been raised by Jones (1983) with regard to race; and social psychology's methodological blindness has been provided by feminist scholars (Lott, 1985; Wallston & Grady, 1985; Westcott, 1979). Newer methodologies and sources of research questions are particularly relevant in studying neglected groups.

Interpersonal Relations

Close relationships, liking and loving. This general topic can be used as a vehicle for introducing a wide range of materials about people who are not traditionally covered in social psychology. Peplau and Gordon's (1983) work on intimate relationships of gays and lesbians provided an opportunity for comparing homosexuals and heterosexuals on questions of friendship and love, exploring comparative values about intimacy as well as different models for close relationships and marriage. Areas of similarities and differences between men and women, homosexual and heterosexual, not only introduce information that is new for the students but also address basic human questions about caring, love, sexual behavior, and long-term commitment.

In addition, a 90-minute videotape, *The Male Couple* (based on the book by the same name by McWhirter and Mattison, 1984), provides a comprehensive look at important issues facing all gay couples. It adds a realistic, human element to the academic background materials. Another film, *Silent Partners: Gay and Lesbian Elders*, addresses stereotypes of age, race, and sexual orientation and considers the nature of intimate relationships.

Black interpersonal relations are richly portrayed in anthropologist John Gwaltney's (1980) powerful oral history, *Drylongso: A Self-Portrait of Black America.* This book can be used as a supplement to a variety of topics in social psychology; ordinary people in it describe aspects of their lives which give insight into more formal social psychological processes. For example, the comment by one of Gwaltney's respondents, "I think this anthropology is just another way to call me a nigger," can serve as an impetus for more fully examining biases in research methods, as well as the uses to which research results are put. For most undergraduate students, these represent new issues to be considered in regard to the research enterprise as a social psychological process in itself.

I have used other materials from Gwaltney (1980) to expand coverage of topics on sexuality and prejudice, as well as an analysis of self-efficacy and personal coping skills. In each case, the oral histories have added new depth and variety to the ideas that social psychologists have formulated. In addition, Gwaltney linked these new insights to the lives of Black people in ways that no contemporary social psychology textbook approaches.

A note of caution should be added with regard to using *Drylongso*, as well as all oral histories. Students, while responding positively to the basic information, seem to need considerable guidance in extracting basic principles from complex oral histories. The most successful technique for me has been to have a class discussion about the readings which is based on questions that are handed out before the students read the personal accounts. The questions help focus the students' reading, and the discussion captures the richness and new insights.

Gwaltney (1986) published a book of interviews with nearly three dozen self-proclaimed "principled dissenters"—nonconformists from different social class, racial, and ethnic groups. He provided fascinating real-life examples of individuals who are given little attention in standard social psychological texts.

Aggression and violence. In addition to covering the extensive theoretical and empirical material social psychology has generated on the topic of aggression, I use the Vietnam War and the effects of the war on the men and women who served in Vietnam as examples. The overwhelming majority of my students were infants or children during the Vietnam War. In effect, I am able to teach some contemporary history, while placing issues of social psychology within that history. This approach fits well with Gergen's (1973) concerns about looking closely at the historical context of our theories or empirical findings. While he argued that historical change leads to fundamental changes in the basic science of social psychology, I claim that knowing the historical circumstances in which a social psychological phenomenon occurs gives one both a deeper understanding of the phenomenon itself and clarifies aspects of the historical event. Social psychology and history supplement each other; one cannot substitute for the other in accounting for complex human social behavior.

To provide this understanding and clarification, I have relied primarily on an oral history of Black soldiers (Terry, 1984), a reporter's intimate account of the lives of five Marines (Klein, 1984), and the work of two clinicians, one of whom is a Black clinical psychologist who is a Vietnam veteran (Brende & Parson, 1985). These reports focus on issues of race, ethnicity, and gender as the soldiers are influenced by living in a highly violent, dehumanizing environment.

Bloods (Terry, 1984) chronicled the lives of 20 Black soldiers chosen as a representative cross-section of Black combat soldiers in Vietnam. Each man gave his own impressions about the war's impact on him, his experiences with discrimination and brotherhood, and his reactions to the horrors of war and killing. Like *Drylongso* (Gwaltney, 1980), *Bloods* may be too overwhelming for an undergraduate class in social psychology. But having small groups of students read one or more of the accounts and look for specific examples of prejudice and aggression provides an excellent vehicle for class discussion based on real-life examples of concepts found in the basic social psychological literature.

Payback (Klein, 1984) can be used similarly. Focusing on the post-Vietnam War adjustment of five White Marines, it addresses questions of how men who have been taught to kill, and who have participated in war, return to civilian life. *Payback* does a good job of linking war experiences to postwar behaviors. Its compelling examples illustrate successful, as well as unsuccessful, adjustment, making *Payback* a useful vehicle for looking at individual differences in reaction to aggressive situations and the stresses of readjustment to nonaggressive situations.

Vietnam Veterans (Brende & Parson, 1985) provided a multifaceted analysis of the role of violence in the lives of young, mostly poor, men, as well as an excellent discussion of the experiences of female military personnel (mostly nurses) and Black, Hispanic, American Indian, and Asian American Vietnam veterans. The reader learns about ethnic and gender differences in response to the aggression and violence of war and how biculturality affects ethnic returnees. The complex issues of identification with one's enemy, masculinity, sexual stereotypes, and guilt are explored in ways that are very different from those in the standard social psychology textbook. In the process, the roles of gender and ethnicity in individuals' lives are presented in compelling ways. Also available are *A Piece of My Heart* (Walker, 1986), an oral history of women's experiences in Vietnam, and *Home Before Morning* (Van Devanter, 1983), a well-received account of one woman's tour of duty as an army nurse.

Two very good documentary films on the Vietnam War have been recommended by Vietnam veterans organizations. *How Far Home: Veterans After Vietnam* looks at the turmoil, problems, and joy both male and female veterans have experienced in their relationships with others since coming home. The film focuses on the struggle for self-awareness after being shaped by a controversial war and the strenuous efforts to form meaningful relationships following the war. A very different perspective on the war is offered in *Warriors' Women: A Film About the Vietnam War and Families.* Revealing the tense reality of living with men who are still upset by memories of the war, it looks at the lives of five wives (and families) of Vietnam veterans. This film can serve as a transition from topics of aggression and violence to aspects of everyday life such as altruism, helping behavior, emotional closeness, and intimacy that are not typically anchored in war. By comparing the ways in which the Vietnam War influenced or changed how these men and women dealt with situations requiring intimacy or helping with the traditional approach presented in the social psychology literature, students may become aware of the lasting effects of the aggression and violence of war on interpersonal behavior and relationships.

Behavior in Groups

Conformity, obedience, and authoritarianism. I use this topical area to teach some history about the Nazi Holocaust, ethnocentrism, and death and survival in concentration camps. Milgram's (1974) series of experimental studies of destructive obedience and the classic study of the authoritarian personality (Adorno, Frenkel-Brunswik, Levinson, & Sanford, 1950) formed the scientific backdrop for a very compelling book by Des Pres (1976) on the structure of social life in the death camps. In combination, Milgram and Adorno et al. showed how strong leaders can order ordinary people to carry out destructive acts and how an ethnocentric culture or personality can facilitate that process. These works tie politics to prejudice and to social psychology in general and, in fact, may be used as models to help analyze the political situation.

Des Pres (1976) took the process one step further and developed a picture of life in the Nazi concentration camps based on personal accounts of survivors. In portraying the behavioral nuances of camp inmates, Des Pres gave new insights into altruism, obedience, and the pursuit of feelings of self-efficacy while living in a highly degrading, life-threatening environment. The setting also provided an unusual and dramatic context for analyzing traditional theories of behavior. For example, how do traditional theories handle the relation between self-actualization or individuation and commitment to groups or significant others, and what does the concentration camp context add to that account? Des Pres not only provided a kind of psychohistory of the Nazi death camps, but also integrated descriptions of the coping strategies of individuals living under the constant threat of death into that account. He related both of those perspectives to social psychological theory.

The American Context of Social Psychology

In recent semesters, I have had my students look at cultural and demographic aspects of the United States over the past 15 to 20 years to help them understand continuity and change, as well as to identify major themes or problems of American life and how social class and ethnicity relate to these problems. My goal is to help them understand the cultural context in which social psychology functions, how their lives are influenced by broad cultural trends, and how cultural trends are played out differently if one is a man or a woman, Black or White, or earning a middle or low income.

Two books have been helpful: *New Rules* (Yankelovich, 1981) and *Habits of the Heart* (Bellah, Madsen, Sullivan, Swidler, & Tipton, 1985). Based primarily on public opinion surveys from the late 1960s to the early 1980s, Yankelovich identified changing views of self-fulfillment and commitment to others. Students have found the information eye-opening but have needed clarification of the material through group discussion or lectures. In *New Rules*, social class and gender are discussed, but little attention is given to racial and ethnic groups. The major value of this book is its examination of the changing behaviors of large numbers of Americans and the social and psychological reasons for these changes.

Part 1, "Private Life" in Bellah et al. (1985), which I have used as supplemental reading, has a White, middle-class orientation, but the questions it raises and addresses are of general interest. Students have responded positively to it. Gender is considered, but the alert instructor has to raise questions at each point of discussion about race and ethnicity (see Chapters 15, 16, and 18 of this volume for resources). Students have been especially helpful in bringing their own ideas, materials, and data about class differences and ethnic diversity into class discussions. In fact, the class has supplemented and countered the middle-class emphasis of the book with considerable insight and energy. The book's value rests on the rich accounts it contains of self-discovery and awareness, self-reliance, individualism, love, marriage, communication with others, and therapy. The authors attempted to identify representative issues we all face in order to make sense of our lives. With the addition of social class and ethnic perspectives, the book has worked very well in my classes.

While students have enjoyed the book's analysis of private life, they need class discussion and lecture supplements to more fully understand the authors' key points and to broaden the coverage to other groups. In this regard, articles by Sampson (1977) and Waterman (1981) are helpful in relating the culture-level books to issues of self-contained individualism and interdependence as psychologists have looked at these topics over the years. Sampson, for example, decried the fact that American social psychology has such a strong individualistic bias and that explorations of interdependence are neglected. Such an individualistic model places responsibility for success or failure on the individual, while a more interdependent perspective would locate it in a group.

On the other hand, Waterman (1981) argued that individualism and interdependence are linked. Interpersonal trust, for example, is more likely to emerge when an individual has high self-esteem, does not see others as a threat, and can voluntarily decide to participate in cooperative activities.

The Sampson–Waterman "debate" has served as a vehicle for bringing together the same issues posed by *New Rules* and *Habits of the Heart* on a cultural level. On balance, the students end up with both a cultural and psychological appreciation of the dynamics of individual advancement versus responsibility for others and how these potentially conflicting demands are balanced.

Concluding Comments

The materials on cultural diversity presented here are illustrations of a particular pedagogical orientation to teaching social psychology. I attempt to relate the scientific content of social psychology to racial and ethnic groups, special and underrepresented groups, life in contemporary United States, and major historical events that illustrate human coping in atypical contexts, and at the same time, teach some social history. In other words, I am attempting to place social behavior in a context that is sensitive to issues of race, gender, socioeconomic status, ethnicity, and age. In order to do this for undergraduate students, I am continually looking for supplemental readings to expand the coverage of social psychology presented in a typical textbook. My search for the additional content is guided by cultural diversity as I have defined it here.

Cazenave (1984) pointed out that we cannot understand the dynamics of the male role in American society without considering the relative position a man occupies in the prestige and power structures of his country. Cazenave's observation can be extended to all social behaviors. Our understanding of behavior will remain incomplete if we do not consider its social and historical context. Also, we will be neglecting many important theoretical, empirical, and applied questions if we remove social psychology from a sociocultural matrix that responds to real world events.

Films

How Far Home: Veterans After Vietnam. Northern Light Productions, 176 Newbury Street, Boston, MA 02116; (617) 267–0391.
Silent Partners: Gay and Lesbian Elders. Filmmakers Library, Inc., 133 East 58th Street, New York, NY 10022; (212) 355–6545.
The Male Couple. Humanus Home Video, 424 North Larchmont Boulevard, Los Angeles, CA 90004; (213) 460–4605.
Warriors' Women: A Film About the Vietnam War and Families. Dorothy Tod Films, PO Box 315, Franklin Lakes, NJ 07417.

References

Adorno, T., Frenkel-Brunswik, E., Levinson, D., & Sanford, R. N. (1950). *The authoritarian personality.* New York: Harper & Row.
Bellah, R., Madsen, R., Sullivan, W., Swidler, A., & Tipton, S. (1985). *Habits of the heart: Individualism and commitment in American life.* Berkeley, CA: University of California Press.
Brende, J. O., & Parson, E. R. (1985). *Vietnam veterans: The road to recovery.* New York: Plenum.
Cazenave, N. A. (1984). Race, socioeconomic status, and age: The social context of American masculinity. *Sex Roles, 11,* 639–656.
Des Pres, T. (1976). *The survivor: An anatomy of life in the death camps.* New York: Oxford.

Gergen, K. (1973). Social psychology as history. *Journal of Personality and Social Psychology, 26,* 309–320.

Gwaltney, J. L. (1980). *Drylongso: A self-portrait of Black America.* New York: Random House.

Gwaltney, J. L. (1986). *The dissenters: Voices from contemporary America.* New York: Random House.

Jones, J. M. (1983). The concept of race in social psychology. In L. Wheeler & P. Shaver (Eds.), *Review of personality and social psychology* (Vol. 4) (pp. 117–149). Beverly Hills, CA: Sage.

Klein, J. (1984). *Payback: Five Marines after Vietnam.* New York: Knopf.

Lott, B. (1985). The potential enrichment of social/personality psychology through feminist research and vice versa. *American Psychologist, 40,* 155–164.

McGuire, W. (1973). The ying and yang of progress in social psychology: Seven koan. *Journal of Personality and Social Psychology, 26,* 446–452.

McWhirter, D., & Mattison, D. (1984). *The male couple.* Englewood Cliffs, NJ: Prentice-Hall.

Milgram, S. (1974). *Obedience to authority.* New York: Harper & Row.

Morin, S. F. (1977). Heterosexual bias in psychological research on lesbian and male homosexuality. *American Psychologist, 32,* 629–637.

Pedersen, P. B., & Inouye, K. (1984). The international/intercultural perspective of the APA. *American Psychologist, 39,* 560–561.

Peplau, L. A., & Gordon, S. L. (1983). The intimate relationships of lesbians and gay men. In E. R. Allegeier & N. B. McCormick (Eds.), *Changing boundaries: Gender roles and sexual behavior* (pp. 226–244). Palo Alto, CA: Mayfield.

Sampson, E. (1977). Psychology and the American ideal. *Journal of Personality and Social Psychology, 37,* 245–257.

Terry, W. (1984). *Bloods: An oral history of the Vietnam War by Black veterans.* New York: Random House.

Van Devanter, L. (1983). *Home before morning: The story of an army nurse in Vietnam.* New York: Beaufort.

Walker, K. (1986). *A piece of my heart: Stories of 26 women who served in Vietnam.* Novato, CA: Presidio.

Wallston, B. S., & Grady, K. E. (1985). Integrating the feminist critique and the crisis of social psychology: Another look at research methods. In V. O'Leary, R. Unger, & B. Wallston (Eds.), *Women, gender, and social psychology* (pp. 7–33). Hillsdale, NJ: Lawrence Erlbaum.

Waterman, A. (1981). Individualism and interdependence. *American Psychologist, 36,* 762–773.

Westkott, M. (1979). Feminist criticism of the social sciences. *Harvard Educational Review, 49,* 422–430.

Yankelovich, D. (1981). *New rules: Searching for self-fulfillment in a world turned upside down.* New York: Bantam.

7

Phyllis Bronstein

Personality From A Sociocultural Perspective

Because it attempts to reveal the underlying nature of human beings, the study of personality is potentially one of the most interesting areas within psychology. Its quest is analogous to that of fiction and drama, whose impact depends on how meaningfully characters are portrayed and to what extent we come to understand their worries, quirks, struggles, and dreams. In literature, however, the motivations, perceptions, and behaviors of memorable characters such as Ibsen's Hedda Gabler (1890) or Alice Walker's Celie (1982) are not developed in a vacuum but are shaped by factors such as gender, race, and socioeconomic level against a backdrop of the particular culture and time in which the stories are set. The study of personality, on the other hand, has tended to ignore the contexts within which individuals develop. Perhaps because of ethnocentrism and androcentrism or in an attempt to make personality psychology as scientific as possible, theorists and researchers have tended to ignore or control for human diversity. Thus, the study of personality has in general become the study of individual differences within select homogeneous groups (such as majority-culture male college students), based on the largely unsupported assumption that such findings are broadly representative of human behavior.

Most texts available for teaching the undergraduate personality course reflect this perspective. They include the traditional march through the graveyard of hallowed historical figures, with some attention to personality measurement techniques and the person–situation controversy. With few exceptions (e.g., Babladelis, 1984; Feshbach & Weiner, 1986; Phares, 1984; Potkay & Allen, 1986), these texts do not consider the ways that culture, ethnicity, socioeconomics, or gender shape the ways we act, feel, and perceive ourselves and our world. It is generally up to the instructor to introduce other viewpoints and materials in order to provide students with a broader perspective on personality psychology. My own approach to teaching the personality course, which I have found is effective both with large lecture classes and smaller discussion sections, is to cover some of the traditional theorists and their approaches and balance them with (a) recent theory and research on gender-related factors in personality development, (b) readings from anthropology on personality development in other cultures, and (c) experiential projects and exercises designed to help students become aware of the ways their own sociocultural backgrounds have affected their personality development.

Psychoanalytic Theory

Providing Gender Balance

Almost all of the texts devote at least a full chapter to Freud, often with chapters on his better known followers as well. The instructor may wish to supplement the traditional material with a feminist critique of Freud's views on women (e.g., see Garner, Kahane, & Sprengnether, 1985; Lewis, 1986; Mead, 1979; or almost any text on the psychology of women), as well as new psychoanalytic perspectives on women (e.g., Bernay & Cantor, 1986; Chodorow, 1978; Dinnerstein, 1976; Lerman, 1986). Weskott (1986) provided a rich discussion of Karen Horney's contributions in this area. The recent controversy over Freud's seduction theory (Masson, 1984; Westerlund, 1986) provided a fascinating example of how sociocultural factors shape theory construction in the psychoanalytic understanding of female personality.

A Cross-Cultural Perspective

Cross-cultural applications have both challenged and supported psychoanalytic theory. Duley, Sinclair, and Edwards (1986) used cross-cultural data to provide a critique of Freud's views on women. Munroe, Munroe, and Whiting (1980) provided persuasive psychoanalytic explanations of male initiation rites at puberty and the *couvade* (male rituals around childbirth) that occur in many nonliterate societies. Whiting and Child (1953; Whiting, 1961) presented strong cross-cultural evidence in support of a theory linking child-rearing practices to personality development and to the society's projective systems. For example, societies that indulge their infants tend to produce adults who believe that the behavior of the gods can be influenced or controlled by the behavior of humans through specific rituals (Spiro & D'Andrade, 1958), whereas societies that treat their infants more harshly tend to produce adults who believe that the gods are more aggressive than benevolent toward human beings (Lambert, Triandis, & Wolf, 1959).

The Nature–Nurture Controversy

Historical Perspective

I devote a section of the personality course to comparing the evidence for biological versus social determinants of personality. I start with a historical overview of biological theories, beginning with the ancient notion of the humours of the body and including physiognomy, phrenology, and body types. This allows students to see that there have historically been numerous attempts to attribute individual differences to immutable genetic factors, and that those theories have not withstood the test of time. Since the Kretschmer/Sheldon theory linking body type to personality often receives substantial coverage in contemporary introductory psychology and personality texts, I use it to demonstrate gender and cultural bias in traditional psychology; for example, I ask students to consider how a *Vogue* fashion model, a full-bodied Polynesian woman, a tall, slim Black man, and a sumo wrestler would fit into Sheldon's three body/personality types. As students realize that the theory seems mainly to reflect popular stereotypes about Caucasian male physiques, I then contrast it with research that has considered the female physique in relation to personality. One study reported in the field's most prestigious journal (Wiggens, Wiggens, & Conger, 1968) considered the size of women's breasts, buttocks, and legs in relation to *men's* personalities: The researchers found, for example, that men preferring large breasts had higher need-for-independence and greater interest in sports than men preferring small breasts, and men preferring large buttocks tended to be more neat and organized than men preferring small buttocks. Another study (Kleinke & Staneski, 1980) asked both male and female subjects to predict women's personalities and abilities based on photographs in which bust size was systematically varied. These examples, particularly when compared with the very different approach to studying male body types, can stimulate discussion of the effects of culture on the choice of research topics. Students can then be asked to consider whether the latter kinds of studies make meaningful contributions to the psychology of personality, or whether the focus of those studies on the sexualized aspects of women's anatomy serves more to perpetuate stereotypic perceptions of women.

Biological Explanations of Gender Differences

Bleier (1984) and Fausto-Sterling (1985) provided excellent critiques of the arguments for biologically based gender differences. They examined the data and persuasively challenged hormonal explanations (e.g., testosterone, premenstrual syndrome, menopause) for gender differences in aggression, dominance, and emotional instability. Genetic explanations (such as the Y chromosome) are similarly examined and refuted. The researchers also effectively refuted sociobiological rationales for traditional gender role behavior and reproductive strategies such as male promiscuity and rape. Lewontin, Rose, and Kamin (1984) presented well-reasoned and documented arguments against biogenetic explanations for racial and social class differences in IQ and mental illness (see Chapter 9 in this volume). On the other hand, Freedman's (1979) cross-cultural studies of newborns provided fascinating evidence for innate ethnic differences in temperament.

Environmental Factors in Personality Development

Ethnographic data from various nonliterate societies reveal interesting links between personality and environmental factors such as geography, climate, and means of subsistence (e.g., Barry, Child, & Bacon, 1959; Berry, 1967; Whiting, 1961; Whiting & Whiting, 1975). For example, in societies in which children participate in the family's food production or household maintenance, they are socialized to be cooperative and obedient. On the other hand, in societies in which children usually have no responsibility for family work, they tend to show more demanding or attention-seeking and less helping behavior than children in the former category (Whiting & Whiting, 1975).

Gender and Personality

Another section of the personality course focuses specifically on issues of gender and personality. I supplement the brief information provided in the text with lectures and readings that help students become more aware of gender-role messages in the family (e.g., Block, 1983; Bronstein, 1988; Rubin, Provenzano, & Luria, 1974), in school (Sadker & Sadker, 1985; Serbin & O'Leary, 1979; Wilkinson & Marrett, 1985), in communication (Mayo & Henley, 1981; Thorne & Henley, 1975), and in the media (Sternglanz & Serbin, 1974). I also assign Gould's (1972) imaginative tale of gender-free childrearing and show a NOVA documentary ("The Pinks and the Blues," 1980) about research on gender role socialization. In addition, I include a discussion of the meaning and measurement of the constructs "masculinity," "femininity," and "androgyny" (Bem, 1976; Lott, 1981; Morawski, 1987; Spence, Helmreich, & Stapp, 1975). Finally, I provide readings on the adult development of both sexes (e.g., selections from Baruch, Barnett, & Rivers, 1983; Belenky, Clinchy, Goldberger, & Tarule, 1986; Doyle, 1983; Gilligan, 1982; Miller, 1976; Pleck & Brannon, 1978; Ruddick & Daniels, 1977).

Sociocultural Factors in Personality Development

I also devote a section of the course to the study of sociocultural factors in personality development. Mead's (1935) classic, *Sex and Temperament in Three Primitive Societies*, provided an excellent example of the ways that values, customs, and child-rearing practices shape gender roles and individual personality within different societies. Other readings from anthropology (e.g., Briggs, 1970; LeVine, 1974; Spindler, 1978) or from autobiography and literature (see Chapters 15, 17, and 21 in this volume for suggestions) can be very useful here in providing students with descriptive, engaging accounts of the effects of socioeconomic level and ethnicity (and often gender) on individual personality development.

The Measurement of Personality

Since most of the personality psychologists students will read about in their text are male, some gender balance can be provided by informing students of the important (and often unrecognized) role played by women in the development of personality measures. For example, important clinical diagnostic instruments, such as the Draw-A-Man test and the Bender's Visual Motor Gestalt test, were developed by women (O'Connell & Russo, 1980; Stevens & Gardner, 1982). Henry Murray is generally credited with the development of the Thematic Apperception Test

(TAT); however, in a letter to the Radcliffe College alumni newsletter, he stated that his colleague Christiana Morgan "had the main role" in developing the TAT, and the original idea for the test in fact came from a Radcliffe student in abnormal psychology (Murray, 1985, p. 2). Janet Taylor Spence, most currently known for her Personal Attributes Questionnaire (Spence, Helmreich, & Stapp, 1975), which measures gender role attributions, is also the author of the widely used Manifest Anxiety Scale (Taylor, 1953).

The Authoritarian Personality study (Adorno, Frenkel-Brunswik, Levinson, & Sanford, 1950; summarized and critiqued in Brown, 1965) provides a good illustration of a multi-instrument approach to personality measurement and is a useful example for teaching about scale construction, reliability, validity, bias, and response set. In addition, in enabling students to examine prejudice and ethnocentrism as personality variables and to discuss them in terms of their social and cultural context, it demonstrates that personality research can be highly relevant to the domain of social issues.

Assignments, Projects, and Exercises

Assignments, projects, and experiential exercises can be designed to enhance students' awareness of sociocultural factors in personality development. One exercise I have found effective is for students to join a small discussion group with people from the same socioeconomic or ethnic background. Each group can be designated to meet either during or outside of class. In these groups, students take turns talking about their own experiences growing up with that particular background—what they are proud of, what they found hard, and what they would like others not of that background to know about them. One person in each group is appointed to take notes, and at the end the group prepares a brief written summary of what was shared and discovered. In the next class, each group is then invited to share its ideas and conclusions with the entire class and to answer questions. Sharing with others from a similar background is often a powerful experience, especially for students who are in a minority at their institution and who may have been trying to downplay or deny their differentness. Similarly, it is eye-opening for the other students to learn, often for the first time, what it may be like to grow up working class, Asian American, or Jewish in this culture. Because of the sensitive nature of the exercise, I have found it best to make it voluntary and ungraded. Students can earn a certain number of points toward their grade (some for the written summary, and additional ones for sharing their conclusions with the class), and they decide what groups they will form and which ones they will join. Thus, the composition of the groups will depend on the diversity in the class and the students' willingness to acknowledge and explore their own backgrounds. To enable exercises such as this to be truly voluntary, I set up course assignments and exercises on a menu principle; some are required, but the rest are offered as choices for varying amounts of points.

As a follow-up to this exercise, students may elect to do one or more related short paper assignments. They may write a self-analysis from a sociocultural perspective, examining how gender role socialization and ethnic and socioeconomic background may have affected their personality development. They may also do one or two taped, half-hour interviews with people from sociocultural backgrounds different from their own and write a paper relating each subject's background to her or his current personality, values, and perspective on life. This assignment encourages students to move beyond what may be a limited circle of family and social relations—to get to know a Vietnamese graduate student, or the Italian American bakery owner in their hometown. They may also learn for the first time about their own grandparents' childhoods, if the grandparents grew up in cultures or socioeconomic environments different from their own. For this assignment, I require that students get my approval in advance on both the subjects they choose and the questions they ask and that they hand in the tapes with their papers. These steps assure that they don't interview their roommates (having perhaps decided that coming from New Jersey is a sufficiently different sociocultural background), that they ask questions that are meaningful and nonoffensive, and that they report the interview information accurately.

I also require students to do an empirical research project, in which they may choose to examine gender and sociocultural issues in relation to personality. As part of the unit on personality measurement, each student becomes both a researcher and subject. As researchers, they each create their own 10–15 item personality trait scale; as subjects, using assigned numbers rather than their names, they each fill out everyone else's scale. In addition, they fill out data sheets providing information about their parents' level of education, occupation, and religion; their own sex, age, ordinal position in the family, and academic performance (e.g., high school math grades and SAT scores); and miscellaneous information about their weekly frequency of such behaviors as crying, feeling and showing anger, comforting someone else, phoning or writing home, and studying with classmates for exams. Then, after some preliminary work to determine each scale's internal consistency and to eliminate weak items, each student uses simple correlations, t-tests, or chi squares to test the hypothesis of a relationship between each trait measure and some variable or variables from the class data sheet. Thus, for example, one student might correlate the scores on an ambitiousness scale with mother's and father's level of education, another might look at differences in an assertiveness scale's scores across religious groups, and a third might look at gender differences on a measure of emotional sensitivity. In addition, for purposes of discussion, I provide a breakdown by gender of the means and standard deviations of the class data sheet variables.

Finally, I have found that course-related journal entries help students to relate the sociocultural information they are learning to their own observations and experiences. They can receive credit for up to two weekly entries, the first of which must discuss or raise a question about a topic from that week's assigned readings, and the second of which must relate some aspect of the week's readings, exercise, or discussion to each student's own life experiences or observations of the world. This ongoing exercise helps students to see that personality psychology, for all its theoretical disputes and scientific methodology, is about real people living in diverse and complex social environments, and also helps them to become more acute observers of their own world.

References

Adorno, T. W., Frenkel-Brunswik, E., Levinson, D. J., & Sanford, R. N. (1950). *The authoritarian personality.* New York: Harper & Row.

Babladelis, G. (1984). *The study of personality.* New York: Holt, Rinehart & Winston.

Barry, H., Child, I. L., & Bacon, M. K. (1959). Relation of child training to subsistence economy. *American Anthropologist, 61,* 51–63.

Baruch, G., Barnett, R., & Rivers, C. (1983). *Lifeprints: New patterns of love and work for today's women.* New York: McGraw-Hill.

Belenky, M. F., Clinchy, B. M., Goldberger, N. R., & Tarule, J. M. (1986). *Women's way of knowing: The development of self, voice, and mind.* New York: Basic Books.

Bem, S. L. (1976). Beyond androgyny: Some presumptuous prescriptions for a liberated sexual identity. In J. Sherman & F. Denmark (Eds.), *Psychology of women: Future directions of research* (pp. 1–23). New York: Psychological Dimensions.

Bernay, T., & Cantor, D. W. (Eds.). (1986). *The psychology of today's women: New psychoanalytic visions.* Hillsdale, NJ: Analytic Press.

Berry, J. W. (1967). Independence and conformity in subsistence-level societies. *Journal of Personality and Social Psychology, 7,* 415–418.

Bleier, R. (1984). *Sex and gender: A critique of biology and its theories on women.* New York: Pergamon Press.

Block, J. H. (1983). Differential premises arising from differential socialization of the sexes: Some conjectures. *Child Development, 54,* 1335–1354.

Briggs, J. L. (1970). *Never in anger.* Cambridge, MA: Harvard University Press.

Bronstein, P. (1988). Father-child interaction: Implications for gender role socialization. In P. Bronstein & C. P. Cowan (Eds.), *Fatherhood today: Men's changing role in the family* (pp. 107–124). New York: Wiley.

Brown, R. W. (1965). *Social psychology.* New York: Free Press.

Chodorow, N. J. (1978). *The reproduction of mothering: Psychoanalysis and the sociology of gender.* Berkeley, CA: University of California Press.

Dinnerstein, D. (1976). *The mermaid and the minotaur: Sexual arrangements and human malaise.* New York: Harper & Row.

Doyle, J. A. (1983). *The male experience.* Dubuque, IA: Wm. C. Brown.

Duley, M. I., Sinclair, K., & Edwards, M. I. (1986). Biology versus culture. In M. I. Duley & M. I. Edwards (Eds.), *The cross-cultural study of women: A comprehensive guide* (pp. 3–25). New York: The Feminist Press.

Fausto-Sterling, A. (1985). *Myths of gender: Biological theories about women and men.* New York: Basic Books.

Feshbach, S., & Weiner, B. (1986). *Personality* (2nd ed.). Lexington, MA: Heath.

Freedman, D. (1979). *Human sociobiology.* New York: Free Press.

Garner, S. N., Kahane, C., & Sprengnether, M. (Eds.). (1985). *The (m)other tongue: Essays in feminist psychoanalytic interpretation.* Ithaca, NY: Cornell University Press.

Gilligan, C. (1982). *In a different voice: Psychological theory and women's development.* Cambridge, MA: Harvard University Press.

Gould, L. (1972). X: A fabulous child's story. *Ms., 1*(6), pp. 74–76, 105–106.

Ibsen, H. (no date). Hedda Gabler. *Eleven plays of Henrik Ibsen.* New York: Modern Library. (Original work published 1890)

Kleinke, C. L., & Staneski, R. A. (1980). First impressions of female bust size. *Journal of Social Psychology, 110,* 123–134.

Lambert, W. W., Triandis, L., & Wolf, M. (1959). Some correlates of beliefs in the malevolence and benevolence of supernatural beings: A cross-cultural study. *Journal of Abnormal and Social Psychology, 58,* 162–169.

Lerman, H. (1986). *A note in Freud's eye: From psychoanalysis to the psychology of women.* New York: Springer Publishers.

LeVine, R. A. (1974). *Culture and personality: Contemporary readings.* New York: Aldine.

Lewis, H. B. (1986). Is Freud an enemy of women's liberation? Some historical considerations. In T. Bernay & D. W. Cantor (Eds.), *The psychology of today's woman: New psychoanalytic visions* (pp. 7–35). Hillsdale, NJ: Analytic Press.

Lewontin, R. C., Rose, S., & Kamin, L. J. (1984). *Not in our genes: Biology, ideology, and human nature.* New York: Pantheon Books.

Lott, B. (1981). A feminist critique of androgyny: Toward the elimination of gender attributions for learned behavior. In C. Mayo & N. M. Henley (Eds.), *Gender and nonverbal behavior* (pp. 171–180). New York: Springer-Verlag.

Masson, J. M. (1984). *The assault on truth: Freud's suppression of the seduction theory.* New York: Farrar, Strauss, & Giroux.

Mayo, C., & Henley, N. M. (Eds.). (1981). *Gender and nonverbal behavior.* New York: Springer-Verlag.

Mead, M. (1979). On Freud's views of female psychology. In J. Williams (Ed.), *Psychology of women: Selected readings* (pp. 53–61). New York: Norton.

Mead, M. (1935). *Sex and temperament in three primitive societies.* New York: William Morrow.

Miller, J. B. (1976). *Toward a new psychology of women.* Boston: Beacon Press.

Morawski, J. G. (1987). The troubled quest for masculinity, femininity, and androgyny. In P. Shaver & C. Hendrick (Eds.), *Sex and gender: Review of personality and social psychology,* Vol. 7. Newbury Park, CA: Sage.

Munroe, R. L., Munroe, R. H., & Whiting, J. W. M. (1980). Male sex-role resolutions. In R. L. Munroe, R. H. Munroe, & B. B. Whiting (Eds.), *Handbook of cross-cultural human development* (pp. 611–632). New York: Garland.

Murray, H. A. (1985, February). Dr. Henry A. Murray replies [Letter to the editor]. *Second Century: Radcliffe News,* p. 2.

O'Connell, A., & Russo, N. F. (1980). *Models of achievement: Reflections of eminent women in psychology.* New York: Columbia University Press.

Phares, E. J. (1984). *Introduction to personality.* Columbus, OH: Charles E. Merrill.

The pinks and the blues (1980). [Videotape]. Boston: WGBH Educational Foundation, NOVA.

Pleck, J. H., & Brannon, R. (Eds.). (1978). Male roles and the male experience [Special issue]. *Journal of Social Issues, 34*(1).

Potkay, C. R., & Allen, B. P. (1986). *Personality: Theory, research, and applications.* Monterey, CA: Brooks/Cole.

Rubin, J. Z., Provenzano, F. J., & Luria, Z. (1974). The eye of the beholder: Parents' views on sex of newborns. *American Journal of Orthopsychiatry, 44*(4), 512–519.

Ruddick, S., & Daniels, P. (Eds.). (1977). *Working it out: 23 women writers, artists, scientists, and scholars talk about their lives and work.* New York: Pantheon Books.

Sadker, M., & Sadker, D. (1985, March). Sexism in the schoolroom of the 80s. *Psychology Today,* pp. 54–57.

Serbin, L. A., & O'Leary, D. K. (1979). How nursery schools teach girls to shut up. In J. H. Williams (Ed.), *Psychology of women: Selected readings* (pp. 183–187). New York: Norton.

Spence, J. T., Helmreich, R., & Stapp, J. (1975). Ratings of self and peers on sex-role attributes and their relation to self-esteem and conceptions of masculinity and femininity. *Journal of Personality and Social Psychology, 32,* 29–39.

Spindler, G. D. (Ed.) (1978). *The making of psychological anthropology.* Berkeley, CA: University of California Press.

Spiro, M. E., & D'Andrade, R. G. (1958). A cross-cultural study of some supernatural beliefs. *American Anthropologist, 60,* 456–466.

Sternglanz, S. H., & Serbin, L. A. (1974). Sex role stereotyping in children's television programs. *Developmental Psychology, 10*(5), 710–715.

Stevens, G., & Gardner, S. (1982). *The women of psychology* (Vols. I and II). Cambridge, MA: Shenkman.

Taylor, J. A. (1953). A personality scale of manifest anxiety. *Journal of Abnormal and Social Psychology, 48,* 285–290.

Thorne, B., & Henley, N. (Eds.). (1975). *Language and sex: Difference and dominance.* Rowley, MA: Newbury House.

Walker, A. (1982). *The color purple.* New York: Washington Square Press.

Weskott, M. (1986). *The feminist legacy of Karen Horney.* New Haven, CT: Yale University Press.

Westerlund, E. (1986). Freud on sexual trauma: An historical review of seduction and betrayal. *Psychology of Women Quarterly, 10*(4), 297–309.

Whiting, J. W. M. (1961). Socialization process and personality. In F. L. K. Hsu (Ed.), *Psychological anthropology: Approaches to culture and personality.* Homewood, IL: Dorsey Press.

Whiting, J. W. M., & Child, I. (1953). *Child training and personality.* New Haven, CT: Yale University Press.

Whiting, B. B., & Whiting, J. W. M. (1975). *Children of six cultures: A psychocultural analysis.* Cambridge, MA: Harvard University Press.

Wiggens, J. S., Wiggens, N., & Conger, J. C. (1968). Correlates of heterosexual somatic preference. *Journal of Personality and Social Psychology, 10,* 82–89.

Wilkinson, L. C., & Marrett, C. B. (1985). *Gender influences in classroom interaction.* Orlando, FL: Academic Press.

8

Kathryn Quina and Janet M. Kulberg

The Experimental Psychology Course

The experimental psychology course provides a powerful arena for exposing gender and racial bias and for promoting a more balanced and diversified psychology of the future. Because psychology departments almost always require that majors take a research methods course, upgrading this course would have a positive effect on the next generation of psychologists. Furthermore, the small set of favorite methods psychologists have tended to use has served to constrict our range of knowledge about human experience; providing students with a broader set of methodologies may increase psychology's knowledge base in the future as some of these students become researchers. Finally, psychological research affects media representations of various groups, public policy, and legal decisions. Thus, sharpening students' skills for detecting and eliminating bias in research and its applications has potentially far-reaching consequences in society.

Philosophical Perspective

The traditional experimental psychology course reviews classical research studies, using them as models from which to abstract the classical methods. Students are often taught that as a science, psychology—and the people who do psychological research—are objective and apolitical. In our revisionist approach, we focus on design and analysis rather than content and introduce recent research. We stress the whole process of acquiring knowledge, in which research methods are imperfect but helpful tools, and discuss the impact of the social and political context on science (Danziger, 1985; Kimble, 1984), using examples from Cook (1984), Gould (1981), Unger (1983), and Wittig (1985). While training students to do laboratory research well, we also question using the experiment as the only means of obtaining psychological knowledge (Bronfenbrenner, 1977; Reinharz, 1984). We teach how to recognize and avoid biases, offering good as well as bad examples of the scientific process (e.g., Kieffer, 1984) to help students appreciate the limitations as well as the opportunities offered by the scientific method (see also Hoffnung, 1986; Quina, 1986).

Makosky (1985) has argued that in the current Information Age, we should try to give students the skills to adapt and change with psychology, because the field's content will certainly evolve. To this end, we consider thinking skills to be a primary objective in our courses and provide practice in information access and synthesis, deduction and induction, and critical evaluation. Our approach benefits all students, whether they are future leaders in or consumers of psychology.

Specific Course Goals

We utilize a variety of instructional techniques to achieve our goals of fostering students' thinking skills. Some of the more important approaches are presented here.

Methodological Breadth

First, we introduce students to a wide range of methodologies, including correlation, quasi-experimental designs, field study, and meta-analysis. These methodologies are illustrated through current as well as classical studies, including research from the women's and minority studies literature. We discuss the kinds of data required, the questions raised, the possible interpretations reached, and the strengths and limitations of each. It is helpful to have students review a current issue of a research journal (including newer journals such as *Psychology of Women Quarterly* or *Journal of Black Psychology*) and report back to the class on the various methods and types of subjects used. This also familiarizes students with literature that interests them personally.

Library Research Skills

Students practice library research skills by tracking down two articles starting from a key word in *Psychological Abstracts* such as *anorexia*. They summarize the theoretical approaches and empirical findings of the articles for the class, often resulting in spirited debate when findings conflict. These discussions not only demonstrate that different views and technical approaches may be applied to a single topic but also increase awareness about an important current issue.

Logical Thinking Skills

The process model, developed by Kulberg, conceptualizes the scientific method as a directional process: a circle moving from theory to test through deductive logic and back to theory through inductive logic. Orderly steps in the process—from drawing out the hypotheses to designing the study to making statistical inferences and interpreting the results—are viewed as methodological decision points for the researcher. As such, these points are vulnerable to logical errors or personal biases.

Using this process model as a guide, logical skills can be practiced through entertaining in-class exercises. For example, to develop deductive skills, we pose everyday sayings as theories: "Success breeds success" or "A clean home is a happy home." Students independently develop hypotheses, predictions, and operationally defined independent and dependent variables and then share them with the class. This exercise also underscores the arbitrary way in which theories are narrowed to real-world tests, often with evident personal or cultural bias; for example, some students will define success as wealth, others as achievement, and still others as satisfaction. We follow with a discussion of how such decisions have influenced research in psychology, such as the emphasis on career goals in the literature on achievement, and how research based on such definitions may have affected conclusions about differences between men and women or between individuals from Western and non-Western cultures.

Evaluation Skills

Students hone evaluation skills by critiquing empirical publications according to specific guidelines, which include ways to avoid gender bias (McHugh, Koeske, & Frieze, 1986). They often report shock and dismay over the extent of gender and racial bias in the literature, as well as other logical flaws such as poorly designed control procedures. At the same time, they report greater confidence in their own judgment and are pleased with being able to question or reject claims such as gender or racial inferiority. By allowing a choice of content and encouraging exploration of nontraditional areas, students are introduced to a wider definition of psychology.

In addition, we provide opportunities for students to confront stereotypes of underrepresented groups, such as "not mathematically or statistically inclined," "don't want to work hard," or "can't reason logically." Students use their new evaluative skills to critique research promoting stereotypes. For example, they discover that Benbow and Stanley's (1980) claims of genetic female inferiority in mathematical ability were based on data from the top half-percent of mathematically talented students—data that also showed dramatic improvement for women over the past 10 years that cannot be attributed to genetics. We then promote a discussion of alternative hypotheses for gender differences based on experience and cultural factors (Fausto-Sterling, 1985; Sherman, 1983).

Application to the Public Domain

The course's usefulness is enhanced by having students apply their emerging skills to the public domain (Russo & Denmark, 1984). Students may debate a public policy issue, for example, "Is pornography harmful?" (Donnerstein, Linz, & Penrod, 1986). The nature–nurture issue in intelligence offers a stimulating lesson in methodology (Eysenck & Kamin, 1981); other resources and topics for debate are found in Walsh (1987). We also have students collect and critique popular representations of psychological research from various media. Often they are alarmed by the misstated or wildly generalized conclusions they uncover. The students then develop a healthy cynicism for such reports.

Mastery Learning

To keep the emphasis on skill development, we use a mastery learning approach, which allows students to learn without the pressure of grading. Homework assignments are ungraded but must be rewritten if there are serious errors. On initial laboratory reports, students have the opportunity to incorporate feedback into a complete revision for a new grade. Although this takes more grading time early in the course, the vast improvement in later papers shows it is worthwhile in the long run.

Role Modeling

Traditionally, fostering professional identity and attitudes has been considered incidental to the classroom and not included among course objectives. In experimental psychology, where the majority of role models have been White, nondisabled men (Howard et al., 1986), professional identity has been a serious problem for many students from underrepresented populations. We provide role models of women and minorities participating in the full range of research and applied psychology. This is done by integrating the work of these new role models into discussions to illustrate important concepts and well-designed research. We also take time to discuss issues of professionalism, including potential barriers and ways to overcome them (see Rose, 1986), and to offer encouragement to all students.

Research Examples: Detecting Cultural and Gender Bias

In this section, examples of cultural and gender bias are presented for each stage of the research process model. We use these to illustrate decision-making errors and in some cases to discuss the policy implications. Other examples of gender bias in the research process are offered in Frieze, Parsons, Johnson, Ruble, and Zellman (1978), Grady (1981), Hyde (1985), and McHugh et al. (1986).

Formulating the Theory

When research is founded on biased or uninformed assumptions, the rest of the process—including the conclusions—will reflect them. Researchers tend to form designs, to reject or accept data, and to review the literature in a selective fashion to support their theories. Greenwald, Pratkanis, Leippe, and Baumgardner (1986) reviewed the history of the sleeper effect from social psychology as an example of this confirmation bias. Other examples of theoretical bias include the following:

- Theories about moral development formed around narrow assumptions and definitions such as Kohlberg's (1976) concern with legal rights and justice. Because it failed to consider other aspects of moral decision making such as the role played by relationships, this research fueled conclusions that women were morally inferior to men (Gilligan, 1982).

- Research on family issues derived from the assumption that a nuclear two-parent structure is the norm against which other structures are compared. Black single parents, for example, often raise their children in an extended family support system not available to many White nuclear families (Joseph & Lewis, 1981), yet research focusing only on the presence of two parents has considered such families deprived (see Fairchild, Chapter 16 in this volume).

- Attributions of a wide range of deviancies and disorders to early childhood experiences, for which the mother but not the father is held responsible (Caplan, 1986). Studies of attachment and child rearing (reviewed by Mussen, Conger, Kagan, & Huston, 1984) often focus only on the mother's role and perpetuate mother-blame.

Deduction of Hypotheses

Publication practices have strongly favored research that supports the research hypothesis of differences among groups (Greenwald, 1975). Thus, researchers have concentrated on hypotheses, situations, and measures that maximize group differences, ignoring the vast array of behaviors and settings in which differences are not likely to be observed. Furthermore, individual studies showing significant gender or race differences have historically been more likely to be published than multiple studies that fail to find such differences. This has in some cases allowed Type 1 errors (statistical significance caused by chance variation) to become widely cited as fact (Greenwald et al., 1986). The implications of testing the null hypothesis may be discussed in terms of limitations to the kinds of statistical conclusions that can be drawn or the specific problem of exaggerating beliefs about gender and race differences (Sommer, 1987).

Defining and Measuring Variables

Independent and dependent variables form the specific exemplars upon which the validity of the general theory rests. If the researcher selects measures or procedures more familiar or appropriate to one gender, ethnic group, or age under comparison, the results may be biased in favor of that group (Eagly, 1978; Labov, 1973). Examples include the following:

- Teacher ratings of aggressiveness show larger gender differences than actual behavioral records (Maccoby & Jacklin, 1974). Frodi, Macauley, and Thorne (1977) documented a tendency in developmental research to measure aggression through tasks that exaggerate the physical aggression of men and underestimate the verbal aggression of women.

- Researchers working with upper-middle-class Jewish children have identified the "difficult" child, whose temperament often leads to maladaptive behaviors (Thomas & Chess, 1977). Yet the same behaviors are adaptive survival strategies in some other cultural groups such as Puerto Rican immigrant families in New York City. Lerner (1985) suggested that "goodness-of-fit" to cultural demands, rather than specific behaviors, should be the independent variable in temperament research.

 • Most measures of gender-role orientation assume a bipolarity of masculinity and femininity, and some of the earlier scales confuse gender role and sexual orientation (Constantinople, 1973). Lott (1981) critiqued recent attempts to define and measure gender role.

Choice of Subjects

Historically, the most readily available subjects were White male college students, and the research areas pursued by psychologists—as well as their results—often reflected this population (Guthrie, 1976; Signorella, Vegega, & Mitchell, 1981). Some research areas, in fact, were based entirely on data regarding White men, including work on achievement motivation (critiqued by Horner, 1970) and moral development (critiqued by Gilligan, 1982). In animal research, there is a consistent bias for testing species in which the degree of male dominance is relatively large, such as rhesus monkeys, instead of other primates phylogenetically closer to humans in which sex differences are not as great (Bleier, 1984; Weisstein, 1971).

Control of Extraneous Variables

Perhaps the most common bias in research is the failure to consider or control extraneous variables that confound the effects of the independent variable. Examples of these extraneous variables include the following:

 • Income is frequently confounded with variables of gender (e.g., studies suggesting single motherhood is detrimental to children, reviewed in Mussen et al., 1984), race (Tate & Gibson, 1980), and disability (Asch, 1984).

 • The appropriate control groups have not been included in many studies on women (Parlee, 1981). To demonstrate this fact, men were included in a study of daily self-reported mood states across the menstrual cycle (Swandby, 1979). When men's moods (over a 35-day cycle) were statistically compared to women's, there were no differences between the men's and women's patterns; in fact, some men showed evidence of premenstrual syndrome!

 • Experimenter-subject differences are an overlooked but important consideration. Minority children perform more poorly on tests given by White experimenters (Hanley & Barclay, 1979). Gallagher and Quina (1987) found that experimenter gender influenced speech patterns and response content in two linguistic tasks, a slide description task and Kohlberg's moral development interview, for both male and female subjects.

Statistical Analyses

The descriptive and inferential statistics chosen for data analysis influence the conclusions drawn from research. This problem can be demonstrated in several ways.

- Classic studies of hereditary versus environmental influences on IQ show how correlation may reveal very different results from experimental comparisons. For example, developmental psychology texts often cite Skodak and Skeels (1949), who found high correlations between adopted children and their biological mothers versus low correlations between these children and their adoptive mothers, to suggest intelligence is inherited. Yet comparisons of the three groups also supported an environmental effect (Honzik, 1957); the adopted children's IQ scores were closer in magnitude to scores of their adoptive mothers. McCall (1980, pp. 250–252) offered a clear, simplified version of this important statistical point.

- Recent reviews of gender studies utilize meta-analytic techniques to dispute claims of large sex difference, notably in cognitive ability (Hyde, 1981) and aggression (Hyde, 1984). Caplan, MacPherson, and Tobin (1985) critiqued claims of sex differences in spatial abilities in terms of level of analysis, made possible by their review approach.

- Rossi (1983) reviewed research findings on mathematics performance of men and women, concluding that gender differences are exaggerated by the statistical techniques utilized. Measures of real-world meaningfulness such as omega squares (Badia & Runyon, 1982) are important to such conclusions. Other approaches such as path analysis allow researchers to compare the relative contributions of a number of important potential variables (see Eccles, 1987). These techniques keep readers and researchers mindful that variability within groups is greater than variability between groups.

Interpretation and Generalization

A range of logical flaws may occur in the conclusions drawn from research, particularly in failing to complete the process of rejecting or revising the original theory.

- When age, gender, race, or other group differences are observed, the simplistic conclusion is often drawn that the primary cause is differing biological age, hormone level, genetic heritage, physical status (Asch, 1984; Lowe & Hubbard, 1983), or other internal attributes (Riger & Galligan, 1980). However, there are some important secondary causal variables that are often not considered. For example, educational experience has been shown to confound apparent age differences in intelligence (Schaie, 1970), gender differences in mathematics (Sherman, 1983), and life chances for disabled adults (Asch, 1984). Furthermore, some behaviors may actually cause physiological differences, such as the increased testosterone levels observed after aggression (Villars, Chapter 9 in this volume).

- Statistically significant differences may be mistakenly interpreted as categorical differences rather than overlapping distributions (Frieze et al., 1978), especially in media reports (Eccles, 1987) and secondary sources describing general findings. Examples are claims that "men are mathematical, women are verbal," or "men are field independent, women are field dependent" (reviewed in Maccoby & Jacklin, 1974).

• Findings based only on White male subjects are more likely to be generalized, while researchers caution against generalizations from data on women and minorities (Allen, 1979; Dan & Beekman, 1972). The titles of publications on women or minority subjects are more likely to include the subjects' gender or race—an interesting fact for students to verify as a class project.

• Subtle but important biases can occur in the terminology used to describe findings. Garai and Scheinfeld (1968) reviewed the literature on sex differences in achievement and found that when men scored higher, the term *superior* appeared in many of the papers, but when women scored higher, as they did in about half of the comparisons, they were more likely to be described as surpassing the men.

• Jensen (1969) used correlations between identical twins to support his theory that IQ differences between Blacks and Whites are genetic in origin. This conclusion requires a flawed leap in logic, applying findings from correlations within a race to separately obtained (and seriously confounded) comparisons between racial groups. These and other critiques of Jensen's methodology are found in Lewontin, Rose, and Kamin (1984) and Mackenzie (1984).

Conclusions

In this chapter, we have laid out a philosophical approach to the research methods course that promotes an appreciation for diversity and equity. We have illustrated where and how bias may enter the process of designing, carrying out, and interpreting experimental research. And we have suggested instructional approaches that help students develop the skills to interpret, evaluate, and later reshape psychological research.

Teaching the experimental course can be a rewarding experience. It is the place where the big picture comes together for many students—the content, statistics, and skills learned in earlier classes start to make sense. The process of active discovery through exercises such as those offered here is exciting to observe and facilitate. Knowing that students will leave the course with a new awareness about the promises and the pitfalls of science, however, is the most exciting outcome of all.

References

Allen, W. R. (1979). Family roles, occupational statuses, and achievement orientations among black women in the United States. *Signs, 4,* 670–686.

Asch, A. (1984). The experience of disability: A challenge for psychology. *American Psychologist, 39,* 529–536.

Badia, P., & Runyon, R. P. (1982). *Fundamentals of behavioral research.* Reading, MA: Addison-Wesley.

Benbow, C. P., & Stanley, J. C. (1980). Sex differences in mathematical ability: Fact or artifact? *Science, 210,* 1262–1264.

Bleier, R. (1984). *Science and gender.* Elmsford, NY: Pergamon.

Bronfenbrenner, U. (1977). Toward an experimental ecology of human development. *American Psychologist, 32,* 513–531.

Caplan, P. J. (1986, October). Take the blame off mother. *Psychology Today, 20,* 70–71.

Caplan, P. J., MacPherson, G. M., & Tobin, P. (1985). Do sex-related differences in spatial abilities exist? A multilevel critique with new data. *American Psychologist, 40,* 786–799.

Constantinople, A. (1973). Masculinity-femininity: An exception to a famous dictum? *Psychological Bulletin, 80,* 389–407.

Cook, S. W. (1984). The 1954 social science statement and school desegregation: A reply to Gerard. *American Psychologist, 39,* 819–832.

Dan, A. J., & Beekman, S. (1972). Male versus female representation in psychological research. *American Psychologist, 27,* 1078.

Danziger, K. (1985). The origins of the psychological experiment as a social institution. *American Psychologist, 40,* 133–140.

Donnerstein, E., Linz, D., & Penrod, S. (1986). *The question of pornography: Research findings and policy implications.* New York: Free Press.

Eagly, A. (1978). Sex differences in influenceability. *Psychological Bulletin, 85,* 86–116.

Eccles, J. S. (1987). Gender roles and women's achievement-related decisions. *Psychology of Women Quarterly, 11*(2), 135–172.

Eysenck, H. J., & Kamin, L. (1981). *The intelligence controversy.* New York: Wiley.

Fausto-Sterling, A. (1985). *Myths of gender: Biological theories about women and men.* New York: Basic Books.

Frieze, I., Parsons, J. E., Johnson, P. B., Ruble, D. N., & Zellman, G. L. (1978). *Women and sex roles: A social psychological perspective.* New York: Norton.

Frodi, A., Macaulay, J., & Thorne, B. R. (1977). Are women always less aggressive than men? A review of the experimental literature. *Psychological Bulletin, 84,* 634–660.

Gallagher, P., & Quina, K. (1987, August). *The effect of listener gender on linguistic patterns.* Presented at the meeting of the American Psychological Association, New York.

Garai, J. E., & Scheinfeld, A. (1968). Sex differences in mental and behavioral traits. *Genetic Psychology Monographs, 17,* 169–299.

Gilligan, C. (1982). *In a different voice: Psychological theory and women's development.* Cambridge, MA: Harvard University Press.

Gould, S. J. (1981). *The mismeasure of man.* New York: Norton.

Grady, K. E. (1981). Sex bias in research design. *Psychology of Women Quarterly, 5,* 628–636.

Greenwald, A. G. (1975). Consequences of prejudice against the null hypothesis. *Psychological Bulletin, 82,* 1–20.

Greenwald, A. G., Pratkanis, A. R., Leippe, M. R., & Baumgardner, M. H. (1986). Under what conditions does theory obstruct research progress? *Psychological Review, 93*(2), 216–229.

Guthrie, R. V. (1976). *Even the rat was white: A historical view of psychology.* New York: Harper & Row.

Hanley, J. H., & Barclay, A. G. (1979). Sensitivity of the WISC and WISC-R to subject and examiner variables. *Journal of Black Psychology, 5*(2), 79–84.

Hoffnung, M. (1986). Feminist transformations: Teaching experimental psychology. *Feminist Teacher, 2,* 31–35.

Honzik, M. P. (1957). Developmental studies of parent-child resemblance in intelligence. *Child Development, 28,* 215–228.

Horner, M. (1970). Femininity and successful achievement: A basic inconsistency. In J. M. Bardwick, E. Douvan, M. S. Horner, & D. Gutmann (Eds.), *Feminine personality and conflict* (pp. 45–76). Belmont, CA: Brooks/Cole.

Howard, A., Pion, G. M., Gottfredson, G. D., Flattau, P. E., Oskamp, S., Pfafflin, S. M., Bray, D. W., & Burstein, A. G. (1986). The changing face of American psychology. *American Psychologist, 39,* 516–517.

Hyde, J. S. (1981). How large are cognitive gender differences? A meta-analysis using w and d. *American Psychologist, 36,* 892–901.

Hyde, J. S. (1984). How large are gender differences in aggression? A developmental meta-analysis. *Developmental Psychology, 20,* 722–736.

Hyde, J. S. (1985). *Half the human experience.* Lexington, MA: Heath.

Jensen, A.(1969).How much can we boost IQ and scholastic achievement? *Harvard Educational Review, 39,* 1–123.

Joseph, G. I., & Lewis, J. (1981). *Common differences: Conflicts in Black and white feminist perspectives.* Garden City, NY: Anchor.

Kieffer, C. H. (1984). Citizen empowerment: A developmental perspective. In J. Rappaport & R. Hess (Eds.), *Studies in empowerment: Steps toward understanding and action* (pp. 9–36). New York: Haworth.

Kimble, G. A. (1984). Psychology's two cultures. *American Psychologist, 39,* 833–839. [See also rejoinder by R. K. Unger (1985), Epistemological consistency and its scientific implications.*American Psychologist, 40,* 1413–1414; and rejoinder by S. B. Messer (1985). Choice of method is value laden too. *American Psychologist, 40,* 1414–1415.]

Kohlberg, L. (1976). Moral stages and moralization: The cognitive-developmental approach. In T. Lickona (Ed.), *Moral development and behavior.* New York: Holt, Rinehart & Winston.

Labov, W. (1973). *Language in the inner city: Studies in the Black English vernacular.* Philadelphia: University of Pennsylvania Press.

Lerner, J. V. (1985). The import of temperament for psychosocial functioning: Tests of a goodness of fit model. *Annual Progress in Child Psychiatry and Child Development,* 268–279.

Lewontin, R. C., Rose, S., & Kamin, L. J. (1984). *Not in our genes: Biology, ideology, and human nature.* New York: Pantheon Books.

Lott, B. (1981). A feminist critique of androgyny. In C. Mayo & N. Henley (Eds.), *Gender and nonverbal behavior* (pp. 171–180). New York: Springer-Verlag.

Lowe, M., & Hubbard, R. (1983).*Woman's nature: Rationalizations of inequality.* Elmsford, NY: Pergamon.

Maccoby, E. E., & Jacklin, C. N. (1974). *Psychology of sex differences.* Stanford, CA: Stanford University Press.

Mackenzie, B. (1984). Explaining race differences in IQ: The logic, the methodology, and the evidence.*American Psychologist, 39*(11), 1214–1233.

Makosky, V. P. (1985). Teaching psychology in the information age. *Teaching of Psychology, 12*(1), 23–26.

McCall, R. B. (1980). *Fundamental statistics for psychology* (3rd ed.). New York: Harcourt Brace Jovanovich.

McHugh, M., Koeske, R., & Frieze, I. (1986). Issues to consider in conducting nonsexist research: A guide for researchers. *American Psychologist, 41,* 879–890.

Mussen, P. H., Conger, J. J., Kagan, J., & Huston, A. C. (1984). *Child development and personality.* New York: Harper & Row.

Parlee, M. B. (1981). Appropriate control groups in feminist research. *Psychology of Women Quarterly, 5,* 637–644.

Quina, K. (1986). *Teaching research methods: A multidimensional feminist curriculum transformation plan.* Working Paper No. 164, Center for Research on Women, Wellesley College, Wellesley, MA 02181.

Reinharz, S. (1984). *On becoming a social scientist.* New Brunswick, NJ: Jossey-Bass.

Riger, S., & Galligan, P. (1980). Women in management: An exploration of competing paradigms. *American Psychologist, 35,* 902–910.

Rose, S. (Ed.). (1986). *Advice for women scholars.* New York: Springer Publishers.

Rossi, J. (1983). Ratios exaggerate gender differences in mathematical ability. *American Psychologist, 38,* 348–349.

Russo, N. F., & Denmark, F. L. (1984). Women, psychology, and public policy: Selected issues. *American Psychologist, 39,* 1161–1165. (See other articles same issue.)

Schaie, K. W. (1970). A reinterpretation of age related changes in cognitive structure and functioning. In L. R. Goulet & P. B. Baltes (Eds.), *Life-span developmental psychology: Research and theory* (pp. 486–508). New York: Academic Press.

Sherman, J. (1983). Factors predicting girls' and boys' enrollment in college preparatory mathematics. *Psychology of Women Quarterly, 7*, 272–281.

Signorella, M. L., Vegega, M. E., & Mitchell, M. E. (1981). Subject selection and analyses for sex-related differences: 1968–70 and 1975–77. *American Psychologist, 36*, 988–990.

Skodak, M., & Skeels, H. M. (1949). A final follow-up study of one hundred adopted children. *Journal of Genetic Psychology, 75*, 85–125.

Sommer, B. (1987). The file drawer effect and publication rates in menstrual cycle research. *Psychology of Women Quarterly, 11*(2), 233–242.

Swandby, J. R. (1979). *Daily and retrospective mood and physical symptom self-reports and their relationship to the menstrual cycle.* Unpublished master's thesis, University of Wisconsin–Milwaukee.

Tate, D., & Gibson, G. (1980). Socioeconomic status and Black and white intelligence revisited. *Social Behavior and Personality, 8*(2), 233–237.

Thomas, A., & Chess, S. (1977). *Temperament and development.* New York: Brunner/Mazel.

Unger, R. K. (1983). Through the looking glass: No wonderland yet! (The reciprocal relationship between methodology and models of reality). *Psychology of Women Quarterly, 8*, 9–32.

Walsh, M. R. (Ed.). (1987). *The psychology of women: Ongoing debates.* New Haven, CT: Yale University Press.

Weisstein, N. (1971). Psychology constructs the female, or the fantasy life of the male psychologist. In M. H. Garskof (Ed.), *Roles women play: Readings toward women's liberation* (pp. 68–83). Belmont, CA: Brooks/Cole.

Wittig, M. A. (1985). Metatheoretical dilemmas in the psychology of gender. *American Psychologist, 40*, 800–811.

9

Trudy Ann Villars

Psychobiology

We cannot truly understand and celebrate our diversity until we appreciate the richness of the psychobiological processes that make us individuals. In many questions in psychology, including sex and gender studies, we are brushing up against if not actively engaging psychobiological issues. Yet, the research of psychobiology is often misunderstood, sometimes because the media misinterpret and popularize incorrect notions and sometimes because scientists themselves draw inappropriate conclusions. Thus, it is especially important that instructors who include psychobiological issues in their courses correct misconceptions—particularly in the areas of sex and gender or race, where incorrect ideas have been used to justify discrimination.

In this chapter, I will discuss several current issues in psychobiology related to race and gender, with a particular focus on the influence of the "sex–gender system" in our society. Sex and gender studies and psychobiology have much to contribute to each other. On the one hand, psychobiology can do much to advance the understanding of gender. At the same time, questions of gender offer psychobiologists a stimulating challenge to develop and refine our theoretical understandings of mind–body and biobehavioral links.

The Either/Or Problem

In discussions of psychobiology, there is a tendency toward polarization. Some would deny or discount our biological heritage, an understandable response given the socially imposed restrictions that have been justified by purported biological limitations. However, although the fact that biology has historically been used to justify gender, racial, and other inequities may reflect fundamental weaknesses in the structure of the scientific enterprise (Gould, 1981; Harding, 1986; Sayers, 1983), we do not alleviate those weaknesses by ignoring biological influences or by viewing our bodies as enemy forces in need of control (Haraway, 1978). I en-

The ideas presented in this paper were developed with the support of the Wheaton College Balanced Curriculum Project; funded by the Fund for the Improvement of Post Secondary Education (FIPSE); and were further stimulated in the 1984–1985 Mellon-funded seminar on women, feminism, and science held at the Wellesley College Center for Research on Women.

courage female students to explore their social concerns along with the biological data, helping them realize that women do not need to deny their biological selves to achieve equity.

On the other hand, students are continually seduced by the idea that there are complete biological explanations for behavior and personality. Thus, psychobiologists have a special obligation to dissuade students from such an extreme belief. Students need to understand that although the genetic code initiates hormone-dependent sex differentiation—the physical differences that lead to the labeling of almost all newborns ("It's a girl!" or "It's a boy!")—it does not determine sexually dimorphic *behavior*. I stress from early in the course that a complex of social, psychological, cognitive, and biological factors mediates the development of those newborns into adult women and men. The question of gender defies simplistic reduction, either biological or psychological, and challenges us to develop a sophisticated framework that accounts for the richness and diversity of gender differences.

Topics in Psychobiology

Methodology

An extensive literature, concisely reviewed by Rosser (1986), critiqued historical abuses caused by inadequate scientific objectivity and proposed alternative perspectives on the scientific process (e.g., Fee, 1981; Harding, 1986; Harding & Hintikka, 1983; Keller, 1985). Longino (1981; Longino & Doell, 1983), for example, proposed that objectivity in science emerges not from science's empirical nature, but from "critical scrutiny of background assumptions" (p. 191) within the scientific community. She illustrated her point with a critique of the cultural views and assumptions influencing the scientific research on male dominance among primates, providing material useful in sociobiology and animal behavior courses. Newspaper articles and other media claims of biologically caused race or sex differences provide fodder for empirical critiques and discussions of how better research might be planned, carried out, and interpreted.

Sociobiology

The major texts on animal behavior all devote considerable space to discussions of sociobiological concepts, and in many cases (e.g., Alcock, 1984) the sociobiological approach is the only approach presented. To the extent that sociobiology is the study of the evolution of social behavior, this might not seem problematic. Unfortunately, as it is often practiced, sociobiology is profoundly ideological, gender-biased, and androcentric, revealing the same cultural bias historically seen in science (Hubbard, in Hubbard, Henifin, & Fried, 1982; Lowe, 1978; Sayers, 1983; Shields, 1975). There is an extensive literature critiquing various dimensions of sociobiology (Bleier, 1984; Hubbard & Lowe, 1979; Sayers, 1983; Tobach & Rosoff,

1977), which could be used as the basis of a very engaging and informative seminar for advanced undergraduates and graduate students.

Addressing the sociobiology controversy in introductory survey courses is sometimes difficult. Before any critique can be appreciated, the students must understand the basic principles of evolution. Those who expect that science courses will teach the "facts" must come to accept the limitations of scientific understanding of behavior, controversy as a quality of science, and the impact of context and culture on science. The common tendency toward anthropomorphism must be corrected, and the biases it creates must be explained and exposed.

In my Introductory Psychology and Animal Behavior courses, I find students can readily appreciate how science biased by personal racism and sexism is bad science. I begin the semester by assigning an exercise called "Facts, Inferences, and Judgments." Students do a 3 to 5 minute observation of the behavior of some animal of their choice. They are asked to describe the behavior three times: (a) in terms of the directly observable events ("the cat moved to the water dish and began lapping vigorously"); (b) using inferences made from those observations ("the cat was thirsty"); and finally (c) imposing an explicit or implicit moral judgment ("the greedy cat guzzled the water," or "the poor deprived cat was desperately thirsty"). Students read material that summarizes the distinction (chapters by Davis, Hayakawa, and Ruby & Yarbur, in Hogins & Yarber, 1979), but considerable discussion is still needed to help clarify the task. Then the students can begin to apply this analysis to their reading by identifying the judgment in statements such as the following. Based on research with scorpion flies, Thornhill (1980) asserted that ". . . rape [is] an appropriate behavior for a male to adopt when he is aggressively excluded" (p. 55), but warns that it is difficult to distinguish rape from "female coyness" (p. 52). He concludes that "male fitness is enhanced by rape" (p. 55). Thornhill and Thornhill (1983) extended this analysis to human rape. Again, however, they warn the researcher that sometimes the term rape is misapplied—for example, to situations such as "the male slave owner with his female slave. . . . [where] the benefits [e.g., higher status to the female slave] . . . exceed the costs to reproduction" (p. 141). (These and other statements are analyzed in Fausto-Sterling, 1985.)

Texts presenting sociobiological concepts are also problematic because of their intensely anthropomorphic tone. It is useful to discuss the problems of anthropomorphism, which are essential to understanding feminist critiques of sociobiology. Drickamer and Vessey (1986) reviewed the history of the study of animal behavior and provided a context for discussing the swings of the pendulum regarding anthropomorphism.

Behavior Genetics and the Nature–Nurture Controversy

The assumption that the genetic code can limit or determine complex behaviors has been used to legitimize a social "hereditarianism," which has limited access for minorities and women to educational and social opportunities. With this history, it is important to help students recognize important facts about the ways in which genes interact with physiological and environmental systems and how gene expression actually occurs. Gould's (1981) *The Mismeasure of Man* reviewed the history of hereditarian attempts to classify and rank races, classes, and sexes. Gould presented and reanalyzed the data on which these attempts were based, offering important lessons about the science of biology and behavior. In his final chapter, he provided an alternative view of human evolution. The style of the book lends itself well for use in undergraduate courses. Sayers (1983) provided an excellent review of historical and current biological arguments against feminism based on claims of women's inferiority. Several articles by Lewontin (1978, 1979; Lewontin, Rose, & Kamin, 1984, chapter 2) are also useful: a review of the history of biological rationalizations of racism (Lewontin et al., 1984), the errors and over-simplifications of sociobiology (1979), and the origins and limitations of the concept of "adaptation" (1978).

Recent debates on the nature–nurture issue, pointing to the inevitable interactions between and intertwining of environmental and genetic factors in the course of behavioral development, can be found in a series of articles with rejoinders in *Brain and Behavioral Science* (e.g., Plomin & Daniels, 1987). Such a sophisticated understanding requires more effort on the part of both student and teacher. I have found the label *epigenesis* helps students' understanding. Epigenesis, a classic concept in animal behavior (Kuo, 1967) and in developmental biology (Moore, 1987), refers to the dynamic interaction between organismic and environmental factors in development. Drickamer and Vessey (1976) discussed the epigenetic approach as a synthetic approach, in contrast to the determinisms seen in ethology, sociobiology, and traditional comparative psychology. Within that framework, students are better able to avoid dichotomous, nature–nurture thinking and to envision their mutuality.

Behavioral Endocrinology

Research on behavior–endocrine relations, as with behavior–genetic research, is often misconstrued and misused to justify gender-based inequality. One common error is the assumption that the correlational relations between the endocrine system and behavior is unidirectional: that hormones affect behavior but not the reverse. A classic example is found in the work on aggressive behavior in monkeys, in which dominant male monkeys were found to have higher testosterone levels than subordinate males (reviewed in Michael, 1968). When this example is presented to undergraduate classes, their initial presumption is like that of early researchers: that the testosterone caused the dominant behavior. After this example is presented and interpreted, instructors can present subsequent work that revealed increases in testosterone levels with experience in agonistic ("aggressive") interactions and with sexual experience (Rose, Gordon, & Bernstein, 1972).

There has been considerable recent animal research demonstrating the dynamic relations between hormones and behavior (Komisaruk, Siegel, Cheng, & Feder, 1986). Thinking about these dynamic relations may be difficult for undergraduate students whose training is limited to unidimensional cause-and-effect research methodology (Parlee, 1981; Wallston, 1981). However, by including work that emphasizes such reciprocal influences, we not only expose our students to the dynamic nature of psychobiological systems, but we also allow them to discover the value of moving into more sophisticated methodologies.

Sexuality

There is much material on women's biology and sexuality that can and should be incorporated into psychology courses of all types, especially psychobiology. *The New Our Bodies, Ourselves* (Boston Women's Health Book Collective, 1984) is an excellent source for much of that material. Rosser (1986) suggested content and format for several different courses dealing with sexuality and women's health issues. Classroom discussion can be stimulated by critical analysis of menstruation and "premenstrual syndrome" (Golub, 1983; Harrison, 1982; Paige, 1973; Parlee, 1973; Ramey, 1972; Rome, 1983), hormones and homosexuality (Birke, in Hubbard, et al, 1982; Tourney, 1980), menopause (Goodman, 1980; Reitz, 1977; Weideger, 1977), pregnancy (Liefer, 1980), and contraceptive technology (Arditti, Klein, & Minden, 1984; Seaman & Seaman, 1977). Another excellent resource is the volume edited by Parsons (1980), which integrates biological, psychological, and sociological approaches to the topics of sexuality, gender, menstruation, reproduction, and menopause.

Sex Differences in the Brain

The endocrinology of sex differentiation is an area of great popular interest. As in other areas of psychobiology, however, popular summaries of the research findings are often simplistic, implying that sex differences are biologically determined. For example, the subtitle of a *Discover* magazine article claimed "Men and women think differently. Science is finding out why" (Weintraub, 1981). The article in fact discussed recent research on hormonally induced differences in brain structures and in behavior, suggesting that early hormone exposure may determine sex differences in the brain that may, in turn, determine sex differences in behavior.

My review of endocrinology research (Villars, 1983) showed that although articles such as the *Discover* piece may not falsify the data, the tone and emphasis of the writing often reflects hidden assumptions that reinforce sexist stereotypes. For example, discussions of sex differentiation of the brain often ignore the fact that brain structure is influenced by environment and experience as well as by physiological factors (Bleier, 1984).

In presenting and discussing these views I present the fact that many behaviors called "sexually dimorphic" do not distinguish all men from all women, but are only statistically obtained. For most behaviors, there is substantial overlap between the sexes and even greater variability within than between sexes. For example, the "male" rodent sexual behavior of mounting is normally seen in female rodents as well, although with less frequency. Furthermore, I point out that sometimes, especially in the popular press, writers fail to distinguish among various areas of the brain and their functions. For example, I point out that the localized sex differences observed in subcortical brain areas are more clearly connected to differences in reproductive physiology, such as control of ovulation, but provide no direct explanation for sex differences in cognitive ability or social roles (see Bleier, 1984, especially chapter 4; and Fausto-Sterling, 1985, especially chapters 2 and 4). Finally, I point out how very similar both brain structures and functions actually are, noting that our emphasis on obtaining "significant differences" has masked the overwhelming commonalities among races and between men and women. Bleier (1984), Lowe (1983), and Villars (1983) all provided reviews and useful critiques of biopsychological research on sex differentiation and would be appropriate as supplementary readings.

Conclusion

There are additional issues in psychobiology that could have been explored here, and I have only given general references to those I did discuss. This abundance of material is evidence of the growing interest in issues of gender, race, and psychobiology, as well as an indicator of the work that needs to be done. One of my course goals is to generate enthusiasm for well-done scientific inquiry so that my students will enter the field and carry out research without the biases of past generations.

There are many ways in which psychobiology has been used in the support of social injustice. Thus, psychobiologists have an important social role. Lay and professional audiences alike turn to us with questions about nature–nurture relations, and we are in a key position to evaluate and explain that conundrum. The media is fascinated with behavioral–biological relations, and we can translate that complicated literature for them. At the same time, we can correct abuses of psychobiological theory and research in the popular press (not to mention the scientific press) that appear to legitimize societal inequities. Through our teaching we may come to transform first ourselves, our courses, and our students, and ultimately our discipline.

References

Alcock, J. (1984). *Animal behavior: An evolutionary approach* (3rd ed.). Sunderland, MA: Sinauer Associates, Inc.

Arditti, R., Klein, R. D., & Minden, S. (Eds.). (1984). *Test-tube women: What future for motherhood?* London: Pandora Press.

Bleier, R. (1984). *Science and gender: A critique of biology and its theories on women.* New York: Pergamon Press.

Boston Women's Health Collective. (1984). *The new our bodies, ourselves.* Boston: The Boston Women's Health Book Collective.

Drickamer, L. C., & Vessey, S. H. (1986). *Animal behavior: Concepts, processes, and methods.* Boston: Prindle, Weber & Schmidt.

Fausto-Sterling, A. (1985). *Myths of gender: Biological theories about women and men.* New York: Basic Books.

Fee, E. (1981). Is feminism a threat to scientific objectivity? *International Journal of Women's Studies, 4*(4), 378–392.

Golub, S. (Ed.). (1983). *Lifting the curse of menstruation.* New York: Haworth Press.

Goodman, M. (1980). Toward a biology of menopause. In C. R. Stimpson & E. S. Person (Eds.), *Women: Sex and sexuality* (pp. 241–255). Chicago: University of Chicago Press.

Gould, S. J. (1981). *The mismeasure of man.* New York: Norton.

Haraway, D. (1978). Animal sociology and a natural economy of the body politic, Part I: A political physiology of dominance. *Signs, 4*(1), 21–36.

Harding, S. (1986). *The science question in feminism.* Ithaca, NY: Cornell University Press.

Harding, S., & Hintikka, M. B. (1983). *Discovering reality: Perspectives on epistemology, methodology and philosophy of science.* Boston: Reidel.

Harrison, M. (1982). *Self-help for premenstrual syndrome.* Cambridge, MA: Matrix Press.

Hogins, J. B., & Yarber, R. E. (Eds.). (1979). *Reading, writing and rhetoric.* Chicago: Science Reading Associates, Inc.

Hubbard, R., Henifin, M. S., & Fried, B. (Eds.). (1982). *Biological woman: The convenient myth.* Cambridge, MA: Shenkman.

Hubbard, R., & Lowe, M. (Eds.). (1979). *Genes and gender II: Pitfalls in research on sex and gender.* New York: Gordian Press.

Keller, E. F. (1985). *Reflections on gender and science.* New Haven, CT: Yale University Press.

Komisaruk, B. R., Siegel, H. I., Cheng, M., & Feder, H. H. (Eds.). (1986). *Reproduction: A behavioral and neuroendocrine perspective.* New York: New York Academy of Sciences.

Kuo, Z. Y. (1967). *Dynamics of behavior development.* New York: Random House.

Lewontin, R. C. (1978, September). Adaptation. *Scientific American,* pp. 212–222.

Lewontin, R. C. (1979). Socibiology as an adaptationist program. *Behavioral Science, 24,* 5–14.

Lewontin, R. C., Rose, S., & Kamin, L. J. (1984). *Not in our genes: Biology, ideology, and human nature.* New York: Pantheon.

Liefer, M. (1980). Pregnancy. In C. R. Stimpson & E. S. Person (Eds.), *Women: Sex and sexuality* (pp. 212–223). Chicago: University of Chicago Press.

Longino, H. E. (1981, Fall). Scientific objectivity and feminist theorizing. *Liberal Education, 187–195.*

Longino, H. E., & Doell, R. (1983). Body, bias and behavior: A comparative analysis of reasoning in two areas of biological science. *Signs, 9*(2), 206–277.

Lowe, M. (1978). Sociobiology and sex differences. *Signs, 4*(1), 118–125.

Lowe, M. (1983). The dialectic of biology and culture. In M. Lowe & R. Hubbard (Eds.), *Women's nature: Rationalizations of inequality* (pp. 39–62). New York: Pergamon Press.

Michael, R. P. (Ed.). (1968). *Endocrinology and human behavior.* London: Oxford University Press.

Moore, J. A. (1987). Science as a way of knowing—Developmental biology. *American Zoologist, 27,* 415–573.

Paige, K. (1973, August). Women learn to sing the menstrual blues. *Psychology Today,* pp. 41–46.

Parlee, M. B. (1973). The premenstrual syndrome. *Psychological Bulletin, 83*(6), 454–465.

Parlee, M. B. (1981). Appropriate control groups in feminist research. *Psychology of Women Quarterly, 5*(4), 637–644.

Parsons, J. E. (1980). *The psychobiology of sex differences and sex roles.* New York: McGraw-Hill.

Plomin, R., & Daniels, D. (1987). Why are children in the same family so different from one another? *Behavioral and Brain Sciences, 10*(1), 1–59. [Includes rebuttals and discussions.]

Ramey, E. (1972, Spring). Men's cycles (They have them too, you know). *Ms.,* pp. 8–14.

Reitz, R. (1977). *Menopause: A positive approach.* New York: Penguin Books.

Rome, E. (1983). *Premenstrual syndrome examined through a feminist lens.* Watertown, MA: The Boston Women's Health Book Collective.

Rose, R. M., Gordon, T. P., & Bernstein, I. S. (1972). Plasma testosterone levels in the male rhesus: Influences of sexual and social stimuli. *Science, 178,* 643–645.

Rosser, S. V. (1986). *Teaching science and health from a feminist perspective.* New York: Pergamon Press.

Sayers, J. (1983). *Biological politics: Feminist and antifeminist perspectives.* New York: Tavistock Publications.

Seaman, B., & Seaman, G. (1977). *Women and the crises of sex hormones.* New York: Bantam Books.

Shields, S. A. (1975). Functionalism, Darwinism, and the psychology of women: A study in social myth. *American Psychologist, 30,* 739–734.

Thornhill, R. (1980). Rape in Panorpa scorpion flies and a general rape hypothesis. *Animal Behavior, 28,* 52–57.

Thornhill, R., & Thornhill, N. W. (1983). Human rape: An evolutionary analysis. *Ethology & Sociobiology, 4*(3) 137–173.

Tobach, E., & Rosoff, B. (1977). *Genes and gender.* New York: Gordian Press.

Tourney, G. (1980). Hormones and homosexuality. In J. Marmor (Ed.), *Homosexual behavior* (pp. 41–58). New York: Basic Books.

Villars, T. A. (1983). Sexual dimorphisms in the brain and behavior: Reflections on the concept. In M. Triplette (Ed.), *Women's studies and the curriculum* (pp. 55–65). Winston-Salem, NC: Salem Press.

Wallston, B. S. (1981). What are the questions in psychology of women? A feminist approach to research. *Psychology of Women Quarterly, 5*(4), 597–617.

Weideger, P. (1977). *Menstruation and menopause.* New York: Dell.

Weintraub, P. (1981, April). The brain: His and hers. *Discover,* pp.15–20.

10

Elizabeth Scarborough

The History of Psychology Course

Several years ago I received, as department chair, a call from a psychologist at a nearby college. He wanted to know whether someone in my department might be available to give a colloquium presentation to students and faculty at his institution. After giving information about several of my faculty, I mentioned that I had developed a lecture on women in the history of psychology for the American Psychological Association (APA) Centennial Lectures Program. He replied that although that topic would be interesting, the colloquium series was meant to feature research in substantive areas. I commented that a majority of our majors were women and they regularly expressed appreciation for being informed that women had played an important role in psychology's history and said they were often surprised and even relieved to discover this. Two weeks later he called again: "We've talked about what you said—and realized that more than half of *our* majors are women. We're a small department, with no women faculty. Could you come to give your lecture here?"

Discussing women's issues in a historical context not only increases understanding of psychology's social history, but also provides the basis for extended consideration of the status of women today. I see this as an important function of any history of psychology course: to help students examine women's participation, contributions, and experiences in psychology and to discover issues relevant in the past that are still influential. I am convinced that this helps women achieve a sense of their legitimacy in psychology.

Current Status of the History of Psychology Course

The history of psychology course is one of the oldest in the psychology curriculum. From its inception as a distinct academic discipline, psychology has held a self-conscious and almost reverential attitude toward its antecedent development. Early psychologists learned psychology by studying its historical roots and its laboratory methods. Their academic training included reading classical works as well as contemporary research reports. As the literature of psychology burgeoned around the turn of the century, however, it became more difficult for a beginning student to cover all the territory, so history of psychology textbooks began to appear as secondary sources. They necessarily compressed information about psychology's past and not only reported but also categorized, organized, and interpreted what was believed to be most important. Several such works had been produced by 1929 when E. G. Boring published the book that gained such widespread acceptance that it became the standard text for classroom instruction. (Three history textbooks were published in 1929, but Boring quickly cornered the market.) Boring's work stood as *the* history of psychology for more than three decades, and even now most writers of new texts are heavily influenced by it.

The predominance of Boring's conception of psychology's history is crucial because of its limitations. Boring defined psychology purely as an experimental science and gave greatest attention to its development in the 19th century European psychophysical laboratories, particularly those located in Germany. Thus, he almost totally ignored equally important developments that arose in other theoretical traditions and other geographical areas, for example, the biological emphasis in Britain and the work on psychopathology in France. By focusing only on the history of ideas important to academic psychology, Boring also bypassed what had already become, by 1929, a central feature of American psychology: its professional outreach in applied forms.

Following Boring's lead, history textbook writers have tended to focus primarily on academic psychology and on the history of particular ideas, selectively discussing only the historical figures deemed to have been prominent in those two areas. In so doing, these writers have almost totally obliterated the facts surrounding the presence and contributions of women, ethnic minorities, and non-Western cultural traditions in psychology's history. Somehow these facts vanished in the process of writing psychology's history.

Given the bias and limitations of current texts, the instructor who determines to teach a responsible course—one that presents the history of modern psychology as the diverse field that it is and thereby acknowledges that a significant proportion of its adherents have been other than White men—must locate materials not present in the textbooks. Fortunately, scholars are currently producing data and interpretations that future textbook writers may incorporate to give a more balanced presentation. Until they do so, however, the burden and satisfaction of extending our understanding of psychology's history lie with the knowledgeable and innovative instructor.

An Integrative Course

The content and methods used in a history course are dependent on several factors, including the purpose of the course in a department's curriculum (e.g., introductory or upper level, emphasis on history or on systems and theories, required or elective), the interests and goals of the instructor, and students' prior preparation. Because of the variation that exists in institutions and curricula, there is no one best outline or method.

I have not yet settled on what I consider the ideal course for my own situation. Rather, I have used a number of texts, sometimes in combination, and have varied the outline and student assignments year by year. My course is full, because I start with the ancient Greeks and consider the premodern period as a necessary background before launching into the emergence of the "new" psychology in the 19th century. The bulk of the course, however, covers the 20th century, with primary emphasis on the various systems that have dominated psychology in the United States. I conclude with material—sometimes limited to a single lecture—on psychology around the world, so that students may be spared a too parochial view. For this latter emphasis, I draw from Sexton and Misiak (1971) and more recent articles describing national and regional psychologies (e.g., Ardila, 1982). *International Psychologist*, the newsletter of the International Council of Psychologists, provides timely information.

I have chosen to integrate women into the course wherever possible, and I also include at least one specific lecture on the status of women in psychology.[1] For that I begin with the early 1890s, acknowledging the first women psychologists, then move to the establishment of the National Council of Women Psychologists in the 1940s and the data collected by the APA survey reported by Bryan and Boring (1944, 1946, 1947; see also Boring's 1951 follow-up), concluding with an explanation of the role played by the three current groups: the Association for Women in Psychology, APA's Division 35, and the APA Committee on Women (see Chapter 8 in Scarborough and Furumoto, 1987; also Walsh, 1985). Students are surprised and puzzled to learn, for example, that Christine Ladd-Franklin and Mary Calkins, after fully meeting all requirements for doctoral degrees, did not receive their PhDs because Johns Hopkins and Harvard refused to grant the doctorate to women; that married women were denied appointments and so marriage removed women from academic employment; and that women's offers of assistance were blatantly ignored when the APA rallied psychologists to serve the nation's defense efforts in World War II. They are also surprised that over the last 15 years, about a third of the doctorates in psychology have gone to women—and they begin to question why they see so few women professors. This lecture may also emphasize that many well-known contributions to the field were made by unacknowledged women. For example, the principal author of the Thematic Apperception Test was Christiana Morgan, and Maude Merrill was L. M. Terman's collaborator in producing the current version of the Stanford Binet (see Bernstein and Russo, 1974, for other examples).

A lecture on APA history, including its inception, development, and influence in the field, makes it possible to include a discussion of women and minorities while considering such things as early members, membership requirements, governance, and award recipients (for a summary of the early years see Fernberger, 1932; for lists of awardees see Russo and Denmark, 1987). Students learn that despite the high proportion of women members through the years, women only rarely served in leadership positions; there were only two women presidents of APA during its first 80 years. The Committee on Women in Psychology (1986) provided an excellent report on the changing status of women psychologists.

Course assignments, either for an entire class or for individual students, may be directed toward learning more about the roles played by women and minorities,

---

1.   At this point, few resources are available on the role of minorities in the history of psychology. It is an area in which research is especially needed.

provided the instructor emphasizes such topics as important and gives students some direction for locating relevant sources. My library exercises, designed to acquaint students with resources used for historical research as well as with the factual material, always provide opportunities for students to deal with content related to women's participation and contributions to psychology. Student projects, especially when reported and discussed in class, are excellent ways of incorporating material on women and minorities and of encouraging student engagement with issues of sexism and racism. A project I have used several times calls for students to do a content analysis of an entire volume of a psychological journal published between 1890 and 1910 and to include in a written report biographical details for one of the authors. (This project is described by Benjamin, 1981.) It always happens that several students choose to study a woman writer, and then typically discover that it is very difficult to learn more about her. They begin to ask why so little has been preserved for the study of women in psychology.

Resources

Because most of these sources I have found especially useful include bibliographies that are also rich in providing leads to other materials, the references that follow are selective. For additional references and ideas, see also Quina (1987), Russo (1982), and Russo and Denmark (1987).

Current texts are generally deficient in dealing with women (Goodman, 1983), minorities, professional and organizational aspects of psychology, non-Western traditions, and the social context within which the discipline of psychology has evolved. Murphy and Kovach's (1972) text, although dated, included some material not usually covered. Brennan (1986) provided a broader understanding of non-German 19th century antecedents. Designed for student use, the book I coauthored with Furumoto (1987) on the history of women in psychology presented the only systematic study of the experiences, as well as the contributions, of the entire group of first women psychologists: those who entered the field by 1906. It includes a collective biography of 25 women and uses detailed studies of 5 of them to examine the gender-specific themes that influenced their lives and careers: institutional barriers to graduate education, obligations of a daughter to her family, the marriage-versus-career dilemma, limited employment opportunities, and discrimination by male colleagues. In addition, we considered the reasons that textbook writers have failed to deal adequately with the subject of women.

For help in organizing a course and devising student projects and exercises, Benjamin (1981) provided the most comprehensive resource available for the teacher of the history of psychology, which includes an annotated list of articles on teaching the history of psychology. More recent articles that may be useful have been published in the journal *Teaching of Psychology:* Cole (1983); Davis, Janzen, and Davis (1982); Furumoto (1985); Harris (1983); Hart (1986); Kushner (1980); Smith (1982); and Terry (1980). Most of these deal with methods that may be adapted to emphasize women and minorities; Furumoto (1985) explicitly described a seminar that focuses on women in the history of psychology. A useful reference volume, both for instructors and for student projects, is that by Viney,

Wertheimer, and Wertheimer (1979), which has an annotated bibliography under the heading "Histories of Women in Psychology." A more recent reference work (Siegel & Finley, 1985) contains short biographical sketches as well as bibliographies of published biographical studies for a fairly comprehensive set of prominent women psychologists.

Lists of the earliest women in psychology and discussions of issues that influenced their lives and careers are provided by Furumoto and Scarborough (1986) and Scarborough and Furumoto (1987). *The Psychological Register* (Murchison, 1929) is a good starting place to learn about women who had entered the profession by 1929 and about psychologists in countries that might be of special interest to minority students; the listings include selected bibliographies as well as biographical data. Benjamin (1980) provided references for information about a number of women psychologists. For autobiographies of an outstanding group of women plus chapters on historical and achievement perspectives, see O'Connell and Russo (1983). Guthrie (1976) is the principal source of information about Black psychologists; Cadwallader (1984) discussed C. H. Turner, an early, important Black psychologist not included in Guthrie's work.

I also recommend the following basic references that an instructor might use for gaining contextual information: Solomon (1985) on the history of women's education, Rossiter (1982) on women scientists, and Lewin (1984) and Rosenberg (1982) on women's issues during the last 100 years. These are also useful for individual students who want to go deeper into a specialized topic than the usual history and systems course allows. Several of my women students have followed the history of psychology course with independent study projects in subsequent semesters and have found these sources particularly valuable.

References

Ardila, R. (1982). Psychology in Latin America today. *Annual Review of Psychology, 33,* 103–122.

Benjamin, L. T., Jr. (1980). Women in psychology: Biography and autobiography. *Psychology of Women Quarterly, 5,* 140–144.

Benjamin, L. T., Jr. (1981). *Teaching history of psychology: A handbook.* New York: Academic Press.

Bernstein, M. D., & Russo, N. F. (1974). The history of psychology revisited: Or, up with our foremothers. *American Psychologist, 29,* 130–134.

Boring, E. G. (1929). *A history of experimental psychology.* New York: Appleton-Century-Crofts.

Boring, E. G. (1951). The woman problem. *American Psychologist, 6,* 679–682.

Brennan, J. F. (1986). *History and systems of psychology* (2nd ed.). Englewood Cliffs, NJ: Prentice-Hall.

Bryan, A. L., & Boring, E. G. (1944). Women in American psychology: Prolegomenon. *Psychological Bulletin, 41,* 447–454.

Bryan, A. L., & Boring, E. G. (1946). Women in American psychology: Statistics from the OPP Questionnaire. *American Psychologist, 1,* 71–79.

Bryan, A. L., & Boring, E. G. (1947). Women in American psychology: Factors affecting their professional careers. *American Psychologist, 2,* 3–20.

Cadwallader, T. C. (1984). Neglected aspects of the evolution of American comparative and animal psychology. In G. Greenberg & E. Tobach (Eds.), *Behavioral evolution and integrative levels* (pp. 15–48). Hillsdale, NJ: Erlbaum.

Cole, D. L. (1983). The way we were: Teaching history of psychology through mock APA conventions. *Teaching of Psychology, 12,* 234–236.

Committee on Women in Psychology. (1986). *Women in the American Psychological Association.* Washington, DC: American Psychological Association.

Davis, S. L., Janzen, W. C., & Davis, R. L. (1982). Teaching and learning the history of psychology need not be boring. *Teaching of Psychology, 9,* 183–184.

Fernberger, S. W. (1932). The American Psychological Association: A historical summary, 1892–1930. *Psychological Bulletin, 29,* 1–89.

Furumoto, L. (1985). Placing women in the history of psychology course. *Teaching of Psychology, 12,* 203–206.

Furumoto, L., & Scarborough, E. (1986). Placing women in the history of psychology: The first generation of American women psychologists. *American Psychologist, 41,* 35–42.

Goodman, E. S. (1983). History's choices [Review of *History and systems of psychology* and *A history of Western psychology*]. *Contemporary Psychology, 28,* 667–669.

Guthrie, R. V. (1976). *Even the rat was white: A historical view of psychology.* New York: Harper & Row.

Harris, B. (1983). Telling students about the history of social psychology. *Teaching of Psychology, 10,* 26–28.

Hart, J. J. (1986). A strategy for teaching the history and systems of psychology. *Teaching of Psychology, 13,* 67–69.

Kushner, R. I. (1980). The prescriptive approach to the teaching of the history of psychology course. *Teaching of Psychology, 7,* 184–185.

Lewin, M. (Ed.). (1984). *In the shadow of the past: Psychology portrays the sexes.* New York: Columbia University Press.

Murchison, C. (Ed.). (1929). *The psychological register.* Worcester, MA: Clark University Press.

Murphy, G., & Kovach, J. K. (1972). *Historical introduction to modern psychology.* New York: Harcourt Brace Jovanovich.

O'Connell, A. N., & Russo, N. F. (1983). *Models of achievement: Reflections of eminent women in psychology.* New York: Columbia University Press.

Quina, K. (1987). Resources for teaching history of psychology. In S. Golub & R. J. Freedman (Eds.), *Psychology of women: Resources for a core curriculum* (pp. 51–55). New York: Garland Press.

Rosenberg, R. (1982). *Beyond separate spheres: Intellectual roots of modern feminism.* New Haven, CT: Yale University Press.

Rossiter, M. W. (1982). *Women scientists in America: Struggles and strategies to 1940.* Baltimore: The Johns Hopkins University Press.

Russo, N. (1982). *Resources for teaching the history of women in psychology.* Washington, DC: American Psychological Association, Office for Women's Programs.

Russo, N., & Denmark, F. (1987). Contributions of women to psychology. *Annual Review of Psychology, 38,* 279–298.

Scarborough, E., & Furumoto, L. (1987). *Untold lives: The first generation of American women psychologists.* New York: Columbia University Press.

Sexton, V. S., & Misiak, H. (1971). *Historical perspectives in psychology: Readings.* Belmont, CA: Brooks/Cole.

Siegel, P. J., & Finley, K. T. (1985). *Women in the scientific search: An American bio-bibliography, 1724–1979.* Metuchen, NJ: Scarecrow Press.

Smith, A. H. (1982). Different approaches for teaching the history of psychology course. *Teaching of Psychology, 9,* 180–182.

Solomon, B. M. (1985). *In the company of educated women: A history of women and higher education in America.* New Haven, CT: Yale University Press.

Terry, W. S. (1980). Tracing psychology's "roots": A project for history and systems courses. *Teaching of Psychology, 7,* 176–177.

Viney, W., Wertheimer, M., & Wertheimer, M. L. (1979). *History of psychology: A guide to information sources.* Detroit, MI: Gale Research Company.

Walsh, M. R. (1985). Academic professional women organizing for change: The struggle in psychology. *Journal of Social Issues, 41,* 17–27.

11

Felipe G. Castro and Delia Magaña

A Course in Health Promotion in Ethnic Minority Populations

The health needs of American ethnic minorities often require considerations beyond the customary applications of good health care. These needs apply most to those ethnics who differ substantially from members of the American middle class in terms of life-style or access to basic medical care. Health promotion among members of such unacculturated ethnic populations requires that health professionals conceptualize and understand the many interacting variables that produce different health needs and levels of health risk.

Whereas promoting health in motivated middle-income Anglo Americans can be difficult, promoting health among lower income ethnic minorities is even more challenging. Members of ethnic minorities often differ from members of the dominant culture in their conceptual models of illness, their values, their health habits, their level of compliance, and their need to cope with stressful social and economic conditions. In addition, many ethnic minority persons also have limited resources for maintaining their personal health and the health of family members.

The course we describe in this chapter was developed for junior and senior undergraduate students who are considering graduate study and a career in one of the helping professions. It has been offered once a year at the University of California, Los Angeles, and this year 100 students were enrolled. We present the course format here and offer suggestions for developing a similar course or for integrating the material into an existing health psychology curriculum.

Background and Rationale for the Course

In the 1980 census, of the 226.5 million Americans living in the United States, 26.5 million (11.7%) were Blacks, 14.6 million (6.4%) were Hispanics, 3.5 million (1.5%) were Asians and Pacific Islanders, and 1.4 million (0.6%) were American Indians, Eskimos, or Aleuts (U.S. Bureau of the Census, 1981). In the 1980s, sociopolitical conflicts or economic upheaval in Mexico, El Salvador, Nicaragua, Southeast Asia, and other regions have resulted in the influx of both documented and undocumented immigrants to the United States, thus inflating the population size for several ethnic minority groups. For example, as of January 1986, the size of the U.S. Hispanic population has been reliably estimated to have increased 16% in less than 6 years ("Latino population," 1986). Thus, from a practical standpoint, students in the health and human service professions will be likely to come in contact with ethnic minority individuals. This is most likely to occur in the nation's major urban centers, where Blacks, Hispanics, and Asians make up a significant proportion of the city's population and are the majority population in some city districts.

In addition, rapid population growth and cultural isolation of ethnic groups mean that many first-generation immigrants are likely to be unacculturated and unfamiliar with the mental health system in the United States. Finally, minority individuals are more likely to be unemployed or living below the poverty level. The complex and devastating effects of isolation and poverty on health problems and on the ability to carry out effective behavior change must be considered throughout any course or discussion on minority health promotion (see U.S. Department of Health and Human Services, 1986).

From a population's perspective, important differences exist among ethnic minority groups in the incidence rates of various disease entities. For example, the incidence rates of coronary heart disease (CHD), the major cause of death in the United States, vary considerably by ethnicity. A recent study conducted in Los Angeles County by Chapman, Frerichs, and Maes (1983) has identified ethnic group differences in age- and sex-adjusted mortality rates per 100,000 for CHD as follows: Blacks 472.0; Whites, 429.5; Hispanics, 390.6; Japanese, 255.3; Chinese, 157.0; Koreans, 143.8; and Filipinos, 84.2. These differences may be attributable to genetic factors, although they more likely suggest group differences in life-style such as dietary habits, exercise habits, rest, and recreation (Blackburn, 1980). Current views of major health agencies and empirical studies suggest that such life-style differences serve as mediators of CHD risk and mortality rates and that longevity as well as quality of life are influenced by health habits (American Heart Association, 1985; Paffenbarger, Hyde, Wing, & Hsieh, 1986; U.S. Department of Health and Human Services, 1983).

Health promotion, as conceptualized in our course, involves an examination of the life-styles and health behavior patterns of various ethnic and social class groups and the use of behavior change principles to encourage and guide health-oriented changes. Such changes must consider culturally valued habits involving diet, recreation, and exercise while also taking into account the limits imposed by a person's sociocultural environment. A basic premise of such behavior change efforts is that almost all persons in the United States have *some* degree of control over the quality of their life in terms of physical fitness and psychological well-being. This course examines such issues related to health-oriented behavior change among the major U.S. ethnic minority populations.

Course Goals and Structure

The focus of the course is on identifying and understanding the factors—cultural, socioeconomic, genetic, psychological, interpersonal, and environmental—which may increase or reduce the risk of chronic degenerative disease and which may encourage or discourage good health habits in ethnic populations. The basic course outline appears before the references at the end of this chapter. The three units in the course are the following.

I. Introduction to Concepts of Health

This unit focuses on health promotion, disease risk factors, psychological and physiological aspects of the stress process, and a multivariate model for effective conceptualization, assessment, and intervention with ethnic minorities. Health promotion is defined as disease prevention and risk factor reduction, plus behavior change for enhancing health status. Health status is described as a product of (a) genetically determined biological processes, (b) environmental conditions, and (c) behavior, that is, life-style and health habits. Because a person has most control over his or her personal health habits, this is the area in which health status may most easily be improved. Stress is seen as a complex person–environment variable that influences health status via cognitive and physiological pathways (Asterita, 1985; Lazarus & Folkman, 1984). Ethnic minorities of lower socioeconomic status are seen as persons most often exposed to uncontrollable life events that are potentially stressful and that can eventually deteriorate good health status.

II. Ethnic Minority Groups

The three largest ethnic minority groups in the United States are Blacks, Hispanics, and Asians and Pacific Islanders. For all groups, we emphasize that there are large within-group differences in living conditions and life-styles and that these differences are mediated by social class, urban versus rural background, current living situation, status as an immigrant, social skills including English-speaking ability, occupational opportunities, and social resources such as the availability of meaningful social support networks.

For Black Americans, we discuss historical issues of prejudice and racial segregation as antecedents of current life issues. We describe the chronic stress due to sociocultural factors, including discrimination and poverty, and the positive effects of supportive extended family networks (Hines & Boyd-Franklin, 1982). Although biobehavioral links are as yet speculative, we focus on personal coping skills and social supports as viable ways to reduce stress and thereby lower the risk of high blood pressure at the individual level—one step toward reducing the incidence rate of high blood pressure for the U.S. Black population.

For many Hispanics, some of the stressors mentioned above are associated with migration to the mainland among Puerto Ricans and with immigration to the United States by various other Hispanics and Latin Americans. We discuss the likelihood that language is a barrier for unacculturated Hispanics in doctor–patient communications and the fact that "personalismo," or cultural expectations of personalized attention in the doctor–patient or client–therapist relationship (Schreiber & Homiak, 1981) may be a critical factor for many Hispanics in compliance with health care regimens (Di Matteo & Di Nicola, 1982). We also make the point that acculturated or bilingual and bicultural Hispanics may or may not share such expectations. In addition, students learn that there is growing epidemiological evidence that diabetes mellitus has higher than average incidence rates in the general Hispanic population (Gardner et al., 1984), making this disease a major health problem that parallels the high incidence rates of high blood pressure among Blacks.

For Asians and Pacific Islanders, students learn about the broad diversity in national backgrounds and life-styles found within this group. Acculturation status is examined as a factor moderating life-style differences—from highly acculturated Japanese Americans who may do better than Anglo Americans in educational and occupational attainments to the many Indochinese refugees who have few economic resources and a poor health status.

Students discover that mental health problems among various Asian American groups may in part be a result of psychological conflicts encountered in the process of adapting to life in the United States. They become aware that such cultural concepts as stigma, shame, and loss of face may be factors preventing Asian Americans from seeking mental health care (Shon & Ja, 1982). They also learn that increasing rates of coronary heart disease correspond with increasing levels of acculturation and associated life-style changes among Japanese and Japanese Americans (Marmot & Syme, 1976).

III.   Health Disorders Affected by Life-Style

This unit presents various health disorders for which life-style (health-related habits) is seen as a major contributor, specifically, cardiovascular disease and the addictive use of cigarettes, alcohol, and drugs (Castro, Newcomb, & Cadish, 1987). Students learn about the cardiopulmonary effects of exercise (McArdle, Katch, & Katch, 1981), which functions as a positive health habit; regular aerobic exercise not only promotes cardiovascular fitness but also tends to discourage cigarette smoking and drug use. In addition, they learn about means of relapse prevention and the maintenance of a healthy life-style (Marlatt & Gordon, 1985).

Prevention of Acquired Immune Deficiency Syndrome (AIDS) is an important topic for this course. In addition to factual information on the virus and its transmission, the behaviors which increase risk of infection (unprotected sex, sharing needles) should be clearly identified. Furthermore, the relationship between these behaviors and the proportionally high rates of Human Immunodeficiency Virus (HIV) infection among Black and Hispanic Americans should be recognized, along with the need for better educational outreach for high-risk minority populations. The *Multicultural Inquiry and Research on AIDS* quarterly newsletter is an excellent resource (6025 Third Street, San Francisco, CA 94124; 415-822-4030).

Course Assignments

The course grade is based on three exams and an independent project. For the project, students have a choice of either completing a behavior change project or writing a term paper on a disease or health problem that affects one or more ethnic minority groups.

Behavior Change Project

Perhaps the best way to understand life-style, health habits, and the issues involved in behavior change is to participate in one's own behavior change project. The behavior change project consists of a 4-week trial in which the student learns about basic principles of behavior change such as contingency contracting and contingent reinforcement[1] while also increasing the frequency (per day or per week) of a desirable behavior such as aerobic exercise, or decreasing the frequency of an undesirable behavior such as salt consumption. As an aid in behavior-change decison making, students use a microcomputer and software developed for this course in order to obtain an automated "health habits profile" (see Castro, 1987). The profile provides the participant with a graph that identifies those behaviors on which he or she is significantly different from his or her peers. The computer profile is normed for age, gender, and ethnicity, so students also have the opportunity to see how these factors affect group norms.

Through daily self-monitoring and other behavioral methods guided by a 4-week behavior change manual, the participant assesses his or her present and ongoing health habits during a baseline period (week 1). The participant attempts to change a discrete target behavior (e.g., jogging for 15 minutes nonstop) during week 2 and then attempts to change a second target behavior (e.g., eating a salad at a meal) during week 3 while maintaining the first target behavior. Finally, during week 4, the participant continues to maintain both target behaviors.

At the end of this project, the participant is asked to evaluate retrospectively, in a brief final report of behavior change progress and analysis, the effects of time constraints, dwindling motivation, fatigue or illness, and competing obligations as these may have acted as barriers to successful behavior change. In this way, this project allows the participant to recognize and appreciate the manner in which one's existing pattern of health-related habits (life-style) and environment (significant others, social pressures, and obligations) can be compatible or incompatible with the incorporation (or the elimination) of any two new target behaviors. Moreover, the participant gains an appreciation for the relative ease or difficulty involved in changing one target behavior (e.g., increasing the frequency of fruit consumption) versus another (e.g., decreasing cigarette smoking). For the project, I emphasize that a student's grade is based not on his or her success at behavior change but rather on the quality of his or her evaluation and final report.

Term Paper

Students may elect to write a 15- to 25-page paper on a disease or health problem that affects an ethnic minority group or groups, using as their sources biomedical and psychological journal articles. Examples of acceptable topic areas are socio-cultural factors affecting incidence rates of non-insulin-dependent diabetes mellitus in Mexican Americans, social and physiological stress pathways in the development of high blood pressure in Blacks, acculturation and other factors

---

1. Details of the behavior contingency reinforcement program as well as the Lifestyle Survey Protocol (Castro, 1987) are available from the author.

associated with high rates of alcohol use among certain American Indians, ways of increasing medication compliance in elderly Chinatown residents, AIDS educational outreach for minority women, and peer influence and neurological factors as determinants of cocaine abuse in minority ghetto youths.

Conclusion

In general, promoting health in ethnic minority populations involves an appreciation of the many cultural, social, and political issues that affect ethnic minority individuals in this country—issues that often have no clear or ideal solution or outcome. Biomedical and epidemiological facts need to be considered within a sociocultural framework, yet such a framework is often complex and is subject to competing or conflicting interpretations. This state of affairs can spark controversy; for example, one question is whether it is preferable for Japanese Americans (or Blacks or Chicanos) to reject their ethnic identity in favor of full assimilation into the American middle class. Open discussion of such issues has added to the richness of this class and increased students' appreciation for the complexity of these social issues.

Course Outline

Unit/topic	Readings
I. *Introduction to concepts of health*	
Health promotion: the concept of health	Taylor, Ureda and Denham (1982)
Risk factors; multivariate model of health behavior and change	U.S. Department of Health, Education and Welfare (1979)
	Spector (1979)
Principles of attitude and behavioral change	Di Matteo and Di Nicola (1982)
	Stuart (1982)
Self-directed behavior change	Watson and Tharp (1981)
Stress and coping: physiological and sociocultural pathways	Asterita (1985)
	Lazarus and Folkman (1984)
II. *Ethnic minority groups*	
Black Americans	Jackson (1981)
	Hines and Boyd-Franklin (1982)
Asians/Pacific Islanders	Gould-Martin and Ngin (1981)
	Shon and Ja (1982)
Hispanics	Schreiber and Homiak (1981)
	Falicov (1982)

Health promotion with ethnic minorities	Harwood (1981)
	McGoldrick, Pearce, and
	Giordano (1982)

III. *Health disorders affected by life-style*

Cardiovascular disease: physiological and psychological factors	Herd (1984)
Exercise physiology	Martin and Dubbert (1982)
Addictive disorders: alcohol abuse, cigarette smoking, cocaine, and polydrug abuse	Brownell (1984)
	Lichtenstein (1982)
	Istvan and Matarazzo (1984)
Life-style: measurement and interpretation	Castro, Newcomb, and Cadish (1987)
Motivation for change; relapse reduction	Marlatt and Gordon (1985)
	Leventhal, Zimmerman, and Gutmann (1984)
Integrative discussion	

References

American Heart Association. (1985). *Heart facts.* Dallas, TX: Author.

Asterita, M. F. (1985). *The physiology of stress.* New York: Human Sciences Press.

Blackburn, H. (1980). Risk factors and cardiovascular disease. In American Heart Association (Eds.), *The American Heart Association heartbook* (pp. 2–20). New York: Dutton.

Brownell, K. D. (1984). The addictive disorders. In G. T. Wilson, C. M. Franks, K. D. Brownell, & P. C. Kendall (Eds.), *Annual review of behavior therapy: Theory and practice* (Vol. 9, pp. 211–258). New York: Guilford Press.

Castro, F. G. (1987). *The lifestyle survey: A manual for self-directed, healthy behavior change.* Unpublished manuscript.

Castro, F. G., Newcomb, M. D., & Cadish, K. (1987). Lifestyle differences between young adult cocaine users and their nonuser peers. *Journal of Drug Education, 17,* 89–111.

Chapman, J. M., Frerichs, R. R., & Maes, E. F. (1983). *Cardiovascular diseases in Los Angeles.* Los Angeles, CA: American Heart Association, Greater Los Angeles Affiliate.

Di Matteo, M. R., & Di Nicola, D. D. (1982). *Achieving patient compliance: The psychology of the medical practitioner's role.* New York: Pergamon Press.

Falicov, C. J. (1982). Mexican families. In M. McGoldrick, J. K. Pearce, & J. Giordano (Eds.), *Ethnicity and family therapy* (pp. 134–163). New York: Guilford Press.

Gardner, L. I., Stern, M. P., Haffner, S. M., Gaskill, S. P., Hazuda, H. P., Relethford, J. H., & Eifter, C. W. (1984). Prevalence of diabetes in Mexican Americans: Relationship to percent of gene pool derived from Native American sources. *Diabetes, 33,* 86–92.

Gould-Martin, K., & Ngin, C. (1981). Chinese Americans. In A. Harwood, (Ed.), *Ethnicity and medical care* (pp. 130–171). Cambridge, MA: Harvard University Press.

Harwood, A. (1981). Guidelines for culturally appropriate health care. In A. Harwood (Ed.), *Ethnicity and medical care* (pp. 482–507). Cambridge, MA: Harvard University Press.

Herd, J. A. (1984). Cardiovascular disease and hypertension. In W. S. Gentry (Ed.), *Handbook of behavioral medicine* (pp. 222–281). New York: Guilford Press.

Hines, P. M., & Boyd-Franklin, N. (1982). Black families. In M. McGoldrick, J. K. Pearce, & J. Giordano (Eds.), *Ethnicity and family therapy.* New York: Guilford Press.

Istvan, J., & Matarazzo, J. D. (1984). Tobacco, alcohol and caffeine use: A review of their interrelationships. *Psychological Bulletin, 95,* 301–326.

Jackson, J. J. (1981). Urban Black Americans. In A. Harwood (Ed.), *Ethnicity and medical care* (pp. 37–129). Cambridge, MA: Harvard University Press.

Lazarus, R. S., & Folkman, S. (1984). Coping and adaptation. In W. B. Gentry (Ed.), *Handbook of behavioral medicine* (pp. 282–325). New York: Guilford Press.

Leventhal, H., Zimmerman, R., & Gutmann, M. (1984). Compliance: A self-regulation perspective. In W. D. Gentry (Ed.), *Handbook of behavioral medicine* (pp. 369–436). New York: Guilford Press.

Lichtenstein, E. (1982). The smoking problem: A behavioral perspective. *Journal of Consulting and Clinical Psychology, 50,* 804–819.

Latino population. (1986, January). *Los Angeles Times.*

Marlatt, G. A., & Gordon, J. R. (1985). Relapse prevention: Maintenance strategies in the treatment of addictive behaviors. New York: Guilford Press.

Marmot, M. G., & Syme, L. S. (1976). Acculturation and coronary heart disease in Japanese Americans. *American Journal of Epidemiology, 104,* 225–247.

Martin, J. E., & Dubbert, P. M. (1982). Exercise applications and promotions in behavioral medicine: Current status and future directions. *Journal of Consulting and Clinical Psychology, 50,* 1004–1017.

McArdle, W. D., Katch, F. I., & Katch, V. L. (1981). *Exercise physiology: Energy, nutrition, and human performance.* Philadelphia, PA: Lea & Febiger.

McGoldrick, M., Pearce, J. K., & Giordano, J. (1982). *Ethnicity and family therapy.* New York: Guilford Press.

Paffenbarger, R. S., Hyde, R. T., Wing, A. L., & Hsieh, C. (1986). Physical activity, all-cause mortality, and longevity of college alumni. *New England Journal of Medicine, 314,* 605–613.

Schreiber, J. M., & Homiak, J. P. (1981). Mexican Americans. In A. Harwood (Ed.), *Ethnicity and medical care* (pp. 264–336). Cambridge, MA: Harvard University Press.

Shon, S. P., & Ja, D. Y. (1982). Asian families. In M. McGoldrick, J. K. Pearce, & J. Giordano (Eds.), *Ethnicity and family therapy* (pp. 208–228). New York: Guilford Press.

Spector, R. E. (1979). *Cultural diversity in health and illness.* New York: Appleton-Century-Crofts.

Stuart, R. B. (1982). *Adherence, compliance and generalization in behavioral medicine.* New York: Brunner/Mazel.

Taylor, R. B., Ureda, J. R., & Denham, J. W. (1982). *Health promotion: Principles and clinical applications.* Norwalk, CT: Appleton-Century-Crofts.

U.S. Bureau of the Census. (1981). *Age, sex, race, and Spanish origin of the population by regions, divisions, and states: 1980.* Washington, DC: Author.

U.S. Department of Health, Education and Welfare. (1979). *Healthy people: The Surgeon General's report on health promotion and disease prevention.* Washington, DC: Author.

U.S. Department of Health and Human Services. (1983). *Promoting health, preventing disease: Objectives for the nation.* Washington, DC: Author.

U.S. Department of Health and Human Services. (1986). Report of the Secretary's task force on Black and minority health, Vol. IV, Part 1. Washington, DC: Author.

Watson, D. L., & Tharp, R. G. (1981). *Self-directed behavior: Self-modification for personal adjustment* (3rd ed.). Monterey, CA: Brooks/Cole.

12

Alice Brown-Collins

Integrating Third World Womanism Into the Psychology of Women Course

Feminist psychology advocates equality of opportunity for women's full development. Writers, scholars, and teachers of feminist psychology are reevaluating traditional psychological premises, theories, methodologies, and studies concerning women, correcting erroneous and value-laden assumptions, developing psychological models that account for female behavior, and integrating women's and men's experiences into a comprehensive model of human behavior. However, a major criticism has emerged which exposes contradictions in the development of the discipline of feminist psychology. A number of scholars (Brown, Goodwin, Hall, & Jackson-Lowman, 1985; Fine, 1985; Hull, Scott, & Smith, 1982; Kahn & Jean, 1983) have pointed out that feminist psychology, as well as other areas of women's studies, either ignores the experiences of Third World women or treats gender issues as relatively uniform for all women regardless of racial, ethnic, or class backgrounds.

Fine (1985) stated, "The experiences of diverse groups of women, particularly those whose lives are neglected by prevailing ideologies and are absent from public view, need to gain further recognition in psychology of women" (p. 171). Thus, while feminist psychologists seek to expose gender-biased ideologies of mainstream psychology in their teaching, they must not fall into the same trap of developing courses that do not reflect multicultural viewpoints.

When a psychology of women course has included Third World women's psychological development, it has generally been limited in scope, focusing only on African American women or selected aspects of Third World women's experiences (Brown et al., 1985). The image presented of the African American woman is often unrealistic: either she is "strong, bold, resilient, and indestructible" or totally victimized (Harper, 1986, p. 1). When course material on the impact of racism and sexism on the gender role development of Third World women is presented, not enough attention is given to the complete individual and the complex interplay of cultural, historical, and social factors (Brown-Collins & Sussewell, 1986; Cole, 1986). Thus, the literature is characterized by limited, stereotypical, overgeneralized explanations of Third World female behavior.

Alice Walker (1983) said, "Womanist is to feminist as purple is to lavender" (p. xii). I offer the same perspective in this chapter: defining feminist as being linked to gender and womanist as being linked to a state and depth of being, "committed to the survival and wholeness of entire people, male and female" (p. xi).

I would like to thank Hortensia Amaro and Anne Fausto-Sterling for discussion on various aspects of this chapter and Donna Mitchell and Gita Greene for assistance in editing and typing.

The rich complexity of the lives of Third World women cannot be conveyed when they are segregated into one chapter in a psychology of women textbook with one week allotted to minority women's issues. If we wish to transform our psychology of women courses to incorporate knowledge of Third World women, we must envision, plan, and teach about a world of women from a multicultural, rather than an ethnocentric, perspective. This chapter presents some guidelines for formulating a course on the psychology of women that would address the diversity among women in a positive, engaging way.

Course Goals

In addition to traditional objectives, I envision five goals in teaching a psychology of women course from a multicultural perspective. They are:

1. To examine commonalities and differences in the psychological development of all women and to develop students' appreciation for and sensitivity to diversity;

2. To familiarize students with the impact of oppression on all women and the special problems created by oppression for Third World women;

3. To incorporate an analysis of economic, social, political, historical, cultural, and racial forces into the psychological literature on women;

4. To develop students' skills in taking multiple cultural perspectives on women's lives and experiences;

5. To promote student empowerment through encouraging students to develop their own critical, independent thinking skills.

Structure of the Course

When teaching about women from minority racial and ethnic groups, there are several guidelines I follow in developing class activities and exercises. First, I acknowledge the importance of students' personal experiences in examining various issues and concerns. Small group activities are utilized to document diversity as well as to reaffirm the importance of individual women's life experiences. Group exercises also provide students with opportunities for meaningful dialogue and significant interaction with their peers. Second, I try to accommodate individual differences in learning styles and personal interests. Individual exercises allow students to demonstrate their learning while pursuing their own interests. Finally, if any activity or exercise is not working for a particular group of students, I empower them by seeking their input and revising the tasks to meet their needs.

In my large classes of 60–70 students, we break into small group discussions once a week. Student moderators lead the discussions within a group of 10 students on a topic of interest. The student moderators are responsible for developing questions and choosing readings on their topic. Although moderators change from one week to the next, the group membership stays the same throughout the semester. This allows students to develop a sense of trust and rapport with each other. In my smaller classes, I allow time for more interaction and feedback. Students are asked to select a journal article or chapter from a book on African American women, present an oral abstract of that paper, and lead a general class discussion.

Students in both large and small classes carry out a number of individual assignments. Writing essays, critiquing lectures, participating in discussions, and reading assigned material are required. Instead of taking a final examination, students may volunteer for a field placement, write an oral history, or develop a research proposal. If they choose a field placement, students meet with me individually to determine a suitable site that addresses Third World women's issues. In an oral history project, the student interviews a Third World woman living outside the university community. Students may develop an original research proposal on a topic of interest which explores the reality of Third World women's lives. I encourage students to interact with individuals in the community, and these assignments are oriented toward achieving that purpose.

Throughout the semester, students are urged to share their insights, as well as information, on the women they view on television, read about in newspapers and magazines, and know in their daily lives. I allow 5–10 minutes at the beginning of each class to address students' concerns. The class is enriched by panel discussions and guest lecturers and informed through debates and discussions of the readings.

Content of the Course

The major topics typically discussed in a psychology of women course are outlined here and include questions and discussion ideas relevant to a multicultural perspective, references, and other resources such as novels, autobiographies, and films.

Introductory Perspectives: What is Psychology of Women?

Is there a single psychology of women? In small groups, students can share their own backgrounds, examine how their backgrounds shape their experience as a woman, and discuss their expectations for this course. As a class, it is helpful to discuss the difficulties involved in developing a course that is able to reflect the diversity of all women and allow the class to suggest strategies to include everyone's experience.

Identify five underrepresented women such as a lesbian mother, a disabled teenager, or an elderly Black woman. Have students list characteristics these women may have in common, and then consider special issues or needs each might face, including the kinds of discrimination or lost opportunity for education, jobs, or growth, each woman may experience. Try to guide students to a recognition that discrimination is real. The following are resources to be included:

Coet, L. J. (1977). Defining the term "handicap": A function of sex, race, religion, and geographic location. *Psychological Reports, 41*(3), 783–787.

Fujitomi, I., & Wong, D. (1981). The new Asian-American woman. In J. S. Cox (Ed.), *Female psychology: The emerging self* (pp. 213–248). New York: St. Martin's Press.

Green, R. (1980). Native American women. *Signs, 6,* 248–267.

Gridley, M. E. (1974). *American Indian woman.* New York: Hawthorne.

Kumagai, G. (1978). The Asian woman in America. *Explorations in Ethnic Studies, 1*(2), 27–39.

Lindsay, B. (Ed.). (1980). *Comparative perspectives on Third World women: The impact of race, sex, and class.* New York: Praeger.

Medicine, B. (1978). *The Native American woman: A perspective.* Las Cruces, NM: New Mexico State University.

Mirande, A., & Enriquez, E. (1979). *La Chicana: The Mexican-American woman.* Chicago: The University of Chicago Press.

Murray, S. R., & Scott, P. B. (Eds.). (1981). A special issue on Black women. *Psychology of Women Quarterly, 6*(3).

Smith, A., & Stewart, A. J. (Eds.). (1983). Racism and sexism in Black women's lives [Entire issue]. *Journal of Social Issues, 39*(3).

Growing Up Female: Socialization Processes

How do socialization practices differ by gender, class, race, religion, and other relevant factors? In a self-study, students can analyze their own childhood and adolescence, including both the positive and negative messages they received from family, friends, school, and the media about being a girl or boy of their particular background. These insights can be used in class to compare and contrast strategies for raising female children. The film *Growing Up Female: As Six Become One* [New Day Films, P. O. Box 315, Franklin Lakes, NJ 07417] shows the influences of forces such as parents, teachers, the media, and pop music in the lives of six women. Novels or autobiographies can be used to reinforce students' awareness of diversity in the socialization and development of women. The following readings may be included:

Fillmore, L. W., & Cheong, J. L. (1980). The early socialization of Asian-American children. In National Institute of Education, *Conference on the Educational and Occupational Needs of Asian-Pacific-American Women.* Washington, DC: U.S. Government Printing Office.

Kingston, M. (1976). *Woman warrior: Memoirs of a girlhood among ghosts.* New York: Knopf.

Ladner, J. (1971). *Tomorrow's tomorrow: The Black woman.* New York: Anchor.

Morrison, T. (1971). *The bluest eye.* New York: Holt, Rinehart & Winston.

Neithammer, C. (1977). *Daughters of the earth: The lives and legends of American Indian women.* New York: Macmillan.

Smith, E. J. (1982). The Black female adolescent: A review of the educational, career and psychological literature. *Psychology of Women Quarterly, 6*(3), 261–288.

Sex Roles

Ask students to generate terms and labels used to define the roles of various women in this culture, including lesbian, African American, Hispanic American, American Indian, Asian American, and disabled women. Explore the stereotypical images that emerge and the ways that society reinforces them. Counteract these with research on actual sex roles. As an individual assignment, students can create a pictorial presentation of representations collected from various magazines about women and analyze the ages and ethnicity of the models, the portrayal of the female role, and potential impact on readers' images of women.

One important subtopic is achievement motivation. Have students critique at least three research articles that cross-culturally examine achievement-related concepts (e.g., learned helplessness, attitudes toward success) using the resources listed, while considering the historical and cultural experiences of the groups studied. Are the conclusions about each group different? Are the concepts valid cross-culturally? The following readings may be included:

Bonner, F. (1975). Black women and white women: A comparative analysis of perceptions of sex roles. In W. D. Johnson & T. L. Green (Eds.), *Perspectives on Afro-American women*. Washington, DC: ECCA Publications.

Brown-Collins, A., & Sussewell, D. (1986). The Afro-American woman's emerging selves. *Journal of Black Psychology, 13*(1), 1–11.

Caudill, W., & DeVos, G. (1956). Achievement, culture and personality: The case of the Japanese Americans. *American Anthropologist, 58*, 1102–1126.

Gonsalves, S. V. (1983). Bibliography of fear of success in Black women: 1970–1982. *Psychological Reports, 53*, 1249–1250.

Houston, J. W. (1980). Beyond manzanar: A personal view of Asian-American womanhood. In R. Endo, S. Sue, & N. Wagner (Eds.), *Asian Americans: Social and psychological perspectives, Vol. II* (pp. 17–25). Palo Alto, CA: Science and Behavior Books.

Kidwell, C. S. (1979). American Indian women: Problems in communicating a cultural/sexual identity. *The Creative Woman, 2*, 33–38.

Lott, J. T., & Pian, C. (1979). *Beyond stereotypes and statistics: Emergence of Asian and Pacific American women*. Washington, DC: Organization of Pan-Asian American women.

Matson, M. R. (1983). Black women's sex roles: The social context for a new ideology. *Journal of Social Issues, 39*(3), 79–100.

Savage, J. E., Jr., Stearns, A. D., Kelley, Y. B., & Williams, J. (1979). Relationship of internal–external locus of control, self-concept, and masculinity-femininity to fear of success in Black freshmen and senior college women. In A. W. Boykin, A. J. Franklin, & J. F. Yates (Eds.), *Research directions of Black Psychologists* (pp. 340–350). New York: Russell Sage.

Women's Lives: The Psychological Impact of Work

What differences occur in the way work impacts women when one considers class, race, and culture? The readings listed and the film, *Nosotras Trabahamos en la Costura: Puerto Rican Women in the Garment Industry* [Center for Puerto Rican Studies, Hunter College, 695 Park Ave., Box 548, New York, NY 10021], may help students understand these differences. Students may interview a working woman from a different ethnic, socioeconomic, or social group and ask her about her work experience, other family members' work history, her perceived place in the work force, her feelings about how her work impacts on her family, and strategies she may have had to develop to deal with sexism, racism, or classism in the workplace.

Almquist, E. M. (1979). *Minorities, gender and work.* Lexington, MA: D. C. Heath.

Center for the Study, Education and Advancement of Women. (1983). *Black working women/ Debunking the myths.* Berkeley: University of California, Berkeley Women's Center.

Kim, E. H., & Otani, J. (1983). *With silk wings: Asian American women at work.* San Francisco: Asian Women United of California.

Krause, N., & Markides, K. S. (1985). Employment and psychological well-being in Mexican-American women. *Journal of Health and Social Behavior, 26*(1), 15–26.

Mullings, L. (1984). Minority women, work and health. In W. Chavkin (Ed.), *Double exposure: Women's health hazards on the job and at home* (pp. 121–139). New York: Monthly Review.

National Institute of Education. (1980). *Conference on the educational and occupational needs of American Indian women.* Washington, DC: U.S. Government Printing Office.

Zambrana, R. E. (1982). *Work, family and health: Latina women in transition.* New York: Fordham University, Hispanic Research Center.

Clinical Psychology and Psychotherapy

As a class, explore the concept of mental health, including characterizations of women in the abnormal psychology literature and whether women of various backgrounds differ in what they consider to be healthy behavior. In small groups, students can compile data from the library on the prevalence of particular diagnoses for women and the approaches used to treat them, focusing on factors such as ethnicity, age, sexual orientation, socioeconomic level, and marital status. A short report and oral group presentation help students compare their findings with those of other groups. Nontraditional approaches to treating women, including religious practices and folk medicine, may be explored. A guest speaker from an ethnically based mental health facility can provide perspectives on dealing with mental health and illness within a particular cultural group. The following are resources:

Amaro, H., & Russo, N. F. (Eds.). (1987). Hispanic women and mental health: Contemporary issues in research and practice [Special Issue]. *Psychology of Women Quarterly, 11*(4).

Comas-Dias, L. (1982). Mental health needs of Puerto Rican women in the United States. In R. E. Zambrana (Ed.), *Work, family and health: Latina women in transition* (pp. 1–10). New York: Fordham University, Hispanic Research Center.

DeMonteflores, C. (1981). Conflicting alliances: Therapy issues with Hispanic lesbians. *Catalyst, 12,* 33–44.

Fullilove, M., Hunt, P., Jackson, S., & Zaretsky, L. (1984). *Women in psychotherapy: Issues of sex, class, and race.* San Francisco: University of California, Tenderloin Mental Health Clinic.

Homma-True, R. (1980). Mental health issues among Asian-American women. In National Institute of Education, *Conference on the educational and occupational needs of Asian-Pacific-American women.* Washington, DC: U.S. Government Printing Office.

Marsella, A. J., & White, G. M. (1982). *Cultural conceptions of mental health and therapy.* Dordrecht, Holland: D. Reidel.

Olmeda, E. L., & Parrow, D. L. (1981). Mental health of minority women: Some special issues. *Professional Psychology, 12,* 103–111.

Rodgers-Rose, L. (1980). *Black woman.* Beverly Hills, CA: Sage. (See pp. 265–284)

Roskies, E. (1978). Sex, culture and illness—An overview. *Social Science and Medicine, 12*(3B), 139–141.

Stoker, D. H., Zurcher, L. A., & Fox, W. (1968). Women in psychotherapy: A cross-cultural comparison. *International Journal of Social Psychiatry, 15*(1), 5–22.

Terrell, F., & Terrell, S. (1984). Race of counselor, client sex, cultural mistrust level and premature termination from counseling among Black clients. *Journal of Counseling Psychology, 31,* 371–375.

Violence Against Women

Limited attention has been given to the concerns of Third World women about violence. One class assignment may be compiling an annotated research bibliography to which all students contribute. This bibliography can be used to identify gaps in existing literature and to point to future research needs. The best examples of the psychological impact of violence is found in novels and autobiographies. Students should read at least one such work and consider how race, social class, and age are related to abuse against women and how they affect women's response to violence. Small groups can discuss race and class stereotypes that interfere with the recognition and prevention of violence against Third World women. The following are recommended readings:

Angelou, M. (1969). *I know why the caged bird sings.* New York: Bantam Books.

Boujouen, N. (1979, March/April). El asalto sexual. *Aegis,* 7–10.

Garcia, C., Destito, C., Mendez, I., & Mercado, M. (1979, March/April). La violacion sexual—The reality of rape. *Aegis,* 18–23.

Lerner, G. (1972). The rape of Black women as a weapon of terror. In G. Lerner (Ed.), *Black women in white America* (pp. 172–192). New York: Vintage Books.

Richie, B. (1985). Battered Black women: A challenge for the Black community. *Black Scholar, 16*(2), 40–44.

Walker, A. (1982). *The color purple.* New York: Pocket Books.

Female Sexuality

The class can explore perceptions of sexuality in the media and in their own lives by examining stereotypes and attitudes toward sexuality of other groups. In addition, issues of reproductive rights in relation to Third World women is an important topic and is graphically detailed in *La Operacion,* [The Cinema Guild, 1697

Broadway, New York, NY 10019], a film about female sterilization. The following are other resources:

Blackwood, E. (1984). Sexuality and gender in certain native American tribes: The case of cross-gender females. *Signs, 10*(1), 27–42.

Davis, A. (1983). Racism, birth control and reproductive rights. In A. Davis (Ed.), *Women, race and class* (pp. 202–221). New York: Random House.

Davis, S. M., & Harris, M. B. (1982). Sexual knowledge, sexual interest, and sources of sexual information of rural and urban adolescents from three cultures. *Adolescence, 17*, 471–492.

Del Castillo, A. R. (1980). Sterilization: An overview. In M. Mora & A. R. Del Castillo (Eds.), *Mexican women in the United States: Struggles, past and present* (pp. 65–70). Los Angeles: University of California, Los Angeles, Chicano Studies Research Center.

Espin, O. (1986). Cultural and historical influences on sexuality in Hispanic/Latin women. In J. B. Cole (Ed.), *All American women: Lines that divide, ties that bind* (pp. 272–284). New York: Free Press.

Hanscombe, G., & Forster, J. (1981). *Rocking the cradle: Lesbian mothers, a challenge in family living.* London: Owen.

Lorde, A. (1978). Scratching the surface: Some notes on barriers to women and loving. *The Black Scholar, 6*, 31–35.

Simpson, R. (1983). The Afro-American female: The historical context of the construction of sexual identity. In A. Snitow, C. Stansell, & S. Thompson (Eds.), *Powers of desire: The politics of sexuality* (pp. 229–235). New York: Monthly Review Press.

Feminist Psychology: Liberation and Change

A class debate helps summarize issues in feminist psychology relevant to Third World women. Ignoring actual race or personal viewpoints, divide the class into a group representing traditional feminist views and a group expressing Third World women's views. Students must research the literature and present their group's definition of feminism and the psychological issues their group believes are important. The debate should help students see the strengths and weaknesses inherent in each position. Follow-up discussion should allow students to formulate strategies for changing feminist psychology in ways that recognize and appreciate diversity as well as commonalities among women. The following are suggested readings:

Anthias, F., & Yuval-Davis, N. (1983). Contextualizing feminism—gender, ethnic and class divisions. *Feminist Review, 15*, 62–75.

Cheng, L. (1984). Asian American women and feminism. *Sojourner, 10*(2), 11–12.

Cole, J. (Ed.). (1986). *All American women: Lines that divide, ties that bind.* New York: Free Press. (See chapters by P. G. Allen on American Indian women [pp. 407–409] and S. Hohri on Asian American women [pp. 420–426].)

Davis, A. (1981). *Women, race, and class.* New York: Random House.

Dill, B. T. (1983). Race, class and gender: Prospects for an all-inclusive sisterhood. *Feminist Studies, 9*, 131–150.

Giddings, P. (1984). *When and where I enter: The impact of Black women on race and sex in America.* New York: William Morrow.

Hooks, B. (1981). *Ain't I a woman.* Boston: South End Press.

Joseph, G. I., & Lewis, J. (1981). *Common differences: Conflicts in Black and white feminist perspectives.* Garden City, NJ: Anchor Press.

Loo, C., & Ong, P. (1982). Slaying demons with a sewing needle: Feminist issues for Chinatown's women. *Berkeley Journal of Sociology, 27,* 77–88.

Noda, B., Kitty, T., & Wong, Z. (1979). Coming out: We are here in the Asian community. A dialog with three Asian women. *Bridge: An Asian American perspective, 7,* 22–24.

Smith, B. (Ed.). (1982). *Home girls: A Black feminist anthology.* New York: Kitchen Table, Women of Color Press.

Additional Resources

Amaro, H. (1987). *Bibliography on the psychology of Hispanic-American women.* Available from author, Boston University Medical School, 818 Harmon Avenue, Boston, MA 02118.

Baca-Zinn, M. (1984). Mexican heritage women: A bibliographic essay. *Sage Race Relations Abstracts, 9* (3, August), 1–12.

Bataille, G. (1980). Bibliography on Native American women. *Concerns: The Newsletter of the MLA's Women's Caucus,* 16–27.

Cabello-Argandona, R., Gomez-Quinones, J, & Duran, P. H. (1976). *The Chicana: A comprehensive bibliographic study.* Los Angeles: University of California, Los Angeles, Chicano Studies Center.

Center for Research on Women. (1984). *Selected bibliography of social science readings on women of color in the United States.* Memphis, TN: Memphis State University.

Cheng, L., Furth, C., & Yip, H. (1982). *Women in China: Bibliography of English language materials.* Berkeley: University of California, Berkeley, Institute of East Asian Studies. (Includes material on Asian women in the United States.)

Chu, J. (1984). Asian American women bibliography. *Network News, 6,* 18–23.

Enabulele, B., & Jones, D. (Eds.). (1978). *A resource guide on Black women in the United States.* Available from the Institute for Urban Affairs and Research, Howard University, 2900 Van Ness Street, Washington, DC 20008.

Fine, M. (1985). Incorporating perspectives on women into the undergraduate curriculum: A Ford Foundation workshop. *Women's Studies Quarterly, 13*(2), 15–17.

Green, R. (1983). *Native American women: A contextual bibliography.* Bloomington: Indiana University Press.

Ito, K. L. (1984). *Selected bibliography: Asian and Pacific American women.* Los Angeles: University of California, Los Angeles.

King, L. M., Moody, S., Thompson, O., & Bennett, M. (1983). Black psychology reconsidered: Notes toward curriculum developments. In J. Chumn, P. Dunston, & F. Ross-Sheriff (Eds.), *Mental health and people of color: Curriculum development and change* (pp. 3–22). Washington, DC: Howard University Press.

Klotman, P., with W. Baatz. (1978). *The Black family and the Black woman: A bibliography.* New York: Arno Press.

Knaster, M. (1977). *Women in Spanish America: An annotated bibliography from preconquest to contemporary times.* Boston: G. K. Hall.

Lindsay, B. (1980). *Comparative perspectives on Third World Women.* New York: Praeger.

Marie, J., & Kaplan, E. B. (1984). Women of color in the United States. In S. Pritchard (Ed.), *The women's annual number four* (pp. 187–201). Boston: G. K. Hall.

Mays, V. (in press). *The Black woman: A bibliographic guide to research materials on Black women in the social sciences and mental health.* New York: Praeger.

Medicine, B. (1975, Summer). The role of women in Native American societies: A bibliography. *The Indian Historian, 8.*

Mortimer, D., & Bryce-Laporte, R. (1981). *Female immigrants to the United States: Caribbean, Latin American and African experiences* (Occasional Papers No. 2). Washington, DC: Smithsonian Instution, Research Institute on Immigration and Ethnic Studies.

Roberts, J. R. (1981). *Black lesbians: An annotated bibliography.* Tallahassee, FL: Naiad Press.

Scott, P. E. (1983). A basic resource list of places where curriculum development on women is done and disseminated. *Sojourner, 8*(5), 12.

Simms, J. L. (1980). *The progress of Afro-American women: A selected guide.* Westport, CT: Greenwood Press.

Young, G. S., & Sims-Wood, J. (1984). *The psychology and mental health of Afro-American women: A selected bibliography.* Temple Hills, MD: Afro-Resources, Inc.

References

Brown, A., Goodwin, B. J., Hall, B. A., & Jackson-Lowman, H. A. (1985). Review of psychology of women textbooks: Focus on the Afro-American woman. *Psychology of Women Quarterly, 9*(1), 29–38.

Brown-Collins, A., & Sussewell, D. (1986). Afro-American woman's emerging selves. *Journal of Black Psychology, 13*(1), 1–11.

Cole, J. B. (1986). *All American women: Lines that divide, ties that bind.* New York: Free Press.

Fine, M. (1985). Reflections on a feminist psychology of women. *Psychology of Women Quarterly, 9*(1), 167–183.

Harper, C. (1986, March). *Themes in psychological and sociological research on African-American women.* Paper presented at the National Council for Black Studies, Boston.

Hull, G., Scott, P. B., & Smith, B. (Eds.). (1982). *All the women are white, all the Blacks are men, but some of us are brave: Black Women's Studies.* Old Westbury, NY: The Feminist Press.

Kahn, A., & Jean, P. (1983). Integration and elimination or separation and redefinition: The future of the psychology of women. *Signs, 8*(4), 659–671.

Walker, A. (1983). *In search of our mothers' gardens.* New York: Harcourt Brace Jovanovich.

Gender and Minority Perspectives: Specialized Courses and Content Areas

13

Alexis Deanne Abernethy, Philip A. Cowan,
Roberto Gurza, Karen Huei-chung Huang,
Mary Ann Yael Kim, Neal King, and B. Jeannie Lum

Psychology Tomorrow:
A Unified Ethnic Psychology Course

Along with the social changes of the 1960s and 1970s came both political and academic demands for new theoretical models in psychology. There was an urgent need for research that would not view ethnic groups and gay or lesbian communities in a context of deviance or disadvantage. In response to this need, students and faculty in the Psychology Department at the University of California at Berkeley established an innovative course, Psychological Research and Third World Americans, designed to explore the issues common to different ethnic groups in America with special emphasis on Black, Asian American, Latino, and American Indian communities. Somewhat later, the graduate section of this course began to explore psychological approaches to gay and lesbian populations. Our focus in this chapter is on the search for a unified ethnic psychology.[1] Teaching about sexual preference is discussed in Chapter 20 by King in this volume.

Overall Design: Our Assumptions and Rationale

Choosing a Multiethnic Approach

In part, the choice of a multiethnic approach was a pragmatic one stemming from ethnic diversity in the group of students who initiated the course and in the students who subsequently enrolled in it. In addition, each group has a different geographical and cultural heritage (Africa, Asia, Latin America) and different current political and psychological status within this country—and traditional psychology has treated each with active prejudice, misinterpretation, or neglect (cf. Guthrie, 1976).

Portions of this material were presented in symposia at the meetings of the Western Psychological Association, April 1983, San Francisco, and of the American Psychological Association, August 1983, Anaheim, CA.

1. The course was originally developed by Professor Stephen Glickman and a group of minority graduate students. This chapter was written by the graduate participants and faculty (Cowan) in the 1982 course, who continued to meet and present symposia at professional meetings over the next 3 years.

Yet an already-fragmented "mainstream psychology" would be inundated by a proliferation of paradigms if each ethnic group or special interest group were to have its own. It was also apparent that the diversity of dialect or language, geography, and culture within each ethnic group challenged the ideal of a unified psychology of Black or Asian or Latino or American Indian peoples. It seemed more reasonable, therefore, to assume that similar principles could be applied to understanding the shared background of economic exploitation, social segregation, and psychological derogation experienced by Third World Americans for more than a century. We make the assumption that a common set of principles and methods could be respectful of and sensitive to cultural differences while at the same time providing a common point of departure for all of us interested in ethnic issues. Furthermore (and this was a potentially radical thought), we hoped that a unified ethnic psychology might provide the guidelines necessary to reshape mainstream psychology, that is, to help shift it from its primary focus on the individual (or individual differences) to an understanding of individuals in their social contexts.

Emphasizing Research

It is important that both White and non-White students become intimately acquainted with the history of neglect and distortion regarding Third World Americans in the field of psychology. However, a historical examination of past improprieties does not necessarily provide students with the tools necessary to create an ethnic psychology of the future. It tends to demoralize them and foster the fatalistic view that psychology has never been and never will be responsive to Third World concerns. After the first trial year of this course, we became convinced that involving students in the task of formulating new research questions and methods would stimulate them to be active participants in the creation of a new ethnic psychology. Through class discussion with speakers and student participants from different ethnic groups, students and teachers could develop an appreciation for the ideas, questions, and methods that could unify this new field of investigation.

Course Structure

There were three "tiers" of interrelated course activities:

1.   Over a period of 10 teaching weeks in an academic quarter, seven or eight psychologists from different ethnic groups were invited to give colloquia describing their research. Because there are relatively few psychologists who are members of ethnic minorities located at any one university, the colloquium series provided excellent and inspiring models of psychologists to an audience of course enrollees and other members of the university community.

2.   Undergraduate students attended the colloquia and also met in weekly lecture and discussion sections led by two advanced-level, graduate student teaching associates. The undergraduates were able to work in close contact with potential mentors, some from the same ethnic group, who were close to them in age.

3. Every other year, the teaching associates and other graduate students were enrolled in a weekly seminar, attended the colloquia, and met with the speakers after each presentation.

The Colloquia

Over the past 7 years, a number of Black, Asian American, Latino, and American Indian psychologists have been invited to give colloquia. Some have been based in academic institutions, others in applied settings; all have written about their work. Three different kinds of presentations have been offered. A few have been directed toward epistemological issues, criticizing past practices, challenging current assumptions, and offering suggestions for rethinking questions and research methods. Most of the speakers, however, gave an account of their own research on topics such as the development of identity in Black children, counseling Asian American clients, and acculturation in Mexican American families. Finally, several talks were given by psychologists working in public agencies. They tended to focus on the service needs of different ethnic groups and the politics and policy issues involved in the health and mental health service delivery system. Both graduate and undergraduate students were assigned readings in connection with each presentation; class discussions were scheduled before and after the colloquium. We did not expect the speakers to deal with the question of creating a unified ethnic psychology; instead, we encouraged them to present their specific point of view and left the task of integration to discussion in the course or seminar.

The Undergraduate Course

Many of the students enrolled in the undergraduate course were psychology majors, but the course content also drew from other fields in the social sciences and humanities. About half of the students were members of the major ethnic groups under discussion. Most of the others identified themselves as members of groups that had experienced some form of discrimination (women, Jews, gays, or lesbians). All were concerned with how to paint an honest picture of "minority" groups that avoids stereotypes held in psychological research as well as in the general culture.

With the exception of a few textbooks focusing on minority mental health, the literature in the field of Third World issues is not easily accessible. Each year, following guidelines for fair use of copyrighted materials, we created a reader with all of the major assigned readings for the course. We always included several general articles to set the study of ethnic issues in psychology in historical and cultural perspective (e.g., Blauner, 1976; Guthrie, 1976). Articles also outlined specific issues faced by researchers and scholars in different ethnic groups (e.g., Jones, 1974; Kitano & Sue, 1973; Padilla & Ruiz, 1973), served as introductions to the colloquium speakers, and focused on the array of traditional and nontraditional research methods available for psychologists (e.g., Golden, 1976). Finally, the instructors provided some exemplars of research on ethnic concerns that could serve as models for student research (e.g., Jones & Zoppel, 1979; Martinez & Mendoza, 1984; Meadow, 1982; Mercer & Lewis, 1978; Sue, 1977).

Several topics chosen for student research proposals illustrate the directions of the course. One student, troubled by the fact that Chicano students' high rate of attrition in college attendance has often been attributed to deficiencies in the Chicano culture, reconceptualized the phenomenon as an interaction between individual factors that lead to dropout and institutional factors that lead to student pushout. Another student examined the difficulties involved in comparing the impact of English-as-a-second-language and bilingual classes on the self-esteem and achievement of Asian-American students, arguing that researchers have ignored the effects of teachers' attitudes and classroom atmosphere. Yet another student proposed that Maitri therapy, an Eastern form of meditation therapy that maintains that accurate reality testing in a hostile environment can lead to personal distress, may have special relevance to the treatment of depression in American gay and lesbian clients.

The Graduate Seminar

A unifying theme has been that of building a base for research on ethnic issues. Graduate participants wrote four position papers, each dealing with an aspect of the guidelines needed to create a general ethnic psychology. The content of the seminar can best be described by outlining three of the central issues that surfaced.

Personal–professional issues. The concerns of the participants were not only intellectual in the broadest sense but intensely personal as well. Personal–professional conflicts were a frequently recurring topic in both graduate and undergraduate courses. The status of ethnic groups in our society and their treatment in traditional psychology make it difficult to motivate ethnic psychologists to be researchers and clinicians when there is an urgent need for political action and advocacy. What role should ethnic psychologists play in relating their data to community needs? What should happen when a psychologist obtains results that might place his or her ethnic group at an apparent or real disadvantage?

Methodological issues. Although the scientific method is designed to keep the observer's perspective and values from influencing his or her observations, this stance has certainly not produced value-free conclusions in traditional ethnic research. In the seminar, we explored the possibility that a "clinical method" based on Piaget's epistemology (see Cowan, 1978) might help to deal with many of the current criticisms of traditional psychological methods as they have been applied to the study of ethnic groups. Using this method, the researcher cannot be objective in the sense that his or her conclusions are independent of a point of view. Rather, he or she attempts to coordinate and synthesize multiple perspectives to obtain a picture of another individual's interpretation of physical and social reality.

Cross-cultural approaches. Our clinical method has much in common with the argument in psychology for an intercultural approach (Jones & Thorne, 1987) and that in anthropology for an emic as opposed to an etic approach (Berry, 1969; Triandis, 1972). The etic approach refers to the tendency of a researcher from a different culture to use categories of experience and instruments derived from his or her own culture under the mistaken assumption that the categories represent universals. By contrast, the emic approach represents an attempt to work with meanings that are indigenous to a given culture but functionally equivalent across cultures. For example, although the specific symptoms of schizophrenia differ from culture to culture, each culture seems to have a category to describe individuals with thought disorders who are isolated from normal social interaction (Murphy, 1976). A number of scholars have argued that ethnic psychology must adopt a cross-cultural point of view (Abernethy, 1983, 1986; Brislin, Lonner, & Thorndike, 1973; Jones & Korchin, 1982; Jones & Zoppel, 1979; Korchin, 1980; Snowden & Todman, 1982).

References

Abernethy, A. D. (1983, August). *Implications for research: A second look at hypertension in Blacks.* Presented at the annual meeting of the American Psychological Association, Anaheim, CA.

Abernethy, A. D. (1986). *Hypertension in Blacks.* Unpublished doctoral dissertation, University of California, Berkeley.

Berry, J. W. (1969). On cross-cultural comparability. *International Journal of Psychology, 4,* 119–128.

Blauner, R. (1976). Colonized and immigrant minorities. In G. Bowker & J. Carrier (Eds.), *Race and ethnic relations: Sociological readings* (pp. 376–412). New York: Holmes & Meier.

Brislin, R. W., Lonner, W. J., & Thorndike, R. M. (1973). *Cross-cultural research methods.* New York: Wiley.

Cowan, P. A. (1978). *Piaget with feeling.* New York: Holt, Rinehart & Winston.

Golden, M. P. (1976). *The research experience.* Itasca, IL: Peacock.

Guthrie, R. V. (1976). *Even the rat was white: A historical view of psychology.* New York: Harper & Row.

Jones, E. E. (1974). Social class and psychotherapy: A critical review of research. *Psychiatry, 37,* 307–320.

Jones, E. E., & Korchin, S. J. (1982). Minority mental health: Perspectives. In E. E. Jones & S. J. Korchin (Eds.), *Minority mental health* (pp. 3–36). New York: Praeger.

Jones, E. E., & Thorne, A. (1987). Rediscovery of the subject: Intercultural approaches to clinical assessment. *Journal of Consulting and Clinical Psychology, 55,* 488–495.

Jones, E. E., & Zoppel, C. L. (1979). Personality differences between Blacks in Jamaica and the United States. *Journal of Cross-Cultural Psychology, 10,* 435–456.

Kitano, H. H. L., & Sue, S. (1973). The model minorities. *Journal of Social Issues, 29,* 1–9.

Korchin, S. J. (1980). Clinical psychology and minority problems. *American Psychologist, 35,* 262–269.

Martinez, J. L., Jr., & Mendoza, R. (Eds.). (1984). *Chicano psychology* (2nd ed.). New York: Academic Press.

Meadow, A. (1982). Psychopathology, psychotherapy, and the Mexican-American patient. In E. E. Jones & S. J. Korchin (Eds.), *Minority mental health* (pp. 331–361). New York: Praeger.

Mercer, J., & Lewis, J. (1978). *System of multicultural pluralistic assessment.* New York: Psychological Corporation.

Murphy, J. M. (1976). Psychiatric labeling in cross-cultural perspective. *Science, 191,* 1019–1028.

Padilla, A. M., & Ruiz, R. A. (1973). *Latino mental health: A review of the literature.* (Department of Health, Education and Welfare Publication No. (HSM) 73–9143). Washington, DC: U.S. Government Printing Office.

Snowden, L., & Todman, P. A. (1982). The psychological assessment of Blacks: New and needed developments. In E. E. Jones & S. J. Korchin (Eds.), *Minority mental health* (pp. 193–226). New York: Praeger.

Sue, S. (1977). Community mental health services to minority groups: Some optimism, some pessimism. *American Psychologist, 32,* 616–624.

Triandis, H. C. (1972). *The analysis of subjective culture.* New York: Wiley.

14

Dan Romero

Teaching Ethnic Psychology to Undergraduates: A Specialized Course

Several years ago the American Psychological Association's (APA) Office of Educational Affairs surveyed by telephone 100 undergraduate psychology department chairs about needs, problems, and issues facing undergraduate psychology education (American Psychological Association, 1983a, 1983b). Although chairpersons reported that student bodies were becoming more culturally diverse, more than half the departments surveyed did not provide any course that incorporated multicultural content. Of those that did incorporate such content, only six focused on ethnic minorities. Thus it is painfully clear that psychology courses that focus on specific ethnic groups in the United States, including Asians, Blacks, Hispanics, and American Indians, are not a priority in the undergraduate curriculum and that these groups continue to be forgotten or ignored. In this chapter, I discuss the need for such courses in general and describe a specific model for a specialized undergraduate course in ethnic psychology.

Course Rationale and Development

Without exposure to racial and ethnic issues in psychology, students may not learn to recognize or value differences among people and may not examine and confront their own assumptions and stereotypic beliefs about ethnic populations. In addition, a vast number of psychology majors may never be exposed to course materials that allow them to understand and respond to the needs of culturally different people they will work with or serve in their eventual careers. Minority undergraduate students interested in psychology may experience a double penalty. These students may never examine personally relevant racial and ethnic psychological issues in their classes or encounter research about ethnic issues that might motivate them to pursue advanced training. This general lack of information may be a major reason why culturally different students do not apply to graduate schools or enter the profession in a variety of specialties. Data reported by Russo, Olmedo, Stapp, and Fulcher (1981) indicated that only two psychology subfields, psycholinguistics and community psychology, had more than 5% racial and ethnic minorities among their membership. More revealing in the data reported is the fact that almost half of the 20 subfields surveyed had no Black members, one third of the subfields had no Hispanic members, one fifth of the subfields had no Asian members, and more than half had no American Indian members. This disturbing reality—that ethnic minority students do not enter a variety of psychology subfields—continues to characterize the profession as we enter the 1990s. Ethnic minority psychologists may become clustered and tracked into particular subfields of psychology much as secondary school ethnic students have been tracked into vocational segments of the school curriculum.

To address the facts that undergraduate students in general know little about ethnic populations and issues in psychology and that ethnic students in particular may know little about a range of subfields in psychology, I designed and coordinated a special-topics course at the University of California at Irvine called Research, Issues, and Trends in Ethnic Psychology. The course was innovative because it brought to campus distinguished psychologists from outside the university who were Hispanic, Black, Asian, and American Indian. The invited presenters had published research or obtained training in a number of psychology specialties including clinical, community, counseling, developmental, educational, experimental, physiological, psycholinguistics, psychometrics, school, and social psychology.

In a personal biographical sketch presented to the class, each lecturer exhibited a strong identity as a psychologist and as a culturally distinct person. Guest lecturers were introduced with comments such as "Today we have one of the six identified American Indian clinical psychologists in the country as our guest presenter" or "Today we have one of the 10 identified Chicanos in counseling psychology as our presenter." Presenters were asked to lecture on the state of the art with regard to cultural issues in their subspecialty and to discuss their current research endeavors relevant to ethnic perspectives in psychology. Finally, they were asked to describe their growth and development as ethnic psychologists. Thus, guest presenters were special role models who provided expertise and consultation to students beyond any resources available on the campus.

Each speaker gave students valuable insights into how psychologists conceptualize research problems and develop strategies to study problems. In addition, many speakers addressed political issues that have impact on the types of acceptable research in various agencies and how research information might be used or misused to make budget and institutional policy decisions. The political nature of psychology was also addressed: obtaining grants and funding for research; getting controversial psychological findings published on subjects such as bilingual education, busing, and desegregation; and examining graduate training and its relation to the ethnic minorities. Course content went beyond the traditional description of research findings and portrayed the life-styles of ethnic minority psychologists by describing realistic hazards and rewards in choosing psychology as a career.

An important element in course development was the willingness for guest participants to provide up to 8 hours of their time to travel to campus, deliver their lecture, and meet informally with instructors, students, and interested faculty. When initial contact was made and the purpose of the course explained, guest lecturers immediately applauded the effort, indicating that it was the quality of the concept and the innovativeness of the class that were the major considerations for consenting to participate.

Although they received a modest honorarium to cover travel expenses, partic-ipants clearly felt there were other benefits from the class. Several reported that the presentation represented an opportunity to consolidate information about re-search and trends in ethnic issues with their latest research concerns; one even wrote an article based on his presentation. Many spoke freely about their personal life experiences in pursuing the doctorate and were pleased that they could talk about their own professional development and growth.

Course Design and Requirements

Course requirements and grade assignments were based on the following three measures:

1.   Attendance. Since an essential aspect of the class was contact with guest presenters, attendance constituted 30% of the final grade.

2.   Term paper. Each student selected a topic of interest relevant to the course content generated from class lectures or materials. Papers were approxi-mately 10 pages in length and accounted for 35% of the final grade. Examples of topics included "Bonds of an Interracially Mixed Couple," "The Social Adjustment of South Vietnamese Refugees," and "Ethnic Identity Between Successive Genera-tions of Japanese Americans." Students were required to meet with me or my teaching assistant to conceptualize their project, review potential resources, and discuss creative ways to present the material.

3.   Final examination. A 70-item, multiple-choice final examination based on lectures and readings accounted for 35% of the final grade.

Because of the unique format of the course, no single text was used. Instead, presenters were asked to submit appropriate readings based on their research and writings about ethnic psychology. Course readings included book chapters, pub-lished articles, and articles in press made available to students in the library re-serve room.

My role as instructor included organizing and coordinating the course, attend-ing lectures, providing some integration of the diverse material, consulting with students on paper topics and questions about course material, and developing the final examination. In addition to coordinating the course, I directed students to-ward information sources for papers and served as an informal advisor by provid-ing suggestions about graduate programs for students to consider.

Because speakers brought diverse orientations, interests, and presentation styles to the course with virtually no overlap in information, integrating the course content became a challenge. To integrate lectures, I summarized main points presented by guest speakers and provided supplemental lecture informa-tion. In addition, I identified a specific body of knowledge as essential information to learn about each lecture from which final examination questions were devel-oped. This approach was designed to decrease student test anxiety and improve performance on the final examination.

Student Response

According to course evaluations, students responded extremely favorably to the course for several reasons. Foremost was the opportunity for contact with psychologists who discussed their current research interests and results or important issues and trends in their fields. Students reported that guest presenters stimulated ideas for term papers and supplied additional resources or supplemental readings for them. Further, they reported that the course format provided understanding and appreciation of the personalities and life-styles of the presenters and the identity of a person choosing psychology for a career. This approach differed from the teaching approach in other courses, in which faculty would typically view the function of classroom interaction as imparting psychological information and not focusing on the identity of the instructor. In addition, teaching styles varied, and students reported they enjoyed contrasting what they learned from a presenter who used an overhead projector compared with one who made detailed outlines on the blackboard and others who were mesmerizing speakers.

Finally, as students became familiar with the existing literature, they discovered that very little research on ethnic issues had been published in psychology journals and that major journals that did focus on such issues were not available in the university library. Students responded by putting in requests to the library to obtain the books and journal subscriptions needed for their projects. Furthermore, on the basis of their growing familiarity with the literature, they also registered complaints about outdated, offensive, and potentially damaging materials discovered in the library. Consequently, they became more active and discerning consumers of educational materials.

Additional Departmental Considerations

For faculty or departments interested in creating a course in ethnic psychology using this format as a model, there are some additional factors to consider. First, courses in ethnic psychology should be carefully labeled so as not to be confused with courses in cross-cultural psychology. Second, the course format could be enhanced by balancing guest lectures with structured small discussion sections. In small heterogeneous groups, students can personally confront significant cultural issues in psychology and learn from each other about cultural differences. Third, it is essential that a faculty member from the department be given responsibility for organizing and synthesizing the course. The temptation exists to bring outside presenters to campus without careful supervision and course monitoring, which could be self-defeating. Fourth, departments should consider the additional uses of the expertise that visiting presenters may bring to campus by providing informal dinners and receptions or formal colloquia to foster faculty and graduate student contact with presenters. Finally, faculty organizers of the course may question the availability of qualified presenters in the community or within a feasible distance from campus. This may be a real problem for rural or isolated campuses, but generally resources can be found if faculty are willing to tap existing networks. For example, the APA's Office of Educational Affairs has developed a Distinguished Lecturers Program of ethnic psychologists who are willing to visit local campuses on a 1-day basis to lecture on areas of their expertise (R. Washington, personal communication, August 4, 1986). In addition, the Office of Ethnic Minority Affairs produces the *Directory of Ethnic Minority Human Resources in Psychology*, which contains information on more than 800 ethnic minority professionals in the field of psychology. A dedicated effort to make use of existing networks and create new ones is essential if psychology is to become responsive to the ethical imperative to recognize and appreciate the differences among people.

References

American Psychological Association. (1983a). *Results: Phase I survey of undergraduate department chairs.* Washington, DC: Author.

American Psychological Association. (1983b). *The undergraduate psychology curriculum from an international perspective: Selected courses.* Washington, DC: Author.

Russo, N. F., Olmedo, E. L., Stapp, J., & Fulcher, R. (1981). Women and minorities in psychology. *American Psychologist, 36,* 1316–1363.

15

Mavis Tsai and Anne Uemura

Asian Americans:
The Struggles, the Conflicts,
and the Successes

Asian Americans comprise heterogeneous groups of people with enormous diversity in ethnicity, language, history, immigration patterns, area of residence, amount of education, competence with English, and socioeconomic level. Yet because of commonalities in racial and cultural backgrounds, these diverse groups have also been considered to be a single large minority group. Although Asian Americans have come to this country at different times under different conditions, each wave of immigrants has faced similar struggles and challenges in trying to build better lives in a new land. After some brief background information on demographics and immigration history, this chapter presents topics and strategies for teaching about the psychology of Asian Americans. In addition, it includes suggestions for assignments, exercises, readings, and audiovisual materials.

Immigration History and Demographics

Initially, the arrival of Asians into the United States was largely influenced by the need for cheap labor. The Chinese were first recruited in the 1840s to work in the West as laborers and then in the 1860s to work on the transcontinental railroads. However, when anti-Chinese sentiment grew, resulting in the Chinese Exclusion Act of 1882, recruiters turned to Japan, Korea, and finally the Philippines. The history of Chinese immigration was then repeated; agitation against the Japanese in California led President Theodore Roosevelt to sign a "Gentlemen's Agreement" with Japan in 1908, which curtailed Japanese immigration. The 1924 National Origins Act set up quotas that effectively ended most Asian immigration until its revocation in 1965 (Yee & Hennessy, 1982).

   After the U.S. immigration laws changed in 1965, the pattern of entering ethnic groups shifted, with a dramatic increase of Asians coming into the country. In particular, when the United States ended its controversial military involvement in Southeast Asia, a mass exodus of refugees from Vietnam, Cambodia, and Laos occurred. In sharp contrast to the period from 1931 to 1960, when Asians constituted 5% of the total immigrants, during the period from 1980 to 1984 they made up 48% of the total. The Asian American population grew from 1.4 million in 1970 to 3.5 million in 1980 and was estimated at 5.1 million in 1985, making it the fastest growing minority group (Gardner, Robey, & Smith, 1985). Included in this group, in order of size based on 1985 data, are Chinese (21%), Filipinos (20%), Japanese (15%), Vietnamese (12%), Koreans (11%), and Asian Indians (10%), plus 22 smaller Asian groups.

From their early beginnings in the United States as laborers, Asian Americans have improved their socioeconomic status impressively. Their median family income reported in the 1980 census was the highest of all groups at $23,600 for the six groups making up 95% of Asian Americans, compared to $20,800 for White families. These figures, however, are somewhat misleading, because a larger percentage of Asian families have two or more workers. In terms of education, 35% of adults 25 years and older in the six major Asian groups had graduated from college, a rate more than double that of White Americans.

Topics and Strategies for Teaching Asian American Psychology

Issues important to an understanding of the Asian American experience are covered in this section, along with resource information and suggestions for presenting these topics in the classroom. These issues not only provide interesting information on Asian American culture but also can be used to illustrate larger psychological and social issues in any classroom. They include cultural values, the consequences of racism, adjustment conflicts, and mental health intervention approaches.

Cultural Values

An examination of the cultural values of Asian Americans is essential to understanding members of these cultures—but it can also add valuable perspectives to any course concerned with socialization processes. In both developmental and social psychology courses, it is important to examine how individuals develop in different cultural value systems. Furthermore, theories and findings in these fields can be evaluated from the perspectives of cultural minorities who were not part of the framework within which they were developed.

Despite their heterogeneity, Asian groups do share some core cultural values and attitudes. Some Asian values seem compatible with American middle-class values, such as the emphasis on achievement and the importance of education. Other values, such as family and group interdependence, interpersonal harmony, and stoicism, often conflict with American norms of individualism, self-sufficiency, and emotional expressiveness. Asian American literature is a particularly rich source of information about cultural values, and excerpts of the writings of many authors are contained in texts by Bruchac (1983), Hsu and Palubinskas (1976), and Kim (1982).

Family and group interdependence. Traditionally in Asian cultures, the family is the primary source of emotional support. It is not defined as just the nuclear family of the present but as extending into the past and the future; one must think of how one's behavior might affect not only the present family but the whole family line as well. Roles and obligations within the family are carried out with the main emphasis on the parent–child relationship rather than on the husband–wife relationship. This strong family orientation can affect Asian Americans in several ways. One is that they come to view the needs and wishes of the family group as more important than their own. Another is that they tend to assume a vertical and deferential rather than an egalitarian stance in significant relationships, as can be seen in Asian American students' deference and courtesy in interacting with teachers. A third is that they tend to be more comfortable in structured situations in which roles and responsibilities are clearly defined.

Interpersonal harmony. The concepts of shame and dignity are important in maintaining harmonious relationships. Shame or threat of shame keeps the individual in line, reinforcing behaviors appropriate to one's role and sensitivity to others' needs. Improprieties result in a loss of "face" or dignity, not only for the culprit and her or his family or group, but also for others in the situation for "causing" the embarrassment. Thus, in order to preserve harmony and dignity, the individual may use indirect and nonconfrontational communication that is sometimes misunderstood to be conforming and passive.

Stoicism. Cultural pressure discourages the direct and open expression of feelings. Restraint of potentially disruptive emotions is strongly emphasized in the development of one's character; emotional maturity is often marked by one's ability to suppress emotions and suffer silently.

Racism and Its Consequences

Ethnic differences, both physical and cultural, make Asian groups obvious targets for prejudice and hatred. Racism is more likely to be expressed when job security is perceived as threatened and is present today as it has been throughout the history of Asian immigration. According to the U.S. Commission on Civil Rights, "anti-Asian activity in the form of violence, vandalism, harassment and intimidation continues to occur across the nation" ("Anti-Asian attacks," 1986, p. A-7). Examples of racism perpetrated against Asian Americans abound and provide important starting points for discussions of the general social psychological concepts of stereotyping, prejudice, and discrimination, as well as for an understanding of the Asian American experience. Examples are the following:

1. Violence targeted against an individual solely because of racial group membership (D. W. Sue, 1973). Reports of recent events are unfortunately easy to obtain from newspapers and can be discussed in terms of the meaning for the individual targeted as well as for members of his or her racial group.

2. The evacuation and internment of Japanese Americans during World War II (Toupin, 1980). The film "Guilty by Reason of Race" (1972) and the book *Desert Exile* (Uchida, 1982) focus on this traumatic social experience and introduce the issue of racism by the majority culture as expressed through the isolation and punishment of the feared group members.

3. Congressional anti-Asian legislation and unresponsive health, education, and welfare policies (Nicks, 1985). Current legislative actions (especially those pending) that would affect Asian Americans may be analyzed for their potential psychological impact.

4. Distorted stereotypes perpetuated by the mass media (S. Sue & Morishima, 1982). The videocassette "Asian Stereotypes in the Mass Media" (1973)

highlights some of these distorted images and provides a starting point for the examination of the pervasiveness and impact of stereotypes for cultural subgroups in general.

5.   Omitted documentation of Asian American contributions (Endo, 1980). Search and rediscovery of some of these contributions can be carried out by students as individual or group projects.

Prejudice and discrimination against a group can lead to racial self-hatred, poor self-esteem, and a sense of helplessness and noncontrol (S. Sue, 1977a). Yet many feel that Asian Americans are no longer victims of racism. In fact, they have been labeled the "model minority." This view, supplemented by statistics regarding high median family incomes and educational attainments, neglects the following facts: (a) These high median incomes are often the combined incomes of several working members of the same family; (b) for the amount of education Asians have, they are underpaid and underemployed; and (c) an ethnic minority group can show upward mobility as a whole, while individual members still experience personal discrimination.

Adjustment Struggles of Immigrants and Later Generations

First-generation immigrants—constituting the majority of Indochinese, Korean, Filipino, and Chinese residents—are particularly vulnerable to emotional and physical illness because they must contend with the multiple problems of language barriers, culture shock, discrimination, unemployment and underemployment, role and status reversal, intergenerational family conflicts, and the lack of community support systems (Tsai, Teng, & S. Sue, 1980). Films such as "Sewing Woman" (1983) and "The Filipino Immigrants" (1973) and autobiographical novels such as *America is in the Heart* (Bulosan, 1973) and *Thousand Pieces of Gold* (McCunn, 1981) can bring these struggles to the fore for nonimmigrant students as well as for those who have shared the immigration experience. Asian Americans born in the United States face different adjustment problems, including cross-generational differences with families, a bicultural existence, and sex role strains. Recognition of these general struggles can contribute to discussions of life span development and social roles, including gender roles. Specific groups and their unique problems and issues are described next.

Southeast Asian refugees. The entry of many former citizens of Vietnam, Cambodia, and Laos into refugee status was involuntary and sudden—more than half indicated they had less than 10 hours to evacuate (Tayabas & Pok, 1983). Although all Southeast Asian refugees faced traumas associated with war, cultural and social transplantation, and sudden and radical life changes, the various groups exhibited considerable differences in terms of urban or rural background, politics, religion, education, and occupation. They also differed in the extent of suffering that they had to endure before arriving in the United States. For example, the earliest refugees had a relatively safe and speedy exodus, whereas later ones who escaped in overcrowded, unseaworthy boats faced a 50% chance of drowning or being murdered. The psychological impact of this sudden and life-threatening departure and entry into a very different world can be illustrated for students by documentary films such as "Farewell to Freedom" (1982) and "Becoming an American" (1982).

The psychological impact of uprooting and resettling is usually more evident after what may appear to be a successful initial adaptation. The single most influential factor in determining severity of refugee trauma is the extent of family separation, which involves feelings of worry and uncertainty over the fate of family members left behind and guilt over surviving when others did not. Other factors associated with emotional trauma include the culture shock of totally unfamiliar social norms and the loss of socioeconomic or cultural status (Nicassio, 1985).

Many refugee children witnessed horrors and experienced perilous escapes and starvation. They suffered from poor health and severe malnutrition and did not attend school for years. In order to ease their suffering and to maximize their potential contributions, special attention must be given to the psychological sequelae of their trauma (Yao, 1985). Consideration of the possible long-term physical and emotional impact of these early stressful events, and of appropriate intervention strategies, can enhance understanding in courses in child development, education, and psychopathology.

Elderly. Instead of the material comfort, esteem, and prestige traditionally accorded them in Asia, most elderly Asians in the United States face poverty, misunderstanding, and social alienation. Their expectations regarding respect, devotion, living arrangements, and financial support often are not met by the actual practices of their middle-aged progeny. Today, two thirds of the immigrant elderly live apart from their families, and their American-born grandchildren speak only English. Recent studies have shown a high rate of psychological dysfunction, depression, and suicide among the Asian American elderly (Kalish & Yuen, 1973; Kiefer et al., 1985). The film "Watariodore: Birds of Passage" (1975) and the book *Through Harsh Winters* (Kikumure, 1981) document not only the obstacles faced by elderly immigrants but also their immense courage and strength.

The later generations. Asians who were born in the United States and who have grown up with American peers face adjustment issues different from those of their immigrant parents or grandparents. Two potentially stressful aspects of being a United States-born Asian American are bicultural existence and sex role conflicts.

- *Bicultural existence*—Growing up within the boundaries of two diverse cultures with incompatible values can create intense inner struggles. The American way of life centers on the individual, emphasizing independence and assertiveness within a youth-oriented perspective. These values clash with Asian values of obedience to parents, respect for elders and for authority, and subordination of individual impulses to the will of the family or group. Further internal conflicts may result from the drive for acceptance by the majority culture. Thus, the Asian American may struggle with feelings of marginality and experience stages of confusion, super-ethnocentricity, or complete denial of ethnicity (D. W. Sue, 1973). The unhappy result of such denial is a poor sense of self and low self-esteem. Yet a bicultural existence can be enriching. It offers opportunities to develop greater sensitivity to and appreciation of differences and to pick and choose from the best of what both cultures have to offer. Powerful accounts of bicultural conflicts and their impact on personal identity can be found in *Roots: An Asian American Reader* (Tachiki, Wong, & Odo, 1971), an anthology of writings by younger generation Asian Americans, and in autobiographical novels such as *The Woman Warrior* (Kingston, 1976).

• *Sex role conflict*—Asian American women are victims of both racial and gender oppression (Asian Women's Journal, 1975; Fujitomi & Wong, 1973; Houston, 1980). One specific conflict they face involves the American emphasis on equality in male–female relationships versus the traditional Asian focus on female subservience. The classic autobiographical novel *Fifth Chinese Daughter* (Wong, 1945) depicts the author's struggle against sex discrimination enforced by family tradition. The quest for self-determination, combined with a devaluation of Asian male traits by the dominant culture, may explain the increasing tendency for many younger Asian American women to marry Whites (S. Sue & Morishima, 1982). This practice, which is not culturally sanctioned, can perpetuate inner turmoil.

Issues in Mental Health Intervention

It is clear that Asian Americans as members of a minority group in America are subjected to a great deal of stress that may negatively affect their mental health. Yet compared to Whites, they underutilize mental health services (S. Sue, 1977b). The traditional explanation is that low use of services reflects their low rate of mental disturbance. This explanation is weakened by findings that Asian Americans who do seek treatment do so only after having endured considerable stress and reaching a point of acute crisis or breakdown, and that they are more severely disturbed than other groups. These facts suggest that because of the cultural stigma and shame over mental disturbance, Asian Americans seek help only when the situation becomes critical or when family and community resources have been exhausted. In addition, available services are often unresponsive to their needs, and the system itself creates barriers to utilization (Chin, 1983; Tsai et al., 1980).

Specific issues for Asian Americans that should be raised in courses on counseling and mental health include the structure and goals of service delivery (Ishisaka & Takagi, 1982; Tsui & Schultz, 1985), the treatment process (Hsu, 1983; Kaneshige, 1973; Leong, 1986; Root, 1985; Shon & Ja, 1982), research paradigms (Doi, Lin, & Vohra-Sahu, 1981; Morishima, S. Sue, Teng, Zane, & Cram, 1979; Washington & McLoyd, 1982), and community empowerment (Rappaport, 1981).

Exercises and Assignments

Structured exercises and assignments can help students develop an awareness of the struggles and successes of Asian Americans. Some sample exercises follow.

Ethnicity and identity. The following exercises can be done as an individual written assignment or as a small group exercise. If the latter approach is used, students generally will be more open about their views and experiences if they are in a group with others from the same ethnic or cultural background; also, the discovery of commonalities can be an enriching experience. The small group then writes up a summary of its common experiences and presents the summary to the class. The following are suggested questions to be included in this exercise:

1. Identify your family origins as far back as you can.

2.   Why did your ancestors come to this country? Speculate on the conditions they left behind and their possible motives for leaving.

3.   When your ancestors arrived here, how do you think they were perceived and treated by others? Describe advantages and disadvantages your ancestors may have experienced because of their ethnicity.

4.   Describe advantages or family strengths that you have enjoyed because of your family's ethnic background.

Adjustment and assimilation. Interview a relative or acquaintance who immigrated here from another country, focusing on the experience of changing cultures as well as issues of adjustment, assimilation, retention of cultural values, and prejudice.

The impact of stereotypes. Identify images portrayed in television, movies, or popular magazines of a cultural, ethnic, religious, socioeconomic, or regional group of which you are a member. Discuss any stereotyped aspects of the portrayal, whether they are negative or positive, and the feelings they arouse in you.

The language barrier. Invite an Asian person who speaks his or her native tongue fluently to come to class and teach about a topic in that language. Alternatively, the person could "teach" an elementary school topic, such as basic arithmetic or reading, as if the audience were, say, a third-grade class. This person should act as if she or he expects the students to understand what is being said. This would provide an opportunity for students to experience some of what newly arrived immigrant children experience in the classroom—confusion, embarrassment, anxiety. Have students discuss their feelings and thoughts or write a reaction paper.

Understanding the Asian American experience. Divide into small groups and pick an event or period in time that was stressful for an Asian American group (e.g., early violence against Chinese immigrant laborers, Japanese American internment, escape and resettlement of Indochinese refugees), and research it by reading or by interviewing knowledgeable persons. Do some role-playing that illustrates the struggles and strengths of the group that you picked. Or read a work (e.g., biography, fiction, drama, history, or poetry) about some aspect of Asian American life, and then write a report discussing what the reading taught you about the Asian American experience.

Audiovisual Resources

Asian stereotypes in the mass media. (1973). Traces 50 years of racial discrimination against Asian performers in the media. Videocassette, 35 minutes. Seattle: Instructional Media Services, University of Washington.

Becoming an American. (1982). The story of a Hmong refugee family. Film, 58 minutes. Franklin Lakes, NJ: New Day Films.

Farewell to freedom. (1982). Immigration struggles of the Hmong refugees of Laos. Videocassette, 55 minutes. Minneapolis: WCCO-TV Media Services.

Guilty by reason of race. (1972). An account of Japanese American evacuation during World War II. Film, 53 minutes. New York: National Broadcasting Company.

The Filipino immigrants. (1973). Chronicles their immigration, problems they faced in the United States, and their development. Film, 31 minutes. Seattle: Instructional Media Services, University of Washington.

Sewing woman. (1983). A story about a woman's determination to survive, from an arranged marriage in old China to the conflicts of acculturation in the United States. Film, 14 minutes. Seattle: Instructional Media Services, University of Washington.

Watariodore: Birds of passage. (1975). A biographical account of the strength and pioneer spirit of three elderly Japanese Americans. Film, 38 minutes. Seattle: Instructional Media Services, University of Washington.

References

Anti-Asian attacks taking place across U.S., says federal report. (1986, April 29). *Seattle Times*, p. A-7.

Asian Women's Journal. (1975). *Asian women.* Los Angeles: University of California, Asian American Studies Center.

Bruchac, J. (Ed). (1983). *Breaking silence.* Greenfield Center, NY: Greenfield Review Press.

Bulosan, C. (1973). *America is in the heart.* Seattle: University of Washington Press.

Chin, J. L. (1983). Diagnostic considerations in working with Asian-Americans. *American Journal of Orthopsychiatry, 53*(1), 100–109.

Doi, M. L., Lin, C., & Vohra-Sahu, I. (1981). *Pacific/Asian American research: An annotated bibliography.* Chicago, IL: Pacific/Asian American Mental Health Research Center.

Endo, R. (1980). Social science and historical materials on the Asian American experience. In R. Endo, S. Sue, & N. Wagner (Eds.), *Asian-Americans: Social and psychological perspectives* (pp. 304–331). Palo Alto, CA: Science and Behavior Books.

Fujitomi, I., & Wong, D. (1973). The new Asian American woman. In S. Sue & N. Wagner (Eds.), *Asian-Americans: Psychological perspectives* (pp. 252–263). Palo Alto, CA: Science and Behavior Books.

Gardner, R. W., Robey, B., & Smith, P. C. (1985). Asian Americans: Growth, change, and diversity. *Population Bulletin, 40*(4), 3–43.

Houston, J. W. (1980). Beyond Manzanar: A personal view of Asian American womanhood. In R. Endo, S. Sue, & N. Wagner (Eds.), *Asian-Americans: Social and psychological perspectives* (pp. 17–25). Palo Alto, CA: Science and Behavior Books.

Hsu, J. (1983). Asian family interaction patterns and their therapeutic implications. *International Journal of Family Psychiatry, 4*, 307–320.

Hsu, J., & Palubinskas, H. (1976). *Asian American authors.* Boston: Houghton Mifflin.

Ishisaka, H. A., & Takagi, C. Y. (1982). Social work with Asian and Pacific Americans. In J. W. Green (Ed.), *Cultural awareness in the human services* (pp. 122–156). Englewood Cliffs, NJ: Prentice-Hall.

Kalish, R., & Yuen, S. (1973). Americans of East Asian ancestry: Aging and the aged. In S. Sue & N. Wagner (Eds.), *Asian-Americans: Psychological perspectives* (pp. 236–251). Palo Alto, CA: Science and Behavior Books.

Kaneshige, E. (1973). Cultural factors in group counseling and interaction. *Personnel and Guidance Journal, 51*, 407–412.

Kiefer, C., Kim, S., Choi, K., Kim, L., Kim, B. L., Shon, S., & Kim, T. (1985). Adjustment problems of Korean American elderly. *The Gerontologist, 25*(5), 477–482.

Kikumure, A. (1981). *Through harsh winters: The life of a Japanese immigrant woman.* Novato, CA: Chandler & Sharp Publishers.

Kim, E. H. (1982). *Asian American literature: An introduction to the writings and their social context.* Philadelphia: Temple University Press.

Kingston, M. H. (1976). *The woman warrior.* New York: Vintage Books.

Leong, F. (1986). Counseling and psychotherapy with Asian-Americans: Review of the literature. *Journal of Counseling Psychology, 33*(2), 196–206.

McCunn, R. L. (1981). *Thousand pieces of gold*. New York: Dell.

Morishima, J., Sue, S., Teng, L. N., Zane, N., & Cram, J. (1979). *Handbook of Asian American/Pacific Islander mental health* (Vol. 1). Washington, DC: U.S. Government Printing Office.

Nicassio, P. M. (1985). The psychosocial adjustment of the Southeast Asian refugee: An overview of empirical findings and theoretical models. *Journal of Cross-Cultural Psychology, 16*(2), 153–173.

Nicks, L. (1985). Inequities in the delivery and financing of mental health services for ethnic minority Americans. *Psychotherapy: Theory, Research, and Practice, 22*(2S), 469–476.

Rappaport, J. (1981). In praise of paradox: A social policy of empowerment over prevention. *American Journal of Community Psychology, 9*, 1–25.

Root, M. (1985). Guidelines for facilitating therapy with Asian American clients. *Psychotherapy: Theory, Research, and Practice, 22*(2S), 349–356.

Shon, S. P., & Ja, D. Y. (1982). Asian families. In M. McGoldrick, J. K. Pearce, & J. Giordano (Eds.), *Ethnicity and family therapy* (pp. 208–228). New York: Guilford Press.

Sue, D. W. (1973). Ethnic identity: The impact of two cultures on the psychological development of Asians in America. In S. Sue & N. Wagner (Eds.), *Asian-Americans: Psychological perspectives* (pp. 140–149). Palo Alto, CA: Science and Behavior Books.

Sue, S. (1977a). Psychological theory and implications for Asian Americans. *Personnel and Guidance Journal, 55*, 381–389.

Sue, S. (1977b). Community mental health services to minority groups: Some optimism, some pessimism. *American Psychologist, 32*, 616–624.

Sue, S., & Morishima, J. (1982). *The mental health of Asian Americans: Contemporary issues in identifying and treating mental problems*. San Francisco: Jossey-Bass.

Tayabas, Y., & Pok, T. (1983). The arrival of the Southeast Asian refugees in America: An overview. In Special Services for Groups (Ed.), *Bridging cultures: Southeast Asian refugees in America* (pp. 3–14). Los Angeles: Asian American Community Mental Health Training Center.

Tachiki, A., Wong, E., & Odo, F. (Eds.), with Wong, B. (1971). *Roots: An Asian American reader*. Los Angeles: University of California Press.

Toupin, E. S. (1980). Counseling Asians: Psychotherapy in the context of racism and Asian-American history. *American Journal of Orthopsychiatry, 50*(1), 76–86.

Tsai, M., Teng, N., & Sue, S. (1980). Mental health status of Chinese in the United States. In A. Kleinman & T. Y. Lin (Eds.), *Normal and abnormal behavior in Chinese culture* (pp. 291–310). Hingham, MA: D. Reidel.

Tsui, P., & Schultz, G. L. (1985). Failure of rapport: Why psychotherapeutic engagement fails in the treatment of Asian clients. *American Journal of Orthopsychiatry, 55*(4), 561–569.

Uchida, Y. (1982). *Desert exile: The uprooting of a Japanese American family*. Seattle: University of Washington Press.

Washington, E. D., & McLoyd, V. (1982). The external validity of research involving American minorities. *Human Development, 25*(5), 324–339.

Wong, J. S. (1945). *Fifth Chinese daughter*. New York: Harper & Row.

Yao, E. (1985). Adjustment needs of Asian immigrant children. *Elementary School Guidance and Counseling, 19*(3), 222–227.

Yee, B., & Hennessy, S. (1982). Pacific/Asian American families and mental health. In F. Munoz & R. Endo (Eds.), *Perspectives in minority group mental health* (pp. 53–70). Washington, DC: University Press of America.

16

Halford H. Fairchild

Curriculum Design for Black (African American) Psychology

In this chapter, Black psychology is defined and a curriculum structure is presented that can be used as the basis for an introductory course; for inclusion in regularly scheduled courses such as introductory, developmental, abnormal, or social psychology; or for the development of over a dozen specialty courses in African American psychology. Emphasis is on the identification of source material that will assist the instructor in designing undergraduate and graduate curriculum content in African American psychology.[1]

What is African American Psychology?

It is easy to say that African American psychology is that body of work that pertains to, and originates from, African Americans. It is more difficult to define the distinctive features of African American psychology, which in fact originate from an African philosophical base (Akbar, 1984; Baldwin, 1986) and can be seen in juxtaposition to a European cosmology or worldview (Baldwin, 1985). This emerging philosophy reflects differences in epistemology.

Instead of the traditional emphasis on the individual, which is characteristic of Caucasian American psychology, African American psychology emphasizes the collective or the tribe. It recognizes the historical connection between generations, rather than the ahistorical "me generation" that is consonant with an individual-oriented psychology (Fairchild & Tucker, 1982). It is concerned with understanding the individual's harmonious relationship with his or her surroundings and how that harmony may be disrupted. Finally, African American psychology deals with the proactive role of the psychologist in bringing about social change (Fairchild & Wright, 1984) rather than the detached perspective of the European American social scientist.

General Source Materials

Before turning to the specifics of curricular design, it is useful to identify a number of general sources of course materials.

---

1. It should be noted that race names evolve, and "African American" is becoming a preferred name for persons of African descent living in the Americas (Fairchild, 1985a).

A number of journals regularly include articles of interest to the instructor of African American psychology. These include *Journal of Black Psychology* (published by the Association of Black Psychologists and the only journal devoted exclusively to this area), *Journal of Black Studies, Western Journal of Black Studies,* and *Journal of Negro Education.* A guide to other scholarly journals in Black studies may be found in a book by the Chicago Center for Afro-American Studies and Research (1981).

The last 10 years have also witnessed a proliferation of books geared specifically to African American psychology. These include edited volumes such as those by Jones (1980) and Boykin, Franklin, and Yates (1980) and several book-length monographs (Jenkins, 1982; Karenga, 1982; White, 1984).

In addition, a number of edited books have appeared that are not necessarily written from a psychological perspective but include chapters of interest to the instructor or student of African American psychology. Most important among these are the edited volumes by Sage Publications on contemporary Black thought (Asante & Vandi, 1980), Black men (Gary, 1981), Black families (H. P. McAdoo, 1981), Black children (McAdoo & McAdoo, 1985), and Black women (Rodgers-Rose, 1980). Other useful books and journals have a more multiethnic focus. For example, a special issue of *Psychotherapy* was devoted to ethnic minorities (Dudley & Rawlins, 1985), and several excellent books address clinical issues from multiethnic perspectives (e.g., Sue & Moore, 1984).

Instructors interested in supplementing reading material with audiovisual aids might consult Mind Productions and Associates (P.O. Box 11221, Tallahassee, FL 32302) for audiotapes by Na'im Akbar (1985) or the Association of Black Psychologists (P.O. Box 55999, Washington, DC 20040-5999) for audio- and videotapes by other prominent African American psychologists. The *Sourcebook on the Teaching of Black Psychology* (Jones, 1978), although somewhat dated, contains a wealth of information in terms of syllabi and classroom activities.

Curriculum Design

An introductory course should include some coverage of the major areas of specialization within African American psychology, specifically developmental, clinical, educational, community, and applied perspectives. In addition, specialized courses should be developed around topics that are of central concern, such as gender (African American men and women and their relationships), employment, health and mental health, criminal justice, personality (with an emphasis on self-concept and identity), race relations, testing, and IQ. In the material that follows, I describe some of these areas and identify representative course materials for each.

Life Span Development

African American developmental psychology has focused on the child (McAdoo & McAdoo, 1985; Spencer, Brookins, & Allen, 1985), the adult (Gary, 1981; Rodgers-Rose, 1980), and the aged (Jackson, 1980, 1982). In addition to this life span perspective, the instructor should identify the intergenerational nature of obstacles confronting the African American community and show how this history is manifested across age groups.

Gender

One of the most active areas of research and theory has been concerned with the African American woman (Allen, 1981, 1982; Murray & Scott, 1982; Rodgers-Rose, 1980; Stevenson, 1985). The African American man has received somewhat less attention, although a number of sources are available (Cazenave, 1984; Gary, 1981). Studies in both areas tend to emphasize the historical and contemporary transmission of gender inequality and its effects on individual functioning. Finally, the most controversial topic in this area is male–female relationships (see Fairchild, 1985b). Issues include imbalanced male–female ratios, the internalization of negative images in the broader culture, and the prescription of superordinate–subordinate gender roles in the broader society (Jewell, 1983; Semaj, 1982).

The Family

The African American family is an area with one of the longest research traditions in the social sciences. Of particular note are edited volumes by H. P. McAdoo (1981) and Staples (1978) and concise analyses by Nobles (1978, 1981). J. L. McAdoo (1981; 1988) provided a rare focus on African American fathers; Simms-Brown (1982) examined the female role in a family context; and DeJarnett and Raven (1981) provided an empirical analysis of power in spousal relationships. In this area, African American psychology counters negative stereotypes and biases while underscoring the strengths and resilience of African American families.

Education

The literature on educational psychology as it pertains to African Americans is also substantial and includes theoretical (Banks, 1982; Boykin, 1982) and empirical (Fairchild, 1984b) analyses. Source material is available on early childhood (Hart, Guthrie, & Winfield, 1980), high school (Hare, 1985), and postsecondary education (Ayres, 1983; Willie & Cunnigen, 1981). Special foci should include the role of Black English in education (Hilliard, 1983a; Troutman & Falk, 1982), school desegregation (Braddock, 1985; Hawley, 1981), the role of African American teachers and faculty (Exum, 1983), and policy analyses (Hilliard, 1984).

Employment and Economics

African American psychology has embraced issues surrounding employment and economics as keys to understanding the life circumstances of African Americans. Useful topics include the effects of job discrimination (Griffith & Griffith, 1986), interracial relations in the workplace (Asante & Davis, 1985), earnings and occupational mobility (Collins, 1983), and unemployment (Bowman, Jackson, Hatchett, & Gurin, 1982).

African American Personality

The study of the African American personality has historically been marked by extreme biases that have endorsed negative racial stereotypes (Banks, McQuater, Ross, & Ward, 1983). In contrast, most of the recent literature in this area has examined such issues as Black identity and activism (Allen, 1984), self-concept and self-esteem (Cross, 1978; Farrell & Olson, 1983; Stephan & Rosenfield, 1979), bi-culturality (Chimezie, 1985), and personality assessment (Baldwin & Bell, 1985; Gynther, 1981).

Clinical Issues

Clinical issues in African American psychology are far ranging, including etiology (Bulhan, 1985), epidemiology (Williams, 1986), diagnosis (Jones & Gray, 1986), and treatment and training (Dudley & Rawlins, 1985). Special topic areas include race of therapist issues (Greene, 1985), gender issues (Smith, 1981), posttraumatic stress disorder among Vietnam veterans (Allen, 1986), drug and alcohol abuse (Tucker, 1985), and suicide (Baker, 1984). African American psychologists have been particularly concerned with societal factors that may affect mental health and with the development of culturally appropriate assessment, diagnostic, and treatment regimens.

Psychological Testing

The debate concerning the relation between race and IQ is one of the most controversial areas in African American psychology and has generated voluminous literature and a lively debate (see Eysenck & Kamin, 1981). It is useful to include and discuss works that have branded African Americans as genetically inferior (e.g., Jensen, 1985) as well as those that sharply rebuke the racial inferiority perspective (e.g., Persell, 1981). Focused topics include race of examiner effects (Hanley & Barclay, 1979), social class effects (Tate & Gibson, 1980), and legal issues (Hilliard, 1983b). Many of the issues surrounding the race and IQ controversy also pertain to general psychological assessment (Cameron, 1980; Wyche & Novick, 1985).

Other Areas

Depending on the interests of the instructor, a number of additional areas may be presented, such as health psychology (Airhihenbuwa, 1985; Boone, 1985), the mass media (Fairchild, 1984c; Fairchild, Stockard, & Bowman, 1986; Staples & Jones, 1985), race relations (Bowser & Hunt, 1981; Fairchild & Gurin, 1978), community psychology (Akbar, 1985; Johnson, 1981), crime and punishment (Benokraitis & Griffin-Keene, 1982; Christianson, 1981; Denno, 1981; Kleck, 1981; Watts & Watts, 1981), and international perspectives (Awanbor, 1982; Binitie, 1984).

Instructors could also develop courses or sections of courses devoted to the work of a single individual.

Conclusion

African American psychology has grown substantially in the last 20 years. Sufficient curricular material now exists to develop a dozen or more specialized courses. This wealth of information greatly facilitates the development of an introductory course (Fairchild, 1984a) and provides opportunities for including relevant material into the traditional psychology curriculum. More important, the field has reached a point where it is now feasible to consider the development of a sequence of courses that would constitute a major or minor in African American psychology in college studies. To apply the African American philosophical base to the teaching of African American psychology, instructors would present the literature within a historical framework, seek understanding of the commonalities as well as the unique qualities of the African American experience, and encourage strategies that would bring about positive structural changes within the broader society.

References

Airhihenbuwa, C. O. (1985). Race and health care in America. *Western Journal of Black Studies, 9*(4), 204–208.

Akbar, N. (1984). Africentric social sciences for human liberation. *Journal of Black Studies, 14*(4), 395–414.

Akbar, N. (1985). *The community of self* (rev. ed.). Tallahassee, FL: Mind Productions & Associates. [P.O. Box 11221, Tallahassee, FL 32302; tapes available].

Allen, I. M. (1986). Posttraumatic stress disorder among Black Vietnam veterans. *Hospital and Community Psychiatry, 37*(1), 55–61.

Allen, R. L. (Ed.). (1981). The best of *The Black Scholar:* The Black woman [Special issue]. *The Black Scholar, 12*(6).

Allen, R. L. (Ed.). (1982). The best of *The Black Scholar:* The Black woman II [Special issue]. *The Black Scholar, 13*(4–5).

Allen, W. R. (1984). Race consciousness and collective commitment among Black students on white campuses. *Western Journal of Black Studies, 8*(3), 156–166.

Asante, M., & Davis, A. (1985). Black and White communication: Analyzing work place encounters. *Journal of Black Studies, 16*(1), 77–93.

Asante, M. K., & Vandi, A. S. (Eds.). (1980). *Contemporary Black thought: Alternative analyses in social and behavioral science.* Beverly Hills, CA: Sage.

Awanbor, D. (1982). The healing process in African psychotherapy. *American Journal of Psychotherapy, 36*(2), 206–213.

Ayres, Q. W. (1983). Student achievement at predominantly White and predominantly Black universities. *American Educational Research Journal, 20*(2), 291–304.

Baker, F. M. (1984). Black suicide attempters in 1980: A preventive focus. *General Hospital Psychiatry, 6*, 131–137.

Baldwin, J. A. (1985). Psychological aspects of European cosmology in American society: African and European cultures. *Western Journal of Black Studies, 9*(4), 216–223.

Baldwin, J. A. (1986). African (Black) psychology: Issues and synthesis. *Journal of Black Studies, 16*(3), 235–250.

Baldwin, J. A., & Bell, Y. R. (1985). The African self-consciousness scale: An Africentric personality questionnaire. *Western Journal of Black Studies, 9*(2), 61–68.

Banks, J. A. (1982). Educating minority youths: An inventory of current theory. *Education and Urban Society, 15*(1), 88–103.

Banks, W. C., McQuater, G. V., Ross, J. A., & Ward, W. (1983). Delayed gratification in Blacks: A critical review. *Journal of Black Psychology, 9*(2), 43–56.

Benokraitis, N., & Griffin-Keene, J. A. (1982). Prejudice and jury selection. *Journal of Black Studies, 12*(4), 427–449.

Binitie, A. O. (1984). The depressed and anxious patient: Care and treatment in Africa. *International Journal of Mental Health, 12*(3), 44–57.

Boone, M. S. (1985). Social and cultural factors in the etiology of low birthweight among disadvantaged Blacks. *Social Science and Medicine, 20*(8), 1001–1012.

Bowman, P. J., Jackson, J. S., Hatchett, S. J., & Gurin, G. (1982). Joblessness and discouragement among Black Americans. *Economic Outlook USA, 9*(4), 85–88.

Bowser, B. P., & Hunt, R. G. (Eds.). (1981). *Impacts of racism on White Americans.* Beverly Hills, CA: Sage.

Boykin, A. W. (1982). Task variability and the performance of Black and White schoolchildren: Vervistic explorations. *Journal of Black Studies, 12*(4), 469–485.

Boykin, A. W., Franklin, A. J., & Yates, J. F. (Eds.). (1980). *Research directions of Black psychologists.* New York: Russell Sage.

Braddock, J. H. II. (1985). School desegregation and Black assimilation. *Journal of Social Issues, 41*(3), 9–22.

Bulhan, H. A. (1985). Black Americans and psychopathology: An overview of research and theory. *Psychotherapy, 22*(2, Supplement), 370–378.

Cameron, H. K. (Ed.). (1980). Critical issues in testing and achievement of Black Americans [Special issue]. *Journal of Negro Education, 44*(3).

Cazenave, N. A. (1984). Race, socioeconomic status, and age: The social context of American masculinity. *Sex Roles, 11*(7–8), 639–656.

Chicago Center for Afro-American Studies and Research, Inc. (1981). *Guide to scholarly journals in Black studies.* Chicago: Peoples College Press.

Chimezie, A. (1985). Black bi-culturality. *Western Journal of Black Studies, 9*(4), 224–235.

Christianson, S. (1981). Our Black prisons. *Crime and Delinquency, 27*(3), 364–375.

Collins, S. M. (1983). The making of the Black middle class. *Social Problems, 30*(4), 369–382.

Cross, W. E. (1978). The Thomas and Cross models of psychological nigrescence: A review. *Journal of Black Psychology, 5*(1), 13–31.

DeJarnett, S., & Raven, B. H. (1981). The balance, bases, and modes of interpersonal power in Black couples: The role of sex and socioeconomic circumstances. *Journal of Black Psychology, 7*(2), 51–66.

Denno, D. (1981). Psychological factors for the Black defendant in a jury trial. *Journal of Black Studies, 11*(3), 313–326.

Dudley, G. R., & Rawlins, M. R. (Eds.). (1985). Psychotherapy with ethnic minorities. [Special issue]. *Psychotherapy, 22*(2, Supplement).

Exum, W. H. (1983). Climbing the crystal stair: Values, affirmative action, and minority faculty. *Social Problems, 30*(4), 383–399.

Eysenck, H. J., & Kamin, L. (1981). The intelligence controversy. New York: Wiley.

Fairchild, H. H. (1984a). Teaching Black psychology. *Western Journal of Black Studies, 8*(1), 55–60.

Fairchild, H. H. (1984b). School size, per-pupil expenditures, and school achievement. *Review of Public Data Use, 12*, 221–229.

Fairchild, H. H. (1984c). Creating, producing, and evaluating prosocial TV. *Journal of Educational Television, 10*(3), 161–183.

Fairchild, H. H. (1985a). Black, Negro, or Afro-American? The differences are crucial! *Journal of Black Studies, 16*(1), 47–55.

Fairchild, H. H. (1985b). Black singles: Gender differences in mate preferences and heterosexual attitudes. *Western Journal of Black Studies, 9*(2), 69–73.

Fairchild, H. H., & Gurin, P. (1978). Traditions in the social psychological analysis of race relations. *American Behavioral Scientist, 21*(5), 757–778.

Fairchild, H. H., Stockard, R., & Bowman, P. (1986). Impact of *Roots:* Evidence from the National Survey of Black Americans. *Journal of Black Studies, 16*(3), 307–318.

Fairchild, H. H., & Tucker, M. B. (1982). Black residential mobility: Trends and characteristics. *Journal of Social Issues, 38*(3), 51–74.

Fairchild, H. H., & Wright, C. (1984). A social-ecological assessment and feedback-intervention of an adolescent treatment agency. *Adolescence, 19*(74), 263–275.

Farrell, W. C., Jr., & Olson, J. L. (1983). Kenneth and Mamie Clark revisited: Racial identification and racial preference in dark-skinned and light-skinned Black children. *Urban Education, 18*(3), 284–297.

Gary, L. E. (Ed.). (1981). *Black men.* Beverly Hills, CA: Sage.

Greene, B. A. (1985). Considerations in the treatment of Black patients by White therapists. *Psychotherapy, 22*(2, Supplement), 389–393.

Griffith, E. E. H., & Griffith, E. J. (1986). Racism, psychological injury, and compensatory damages. *Hospital and Community Psychiatry, 37*(1), 71–75.

Gynther, M. D. (1981). Is the MMPI an appropriate assessment device for Blacks? *Journal of Black Psychology, 7*(2), 67–76.

Hanley, J. H., & Barclay, A. G. (1979). Sensitivity of the WISC and WISC-R to subject and examiner variables. *Journal of Black Psychology, 5*(2), 79–84.

Hare, B. R. (1985). Stability and change in self-perception and achievement among Black adolescents: A longitudinal study. *Journal of Black Psychology, 11*(2), 29–42.

Hart, J. T., Guthrie, J. T., & Winfield, L. (1980). Black English phonology and learning to read. *Journal of Educational Psychology, 72*(5), 636–646.

Hawley, W. D. (Ed.). (1981). *Effective school desegregation: Equity, quality, and feasibility.* Beverly Hills, CA: Sage.

Hilliard, A. G. III. (1983a). Psychological factors associated with language in the education of the African-American child. *Journal of Negro Education, 52*(1), 24–34.

Hilliard, A. G. III. (1983b). IQ and the courts: Larry P. v. Wilson Riles and PASE v. Hannon. *Journal of Black Psychology, 10*(1), 1–18.

Hilliard, A. G. III. (1984). Democratizing the common school in a multicultural society. *Education and Urban Society, 16*(3), 262–273.

Jackson, J. J. (1980). *Minorities and aging.* Belmont, CA: Wadsworth.

Jackson, J. J. (Ed.). (1982). The Black elderly [Special issue]. *The Black Scholar, 13*(1).

Jenkins, A. H. (1982). *The psychology of the Afro-American: A humanistic approach.* New York: Pergamon Press.

Jensen, A. R. (1985). The nature of Black–White difference on various psychometric tests: Spearman's hypothesis. *Behavioral and Brain Sciences, 8*(2), 193–218.

Jewell, K. S. (1983). Black male/female conflict: Internalization of negative definitions transmitted through imagery. *Western Journal of Black Studies, 7*(1), 43–48.

Johnson, R. C. (1981). The Black family and Black community development. *Journal of Black Psychology, 8*(1), 35–52.

Jones, B. E., & Gray, B. A. (1986). Problems in diagnosing schizophrenia and affective disorders among Blacks. *Hospital and Community Psychiatry, 37*(1), 61–64.

Jones, R. L. (Ed.). (1978). *Sourcebook on the teaching of Black psychology.* Washington, DC: Association of Black Psychologists.

Jones, R. L. (Ed.). (1980). *Black psychology* (2nd ed.). New York: Harper & Row.

Karenga, M. (1982). *Introduction to Black Studies.* Los Angeles: Kawaida Publications. [2560 West 54th Street, Los Angeles, CA 90043.]

Kleck, G. (1981). Racial discrimination in criminal sentencing: A critical evaluation of the evidence with additional evidence on the death penalty. *American Sociological Review, 46,* 783–805.

McAdoo, H. P. (Ed.). (1981). *Black families.* Beverly Hills, CA: Sage.

McAdoo, J. L. (1981). Involvement of fathers in the socialization of Black children. In H. P. McAdoo (Ed.), *Black families* (pp. 225–237). Beverly Hills, CA: Sage.

McAdoo, J. L. (1988). The changing role of Black fathers in the family. In P. Bronstein & C. P. Cowan (Eds.), *Fatherhood today: Men's changing role in the family* (pp. 79–92). New York: Wiley.

McAdoo, H. P., & McAdoo, J. L. (Eds.). (1985). *Black children: Social, educational, and parental environments.* Beverly Hills, CA: Sage.

Murray, S. R., & Scott, P. B. (Eds.). (1982). A special issue on Black women [Special issue]. *Psychology of Women Quarterly, 6*(3).

Nobles, W. W. (1978). Toward an empirical and theoretical framework for defining Black families. *Journal of Marriage and the Family, 40,* 679–687.

Nobles, W. W. (1981). African-American family life: An instrument of culture. In H. P. McAdoo (Ed.), *Black families* (pp. 77–86). Beverly Hills, CA: Sage.

Persell, C. H. (1981). Genetic and cultural deficit theories: Two sides of the same racist coin. *Journal of Black Studies, 12*(1), 19–37.

Rodgers-Rose, L. (Ed.). (1980). *The Black woman.* Beverly Hills, CA: Sage.

Semaj, L. T. (1982). Polygamy reconsidered: Causes and consequences of declining sex ratio in African-American society. *Journal of Black Psychology, 9*(1), 29–44.

Simms-Brown, R. J. (1982). The female in the Black family: Dominant mate or helpmate? *Journal of Black Psychology, 9*(1), 45–55.

Smith, E. J. (1981). Mental health and service delivery systems for Black women. *Journal of Black Studies, 12*(2), 126–141.

Spencer, M. B., Brookins, G. K., & Allen, W. R. (Eds.). (1985). *Beginnings: The social and affective development of Black children.* Hillsdale, NJ: Erlbaum.

Staples, R. (Ed.). (1978). *The Black family: Essays and studies* (2nd ed.) Belmont, CA: Wadsworth.

Staples, R., & Jones, T. (1985). Culture, ideology and Black television images. *The Black Scholar, 16*(3), 10–20.

Stephan, W. G., & Rosenfield, D. (1979). Black self-rejection: Another look. *Journal of Educational Psychology, 71*(5), 708–716.

Stevenson, R. (1985). Black women in the United States: A bibliography of recent works. *The Black Scholar, 16*(2), 45–55.

Sue, S., & Moore, T. (Eds.). (1984). *The pluralistic society: A community mental health perspective.* New York: Human Sciences Press.

Tate, D., & Gibson, G. (1980). Socioeconomic status and Black and White intelligence revisited. *Social Behavior and Personality, 8*(2), 233–237.

Troutman, D. E., & Falk, J. S. (1982). Speaking Black English and reading: Is there a problem of interference? *Journal of Negro Education, 51*(2), 123–133.

Tucker, M. B. (1985). U.S. ethnic minorities and drug abuse: An assessment of the science and practice. *International Journal of the Addictions, 20*(6 & 7), 1021–1047.

Watts, A. D., & Watts, T. M. (1981). Minorities and urban crime: Are they the cause or the victims? *Urban Affairs Quarterly, 16*(4), 423–436.

White, J. L. (1984). *The psychology of Blacks: An Afro-American perspective.* Englewood Cliffs, NJ: Prentice Hall.

Williams, D. H. (1986). The epidemiology of mental illness in Afro-Americans. *Hospital and Community Psychiatry, 37*(1), 42–49.

Willie, C. V., & Cunnigen, D. (1981). Black students in higher education: A review of studies, 1965–1980. *Annual Review of Sociology, 7,* 177–198.

Wyche, L. G., & Novick, M. R. (1985). Standards for educational and psychological testing: The issue of testing bias from the perspective of school psychology and psychometrics. *Journal of Black Psychology, 11*(2), 43–48.

17

Vickie M. Mays

Even the Rat was White and Male: Teaching the Psychology of Black Women

The education of psychologists and mental health specialists has long been inadequate in its attention to the unique experiences of Black women. Historically, the psychology of Black women has been buried either within Black psychology, in which race relations assume primary importance, or in feminist scholarship, with its emphasis on sexism (Zinn, Cannon, & Dill, 1984). In this chapter, I shall discuss some of the issues involved in teaching in the newly emerging area of the psychology of Black women.

The study of Black women needs to emphasize the interrelatedness of gender and ethnicity (Mays, in press). Black women should be studied and taught about as Black women, not as individuals separately experiencing being Black and female. This then raises such fundamental questions as, How does the inclusion of Black women's experiences change our understanding of psychological theories of socialization processes, moral development, autonomy or attachment? The task is not simply to add race to the female experience or gender to the Black experience. Instead the intent is to uncover the complex diversity of Black women's psychological experiences resulting from interdependent systems of oppression.

Developing a Course

Curriculum development is hampered by the paucity of empirical research on Black women. Examining the research literature, I found that until 1983 only 50 articles on this subject had been published in all the American Psychological Association (APA) journals (Mays, 1988a). The majority of these were race comparative rather than interactionist in approach.

Initial work on this chapter was funded by a National Institute of Mental Health New Investigator Research Award to the author at the Program for Research on Black Americans, Institute of Social Research, Ann Arbor, Michigan. The inspiration for the title came from Guthries' (1976) reexamination of the history of the field, *Even the Rat Was White: A Historical View of Psychology.*

An additional difficulty is the lack of organized curriculum materials, though there have been recent efforts to remedy this. A bibliography on Black women by the APA Division 35's Task Force on Black Women's Concerns, compiled into a forthcoming book (Mays, in press), contains more than 2,000 references on Black women. Drawn from the social sciences and the humanities, these resources examine the psychocultural behaviors of Black women from an African American perspective. For example, *Coming of Age in Mississippi* (Moody, 1968) can be used to teach the psychological theory of social movements, although it is a biographical account.

Course Content

Currently, I teach a course titled The Afro-American Woman in the United States. The confluence of oppression experienced by Black women results in a social consciousness differing from that of Black men or White women. This consciousness, in turn, yields a different experience of work, love, growth, change, time, and cooperation (Aptheker, 1981). It is this consciousness and the factors that have given rise to its development that the course attempts to illuminate. Topics covered include (a) social movements; (b) ethnicity, gender, class, and caste; and (c) interpersonal roles (see the schedule for lecture topics listed before the references at the end of this chapter).

The course begins with a focus on social movements, including the early abolitionists, Black women's clubs, Seneca Falls, the civil rights movement, and the recent women's movement. Although historical and sociological reading dominate this section, students learn about racial attitudes from a psychological framework. An organizing framework I use is the question of whether there is a national Black women's movement and, if not, what conditions would be likely to produce one.

In the second section, we examine each social status separately and then in combination. I often ask students to make comparisons with other gender or ethnic groups, as a way of discovering similarities and differences. Although the aim is to get students to understand the contribution of each status to the unique experiences of Black women, it is also important to discover those values, attitudes, or motivations that hold across gender, ethnic group, age, or class. My current reading list in this section includes Morrison's (1970) *The Bluest Eye* (ethnicity); Chafe's (1977) analysis of social class and control; selections dealing with color and caste from Washington's (1977) edited book *Black-Eyed Susans* ("The Coming of Maureen Peel" and "If You're Light and Have Long Hair"); and the excellent Zora Neale Hurston essays edited by Walker (1979).

In the final section, we explore interpersonal roles in the lives of Black women, examining each of these roles for its demands and provisions of support. Age, gender, ethnic group, and class differences among the students help to highlight diversity of experiences. The goals are to delineate differences in expectations of Black women's behavior in specific roles and to uncover the biases associated with those expectations. Students read *Tar Baby* and *Sula* by Morrison (1974, 1981) to explore family roles and female–female relationships, respectively. I have also used selections from Rodgers-Rose's (1980) edited book *The Black Woman;* however, the relationships described in these articles are outdated in that they are no longer representative of relationships in the 1980s.

Selecting material for this last section is a sensitive issue. There are few scholarly articles on Black heterosexual or homosexual close relationships (Mays, 1988b), and these often take biased positions. In addition, discussions of sexual relationships outside of marriage, or lesbian relationships, at times present difficulties for some class participants.

Method of Teaching

In teaching the course, I use group dynamics principles. The classroom is viewed as a large group, learning about the psychology of Black women through personal exploration and guidance from the instructor. As such, it is essential to establish an atmosphere of openness and trust. Explicit guidelines for students' behavior are clearly specified at the beginning. Women students are reminded that the men in class are not there to represent all men, and their presence in class indicates some interest in better understanding Black women. Men are reminded that they are not authorities on women's experiences. Similarly, Black students are not allowed to blame non-Black students, while White students are cautioned that the class is not interested in any demonstrations of "liberalism."

The size of the class can vary, but 60 seems a good upper limit in order to maintain an intimacy within the class. The course is offered simultaneously on a graduate and undergraduate level with minor differences in workload. In the undergraduate curriculum, it is offered to juniors and seniors through three majors: psychology, Afro-American studies, and women's studies. The result is a diverse group of students.

Each class begins with a lecture and is followed by a lengthy question and comment period. During the lecture, I raise several questions for the students to contemplate and address in the latter part of the class session. Over the years, I have decreased my use of guest lecturers. My interactionist perspective precludes devoting an entire class period to only one aspect of an issue. Instead, because of the time constraints, videotaped interviews and television specials integrated into classroom presentations have been more useful.

Course Requirements

I assign three take-home essay exams, one for each section, and encourage cooperative work, although the final product must be an individual one. Exams can be a source of conflict. Some students will be quite articulate in class, have a good grasp of the answers for the exam, but be hampered in their performance by poor writing ability. For ethnic students, it is a shock to be told by an ethnic minority professor that they have writing problems. Many previously had attributed such comments to racism on the part of Anglo professors. To encourage work on writing skills, I sometimes allow students to raise their grades by rewriting answers to the exam.

Students also are required to do a group visual medium project for a 15-minute class presentation, which they often use subsequently during Black History Month or International Women's Week. Projects have included calendars highlighting important Black women's events, a prosocial comic book with a Black woman heroine, board games, a play, and surveys. Students work in groups and meet with the instructor prior to presentation. Grades for the projects are assigned by the class members, who evaluate each project on the three dimensions of new information, ability to teach, and creativity.

Schedule of Lecture Topics for Course Titled The Afro-American Woman in the United States

Section 1: *Social Movement*

> Course introduction—Development of a social movement. Book: Anne Moody, *Coming of Age in Mississippi.*
> Development of a social movement/civil rights movement.
> Civil rights movement/women's movement.
> The creation of a Black women's movement.
> The Black women's movement and feminism.

Section 2: *Ethnicity, gender, class, and caste*

> Ethnicity/race/culture. Book: Toni Morrison's *The Bluest Eye.*
> Gender.
> Class.
> Caste/color.

Section 3: *Interpersonal roles—supportive and conflictual functions*

> Family roles. Book: Toni Morrison's *Tar Baby.*
> Grandmother/mother/daughter relationships.
> Mate relationships.
> Male–female relationships. Book: Toni Morrison's *Sula.*
> Alternative relationships/celibacy–singlehood–polygamy.
> Female friendships.
> Alternative relationships/lesbian relationships.

References

Aptheker, B. (1981). *Strong is what we make each other: Unlearning racism within women's studies.* Unpublished manuscript.

Chafe, W. H. (1977). Sex and race: An analogy of social control. In W. H. Chafe (Ed.), *Women and equality: Changing patterns in American culture* (pp. 81–113). New York: Oxford University Press.

Mays, V. M. (1988a). *The psychology of Black women: A view from mainstream psychology journals.* Manuscript submitted for publication.

Mays, V. M. (1988b). *The impact of perceived discrimination on Black women's relationships*. Manuscript submitted for publication.

Mays, V. M. (in press). *The Black woman: A bibliographic guide to research materials on Black women in the social sciences and mental health*. New York: Praeger.

Moody, A. (1968). *Coming of age in Mississippi*. New York: Dial Press.

Morrison, T. (1970). *The bluest eye*. New York: Holt, Rinehart & Winston.

Morrison, T. (1974). *Sula*. New York: Knopf.

Morrison, T. (1981). *Tar baby*. New York: Knopf.

Rodgers-Rose, L. F. (1980). *The Black woman*. Beverly Hills, CA: Sage.

Walker, A. (Ed.). (1979). *I love myself when I am laughing . . . & then again when I am looking mean and impressive: A Zora Neale Hurston reader*. New York: Feminist Press.

Washington, M. H. (Ed.). (1977). *Black-eyed Susans*. New York: Anchor Books.

Zinn, M. B., Cannon, L. W., & Dill, B. T. (1984). *The costs of exclusionary practices in women's studies*. Unpublished manuscript, Memphis State University.

18

Melba J. T. Vasquez and Augustine Barón, Jr.

The Psychology of the Chicano Experience: A Sample Course Structure

A particularly important element in our understanding of human behavior is the consideration of cultural context. The norms and mores of a society affect the growth and development of all those reared in it. For ethnic minority groups within that society, additional norms and mores contribute to behavior, values, attitudes, and worldview. Whether reared in a traditional ethnic family or in a family more nearly assimilated into the American culture, the members of ethnic minorities—to differing degrees and in different ways—necessarily experience dual cultural influences.

Social and political conditions in a society profoundly influence the ethnic minority individual. Media stereotypes, for example, may promote discrimination and prejudice toward a minority group, and the internalization of those negative messages affects the self-concept of minority group members. Low levels of educational, economic, and occupational attainment (relative to the majority group) further reduce minority individuals' sense of self-worth, and the lack of access to key resources diminishes their overall well-being. Only through recognition of these and other elements in American society that deter and devalue ethnic minority groups, and realization of the effects such elements exert, can we come to understand the psychology of minority groups in general and of their members individually.

Hispanic Americans

Currently the second largest minority group, Hispanic Americans are expected to be the United States' largest minority by the year 2000 (Newton & Arciniega, 1983). They have a high birth rate and high immigration rates, and both trends are predicted to continue. The 1982 current population survey by the U.S. Bureau of the Census (1985) developed a national postcensus estimate of 15.4 million Hispanics, including Cubans, Mexican Americans, Puerto Ricans, and others, the largest group being persons of Mexican descent (8.7 million, according to the U.S. Bureau of the Census, 1980).

Although the various Hispanic subcultures have much in common (e.g., language, values, customs), each Hispanic group also has its own history and experience. Thus, we recommend that a course structure include a brief overview of all Hispanic groups and then focus on one specific group. The target group would generally be that group most widely represented in the local geographic region. For purposes of illustration, the course described here focuses on the Mexican American or Chicano[1] population, although the overall course structure could apply to any group.

A Course on Chicano Psychology

The present course is an advanced undergraduate seminar that has been offered on a number of occasions in the Educational Psychology Department of the University of Texas at Austin. Cross-listed in the School of Social Work and in the Center for Mexican-American Studies, it has had special appeal to liberal arts and education majors wanting to learn more about the psychological literature on Chicanos, a significant ethnic group in Texas. Ideally, the student has had introductory courses in general psychology and social psychology and some additional courses in anthropology, sociology, and ethnic or Chicano studies. Classes have typically been limited to 15 students, which greatly enhances class interchange and discussions.

Although offered to undergraduates, the seminar can easily be directed toward graduate students; in fact, the core readings may be more suited to the latter. Four books have served as texts for the course: *Explorations in Chicano Psychology* (Barón, 1981), *Chicanos: Social and Psychological Perspectives* (Hernandez, Haug, & Wagner, 1976), *Chicano Psychology* (Martinez & Mendoza, 1984), and *Blaming the Victim* (Ryan, 1972).

Course requirements include a midterm and final essay exam based on the readings and a term paper on individually selected topics. Topics for the term paper have varied widely in conjuction with the students' interests; the only requirement has been that they relate in some way to the cultural issues addressed in the course and highlight appreciation of ethnic and cultural factors. They have included teenage pregnancy among Hispanics, patterns and practices of alcohol use, language orientation and mental health, ethnic dialects in sign language, ethnic factors determining the actuarial tables used by life insurance companies, and Mexican-American mythology as expressed in various art forms in the Austin–San Antonio area (presented as a slide show). Students present oral summaries of their papers to the class during the final weeks of the semester.

Course content includes the following: history and overview of Hispanic psychology, narrowing to a focus on Chicano psychology; life span development within a Chicano cultural context; Chicano personality and social psychology; issues of intelligence and learning; psychological services for Chicanos; and the future of Chicano psychology.

---

1. The terms *Chicano* and *Mexican American* are used interchangeably and, for the purposes of this chapter, are defined as Americans of Mexican descent.

History and Overview of Psychology

Hispanics. The first section of the course serves as an introduction to a range of basic subjects, including a historical overview of the experiences of Hispanic Americans, current demographics, the field of Hispanic psychology (including a critical examination of existing research), and stereotyping.

In discussing history and demographics, instructors need to spend time defining *Hispanic*, which is "a generic label including all people of Spanish origin and descent" (Ruiz & Padilla, 1977, p. 401). Although Hispanics share language, values, and customs, they are not a homogeneous group: The Spaniards' arrival in the New World and their subsequent exploration and colonization resulted in an aggregate of distinct subcultures across different geographic areas (Ruiz, 1981). The earliest subculture to develop was Chicano. Students may not know that by the middle of the 16th century, the original immigrants from Spain, the native Indians from Mexico, and their *mestizo* or "mixed-blood" progeny had settled in all of what is known as the Southwestern United States. Ruiz (1981) described contemporary Chicano culture as the "end point" of this historical, immensely varied, genetic and cultural interaction. Puerto Rico and Cuba were also colonized by Spain in the 16th century, with Puerto Rican and Cuban subcultures developing in this country mainly in the 20th century. LeVine and Padilla (1980) have provided a succinct historical sketch of Cubans and Puerto Ricans.

Hispanic Americans tend to be urban dwellers—82.5%, compared with 76% of Blacks and 67.8% of the total population. Ruiz (1981) described the subgroup distribution as follows: 87% of the Chicanos reside in the Southwest (California, Texas, Arizona, New Mexico, and Colorado), 76% of the Puerto Ricans reside in Connecticut, New Jersey, or New York; and most Cubans reside in Florida. These demographic patterns may continue to change with the infusion of new immigrants and refugees from Latin America.

With regard to Hispanic psychology, the course includes both Old and New World concerns about human behavior from a Hispanic perspective. The primary source for this section is a valuable synopsis of the history of psychology by Padilla (in Martinez & Mendoza, 1984). The origins of Hispanic psychology are discussed, in particular the historical interrelation between psychology and medicine in Spain and the New World. Spain's humane care of the mentally ill has long gone unrecognized, and remarkable figures such as Juan Luis Vives, called the father of modern psychology by at least one scholar, are largely unknown outside of the Spanish-speaking world (LaCroce, 1984). In our analysis of psychology in the New World prior to the Conquest, we point out the advanced system of medical care and knowledge of the medicinal value of plants and herbs that had accumulated over centuries, both of which were subsequently lost. *Curanderismo*, a form of folk healing still practiced in Mexico, Latin America, and the United States, appears to be one of several therapies for mental illness once used by Aztec healers. We also describe the advances in mental health and psychotherapy in Mexico in the past four centuries, highlighting contributions of key Mexican psychologists.

The first part of the history and overview ends with a critical examination of the research methodology on which early social science literature on Hispanic Americans was based. Various critiques (Casas, 1984, 1985; Hernandez, 1974; Padilla, 1981) have pointed out ways in which stereotyping and misperceptions have shaped the literature on Hispanics' values, attitudes, and behaviors, and offer recommendations for methodological improvements in future research.

Chicanos. The second part of the overview focuses on the historical experience of Mexican Americans, from those living in the Southwest prior to U.S. acquisition of that land to recent immigrants. It includes the key experiences of Chicanos in American society and the history of Chicano psychology. Ruiz (1981) is a good source of historical information, and Hernandez et al.'s (1976) first nine chapters provide a thorough immersion in key issues related to the social experience of Mexican Americans in the United States. Chapter 4 of Hernandez et al. analyzes the unique evolution of new modes of thought and action by Mexican Americans, demonstrating clearly how Chicanos are different from Anglos in the United States and from Mexicans in Mexico. They point out that cultures are dynamic, not static, so that when groups from various backgrounds come in contact, cultural hybridization often occurs. Thus, for example, Chicano family structure may become less patriarchal than traditional Mexican family structure, yet the underlying values of family loyalty remain and are different from those of the Anglo culture. The first five chapters of Ryan (1972) provide another important perspective.

In reviewing the history of Chicano psychology, we focus on Chicano psychologists and their contributions. Martinez and Mendoza's (1984) text (Chapters 1 through 3 and 13) is a helpful resource for exploring the foundations for a Chicano psychology. Chapter 7 provides a critique of the "damaging-culture" model (that Mexican-American culture itself is the source of problems for this group) and presents an alternative account of Mexican-American culture as a positive example of sociocultural adjustment.

Effect of Culture on Development Over the Life Span

In this section, the focus is on major topics in developmental psychology as they apply to Chicanos. One topic is bilingualism: the process of bilingual language development, the consequences of being familiar with two language systems, and the politicizing of educational interventions for children from non-English-speaking homes. The research in bilingualism is extensive, and resources include Hernandez et al.'s (1976) Chapter 15 and Martinez and Mendoza's (1984) Chapters 17-through 19.

A second topic is the family (Barón, 1981, Chapter 1). Students learn the importance of *la familia* as the central focus for Chicano life, the high value traditional Hispanics place on affiliation, and their need for warm, mutually supportive relationships; thus, students come to see that the family and community are generally much more highly valued in Chicano culture than in American culture (LeVine & Padilla, 1980). In discussions of marriage and family dynamics, we attempt to correct erroneous assumptions such as the notion that Hispanic culture is homogeneous. Regarding sex roles within the family, we point out that many writings in this area suggest that Hispanic sex roles are rigidly defined (LeVine & Padilla, 1980), resulting in unflattering and unrealistic notions. As Ruiz (1981) explained, the word *macho* translates from Spanish as "male" and is used among Hispanics as a flattering term to denote masculinity. It connotes physical strength, sexual attractiveness, virtue, and potency. . . . At a more subtle level of analysis, "real" masculinity among Hispanics involves dignity in personal conduct, respect for others, love for the family, and affection for children. When applied by non-Hispanics to Hispanic males, however, "macho" is often defined in terms of physical aggression, sexual promiscuity, dominance of women, and excessive use of alcohol. In reaction to this abuse, Hispanic women are assumed to be submissive, nurturant, and virtuous thereby maintaining the unity of the Hispanic family despite all this disruption from their fathers, husbands, and sons. (pp. 191–192)

Other topics addressed in this section are children's social development, including the tendency to show more cooperative responding at younger ages (Hernandez et al., 1976, Chapter 10; Martinez & Mendoza, 1984, Chapter 15); gender role development and differences; social support networks; and the effects of poverty. Although little research has been done on the topic, we examine the life span variations of Chicano men and women compared with Anglo men and women, from adolescence to middle age. Finally, using Chapter 2 in Barón's (1981) text and Chapter 11 in the Martinez and Mendoza (1984) text, we address the needs and life-styles of the Chicano elderly.

Personality and Social Psychology

The third section of the course focuses on specific social–psychological concepts of Chicanos. Although related issues appear throughout the course, it is important to address such salient topics as pluralism, gender issues, acculturation, and oppression from the perspective of social psychology. Pluralism is a recognition and appreciation of ethnic and cultural differences; a pluralistic society values and recognizes the unique contributions diverse groups bring to its cultural milieu. Hernandez et al. (1976; Chapters 11 through 14 and 18), Ryan (1972; last five chapters), and Martinez and Mendoza (1984; Chapters 6, 13, and 16) are useful in providing an understanding of this concept.

Gender issues, with special focus on the double minority status of Mexican-American women, are addressed using Barón's Chapter 3 and Martinez and Mendoza's Chapter 14 as primary resources. Specific topics include women's relative lack of power and status in the educational, occupational, economic, and political arenas; the unique conflicts and stresses of employed Mexican-American women, given the culture's strong family values; single motherhood; and the high incidence of depression among Chicanas. Melville's (1980) *Twice a Minority: Mexican-American Women* is a unique compilation of articles presenting a range of perspectives about the Chicana that can serve as an additional resource.

Acculturation is the process of incorporating the beliefs and customs of an alternate culture. We address such issues as the consequences of cultural transition and change, the importance of maintaining one's ethnic identity, and ways of measuring the degree of acculturation (Barón, Chapter 4; Martinez & Mendoza,

Chapters 5 and 7). Examples of acculturation are discussed in the areas of food, language, dress, and customs.

Our discussion of oppression reviews important theoretical and philosophical viewpoints, with special reference to the major issues of bias and stereotyping, as directed toward Chicanos and other minorities. The animated film, *A Tale of O*, which illustrates some of the experiences of being a minority "O" in a majority "X" group setting, is helpful in making students aware of the dynamics that can occur when someone "different" enters a group. We have also found it effective to intersperse our presentation with group experiences designed to raise consciousness about oppression and second-class citizenship. Often presentations on such topics elicit a wide range of affect, including anger and depression on the part of ethnic group members and anger, guilt, and defensive reactions from nonminority students. We have found it helpful to establish norms of openness to promote self-awareness early in the course. Equally important is helping students become aware that we have all internalized racist, sexist, and classist attitudes, by virtue of growing up in American society. The cross-cultural simulation activity, BAFA-BAFA (Gudykunst & Hammer, 1983; Shirts, 1973), is designed to provide an experiential understanding of discriminatory dynamics. Other films which may be helpful on this topic include *El Norte, La Bamba!, Salt of the Earth, Soy Chicano*, and *Zoot Suit*.

Intelligence and Learning: Assessment and Prediction

The section on issues of intelligence and learning begins with a critique of the nature–nurture controversy as it relates to Mexican Americans. Next, we try to help students develop an understanding of issues in educational attainment important for Chicanos, specifically, the measurement of intelligence, academic performance, and achievement. Hernandez et al. (1976) provided unique strategies for assessing and diagnosing intellectual patterns of minority children. As an example, the System of Multicultural Pluralistic Assessments by Mercer (1977), although controversial, is discussed as an alternative strategy. Chapter 4 in the Martinez and Mendoza (1984) text provided an overview of the issues involved in aptitude testing for Hispanic individuals. Barón (1981; Chapters 5 and 6) dealt with aptitude testing and admissions issues. Duran (1983) provided an overview of the appropriate and inappropriate uses of predictors of college achievement for Hispanics and of research indicating that traditional indices (standardized tests, grade point average) do not predict well for Hispanics. Moderating variables, such as social commitment and involvement, motivation levels, overall language proficiency, concern about families' well-being, and parental interest in educational goals, are key factors influencing prediction. As the condition of Hispanic education continues to worsen, an understanding of the complexities of educational attainment, preparation for college, and aptitude assessment acquires greater significance.

Psychological Services: Models, Methods, and Issues

The final section of the course considers mental health services provided to Chicanos. Students learn that, in general, ethnic minorities do not fare well in the mental health system. Special emphasis is given to epidemiological research on psychological disorders, unique stresses on Chicanos, utilization rates of mental health services, and the importance of cultural knowledge and culture-specific techniques for assessment and treatment of Chicanos. Visiting a mental health center especially designed to service a Chicano population, if one exists in the area, can be a very worthwhile experience, with adequate opportunity for follow-up discussion. Goals for such a visit would include the opportunity to observe services that are culturally sensitive, to note community needs, and to meet minority professionals.

The study of unique stresses among Chicanos can provide insights helpful to effective mental health care. Various theories of stress, including those that view psychological distress as stemming from social–environmental factors such as poverty and discrimination, are addressed by Barón (1981; Chapters 7 and 10) and Martinez and Mendoza (1981; Chapter 12). Martinez and Mendoza (Chapter 8) summarized the available research on symptomatology and syndromes unique to Chicanos, including high degrees of depression, culturally influenced hallucinations, somatization of stress, high incidence of alcoholism and drug abuse. Amaro and Russo (1987) offered contemporary research and treatment on Hispanic women. Barón (Chapter 8) reviewed studies of Mexican American usage of mental health facilities. Finally, various issues and special models relevant to providing appropriate mental health services are addressed by Barón (Chapter 9), Hernandez et al. (1976; Chapters 19 through 28), and Martinez and Mendoza (Chapters 9 and 10), and LeVine and Padilla (1980) described counseling approaches geared to the culture, language, and socioeconomic position of Hispanic individuals. Again, we emphasize the wide variation among Chicanos such as in level of acculturation and linguistic skill and the difficulty and dangers in generalizing from the few studies in these areas to all Mexican Americans.

Summary

After student presentations, the course ends with a discussion of directions for future research and the development of Chicano psychology. The instructor may wish to outline and review major themes and issues that have emerged during the course of the semester.

The seminar is designed to sensitize students to ways in which psychological research has both helped and hindered understanding of Chicanos. Although larger classes are possible, the small class size allows for both a lively intellectual exchange and the sharing of personal experience, which we believe is more conducive to our major goal—a working knowledge and a deepened understanding of Chicanos and Chicano psychology.

Resources

Films

A Tale of O. (1979). Cambridge, MA: Goodmeasure.

Additional Readings

Barón, A., Jr. (1979). *The utilization of mental health services by Mexican-Americans: A critical analysis.* Palo Alto, CA: R & E Research Associates.

Olivas, M. A. (Ed.). (1986). *Latino college students.* New York: Columbia University, Teachers College Press.

Padilla, A. M., & Ruiz, R. A. (1973). *Latino mental health: A review of literature.* Washington, DC: U.S. Government Printing Office.

Ramirez, M. (1983). *Psychology of the Americas: Multicultural perspectives in personality and mental health.* New York: Pergamon Press.

Ramirez, M., & Castaneda, A. (1974). *Cultural democracy, bicognitive development and education.* New York: Academic Press.

Smith, E., & Vasquez, M. J. T. (Eds.). (1985). Cross-cultural counseling [Special issue]. *The Counseling Psychologist, 12*(4).

Vaca, N. C. (1970). The Mexican-American in the social sciences, 1912–1970. Part I: 1912–1935. *El Grito, 3*(3), 3–24.

Vaca, N. C. (1970). The Mexican-American in the social sciences, 1912–1970. Part II: 1936–1970. *El Grito, 4*(1), 17–51.

References

Amaro, H., & Russo, N. F. (Eds.). (1987). Hispanic women and mental health: Contemporary issues in research and practice. *Psychology of Women Quarterly* [Special issue], *11*(4).

Barón, A., Jr. (Ed.). (1981). *Explorations in Chicano psychology.* New York: Praeger.

Casas, J. M. (1984). Policy, training and research in counseling psychology: The racial/ethnic minority perspective. In S. Brown & R. Lent (Eds.), *Handbook of counseling psychology* (pp. 785–831). New York: Wiley.

Casas, J. M. (1985). A reflection on the status of racial/ethnic minority research. *The Counseling Psychologist, 13*(4), 581–598.

Duran, R. P. (1983). *Hispanics' education and background: Predictors of college achievement.* New York: College Board Publications.

Gudykunst, W. B., & Hammer, M. R. (1983). Basic training design: Approaches to intercultural training. In D. Landis & R. W. Brislin (Eds.), *Handbook of intercultural training, Volume I: Issues in theory and design* (pp. 118–154). New York: Pergamon Press.

Hernandez, C. A., Haug, M. J., & Wagner, N. N. (Eds.). (1976). *Chicanos: Social and psychological perspectives.* St. Louis, MO: C. V. Mosby.

Hernandez, D. (1974). *Mexican American challenge to a sacred cow.* Los Angeles: Atzlan Publications (University of California).

LaCroce, M. (1984). Juan Luis Vives. In R. J. Corsini (Ed.), *Encyclopedia of psychology* (p. 458). New York: Wiley.

LeVine, E. S., & Padilla, A. M. (1980). *Crossing cultures in therapy: Pluralistic counseling for the Hispanic.* Monterey, CA: Brooks/Cole.

Martinez, J. L., Jr., & Mendoza, R. H. (Eds.). (1984). *Chicano psychology* (2nd ed.). New York: Academic Press.

Melville, M. D. (Ed.). (1980). *Twice a minority: Mexican-American women.* St. Louis, MO: C. V. Mosby.

Mercer, J. R. (1977). *SOMPA, System of multicultural pluralistic assessment.* New York: Psychological Corporation.

Newton, B. J., & Arciniega, M. (1983). Counseling minority families: An Adlerian perspective. *Counseling and Human Development, 16*(4), 1–12.

Padilla, A. M. (1981). Competent communities: A critical analysis of theories and public policy. In O. A. Barbarin, P. R. Good, O. M. Pharr, & J. A. Siskind (Eds.), *Institutional racism and community competence* (pp. 20–29). Rockville, MD: U.S. Department of Health and Human Services.

Ruiz, R. A. (1981). Cultural and historical perspectives in counseling Hispanics. In D. W. Sue (Ed.), *Counseling the culturally different: Theory and practice* (pp. 186–215). New York: Wiley.

Ruiz, R. A., & Padilla, A. M. (1977). Counseling Latinos. *Personnel & Guidance Journal, 55,* 401–408.

Ryan, W. (1972). *Blaming the victim.* New York: Random House.

Shirts, G. (1973). *BAFA-BAFA: A cross-cultural simulation.* Delmar, CA: Simile II.

U.S. Bureau of the Census. (1980). *Census of the population: Supplementary report* (PC80-S13). Washington, DC: U.S. Government Printing Office.

U.S. Bureau of the Census. (1985). *Current population reports: Persons of Spanish origin in the United States, March 1982* (P20 No. 396). Washington, DC: U.S. Government Printing Office.

19

Adrienne Asch

Disability:
Its Place in the
Psychology Curriculum

Reviews of textbooks (Kahn, 1984) and research (Asch, 1984a) confirm that in psychology, persons with disabilities are an "invisible" minority. Yet psychology could significantly contribute to improving the lives of persons who are disabled—as well as those who are not, whose lives would be enriched by knowing them (American Psychological Association [APA] Task Force on Psychology and the Handicapped, 1984). Psychology can help students shift from thinking of disabilities as "flaws to be rehabilitated" to viewing the disabled as a minority group with civil rights (Kahn, 1984). Psychology can also identify and challenge psychological barriers, which are as important to people with disabilities as physical barriers (Fenderson, 1984). At the same time, disability rights issues offer insights into a wide range of more general psychological phenomena (Fine & Asch, 1981). This chapter reviews the literature on persons with disabilities and offers ideas for integrating this material into psychology courses, exercises to increase awareness and sensitivity, and resources for a course on disability in American society.

Profile of the Population

The mere attempt to define disability, or to measure its prevalence, underscores that disability is a social construct (Roth, 1983). The Rehabilitation Act of 1973, as amended in 1978, defines a disabled individual as "any person who (i) has a physical or mental impairment which substantially limits one or more of such person's major life activities, (ii) has a record of such an impairment, or (iii) is regarded as having such an impairment" (Rehabilitation Act of 1973, 7(7)(B)). Although many think of the disabled as those who are deaf, blind, orthopedically impaired, mentally retarded, or mentally ill, many relatively hidden conditions such as arthritis, diabetes, heart and back problems, and cancer, as well as past impairments, are also covered by the legal definitions. Some people, such as those who are cosmetically disfigured or obese, may not have any physical characteristics that affect their performance of tasks but are regarded as disabled by others.

The U.S. Census ("Census Study," 1986) estimated the number of people over 15 years of age with disabilities at 37 million, or about 15% of the population. Gliedman and Roth (1980) suggested that 10% of children under age 21 are disabled. Of adults age 65 and older, 46% report a health impairment (DeJong & Lifchez, 1983). These data may underestimate the size of the population, because these national surveys are restricted to conditions that limit or prevent a person from fulfilling a major social role—attending school, maintaining a home, or working at a job (Haber & McNeil, 1983).

People with disabilities are much more likely than nondisabled people to live at or below the poverty level. Although education substantially narrows the income gap between those with and without disabilities (Asch, 1984a), the disabled at all educational levels still experience lower income and lower rates of workforce participation than nondisabled cohorts, and effects are most severe for disabled women and Black men (Asch & Fine, in Fine & Asch, 1988). The income disadvantage is often compounded by the fact that work-disabled people disproportionately live alone or with unrelated individuals and are disproportionately widowed, divorced, or separated (U.S. Bureau of the Census, 1983).

Integrating Disability Issues Into Mainstream Courses

Disability issues can be integrated into any psychology course, with shifts in emphasis to fit the specific content. Disabilities should *not* be presented as a separate section on "abnormal" or "exceptional" people, or only addressed in those sections, which serves only to perpetuate myths and stereotypes (APA Task Force, 1984). Rather, instructors should include disability as a fact of many lives, a normal aspect of diversity, for example, including data on disabilities in population statistics where race, gender, or other distinctions are provided. A discussion of the psychological, social, and physical barriers facing the disabled can be adapted to any content area, such as school adjustment in developmental psychology or prejudice in social psychology.

Developmental Psychology

Issues related to disability are relevant to many areas of developmental psychology and can be integrated effectively through discussion and debate. Topics include developmental stages, social learning, education, and life span development, as discussed below.

1. *Developmental stages.* Much of developmental theory has evolved from studies of nondisabled children. Thus, much can be learned about both developmental stages and disability, by examining how major stage theories apply or do not apply to the lives of disabled children (Gliedman & Roth, 1980, Chapters 4 through 7). In addition, students can be asked to consider how understanding these stages can help development proceed as positively and effectively as possible for a disabled person.

2. *Social learning.* Theories of social learning (such as Bandura, 1969) maintain that young people learn adult roles by observing the models around them. For disabled youngsters this may pose a problem, because few have the opportunity to interact frequently with disabled adults or view them in the media. Some contend that disabled role models are necessary for young people with disabilities

to develop healthy self-esteem and high aspirations. By discussing the value of disability, race, or gender similarity in role models, students can consider what qualities may be essential for modeling to take place. Fine and Asch (1981) offered other discussion questions on this topic.

3. Education. Federal laws mandating equal access to education require that special services be provided for children with disabilities. However, the disabled are still disproportionately achieving low levels of education. It is important to make students aware of the public and professional attitudes that may prevent equality in education and consider them in light of psychological and economic data on the long-term impact of education on independent living for disabled persons (Asch, 1984a). Students can be asked to think of services that could help parents, teachers, vocational rehabilitation employees, and society provide a healthy, integrated experience for disabled children (Biklen, 1985; Darling, 1979; Turnbull & Turnbull, 1985).

4. Life span development. Since the proportion of individuals experiencing disability increases dramatically with age, consideration of disabilities is crucial to a life span perspective. Students can suggest strategies for effective coping with age-related disabilities, both for elderly individuals and for their families (Ainlay, in Asch & Fine, 1988; Becker, 1980).

Social Psychology

In the social psychology class, basic social–psychological processes can be illuminated through examples from the experiences of people with disabilities. At the same time, students can develop an appreciation of the social–psychological reality experienced by disabled persons. Discussion topics, reviewed in Asch (1984a), include the impact of labeling, stereotyping, role acquisition, "blaming the victim," social interactions with disabled people, altruism, and gender and race issues. Each is briefly discussed below.

1. Labels and their impact on group members. The label "handicapped" dominates over other labels of race, gender, and sexual preference (Asch, 1984b; Fine & Asch, 1981; O'Toole & Weeks, 1978; Scott, 1969). Students can consider the effects labels have on the self-image (Asch, 1984a; Asch & Fine, 1988; Weinberg, 1976).

2. Stereotyping and the disabled. Stereotypes of the disabled are usually negative (Miller, 1970), with disabled people often viewed as unable to perform any adult function (Gliedman & Roth, 1980; Katz, 1981; Lukoff, 1960) and likely to suffer severe emotional consequences (Asch & Rousso, 1985). Positive attitudes tend to be equally distorted (Siller, Ferguson, Vann, & Holland, 1967; Yuker, Block, & Young, 1966). Stereotypes of the disabled are particularly restrictive in the areas of sexuality and reproduction, with disabled individuals often seen as asexual and unfit as parents (Fine & Asch, 1988). Disabled men tend to be gender stereotyped as feminine (Anderson, Lepper, & Ross, 1980; Baker & Reitz, 1978; Schroedel, 1978). The disabled are more often targets of hostility than the nondisabled (Titley & Viney, 1969), and men are more likely than women to apply stereotypes to the disabled (Fine & Asch, 1981). Students can find examples of these stereotypes in the media, literature, and the arts, and discuss questions raised by these data such as "What does this suggest about society's views of 'masculine' and 'feminine'?" and "How is sexuality defined in our culture?".

3. *Role acquisition.* Our society lacks social roles (Blauner, 1964; Merton, 1967), role models (e.g., in the media, Gillespie & Fink, 1974), and opportunities for social comparison (Strauss, 1968) for the disabled, especially for disabled women (Cook & Rossett, 1975; Fine & Asch, 1981). Students can consider how these difficulties may be similar to those experienced by many nondisabled women over the past 20 years, as they have moved away from a traditional gender role definition. It is also helpful to contrast the roles disabled people actually play in society with the restricted range of models offered in the media.

4. *"Blaming the victim."* Nondisabled people may on some level blame the disabled for their disabilities, for example, regarding a disability as punishment for sins of the parents. "Just world" attributions (Lerner, 1980), in which victims of rape, accidents, or illnesses are blamed for their misfortunes, are often applied to people with disabilities (Rubin & Peplau, 1975), most likely as a mechanism for distancing oneself from an awareness of one's own weakness or the possibility of becoming disabled oneself (Asch & Rousso, 1985). An examination of these attitudes can help define more general attitude structures (Fenderson, 1984). Students can discuss the tendency to attribute social and economic disadvantages experienced by the disabled to an inferred biological inferiority and draw parallels to attributions about minorities and women (Asch, 1984a).

5. *Social interactions with disabled people.* Studies of the behavior of the nondisabled toward the disabled demonstrate a variety of responses that, at the very least, hinder ordinary social interaction. These include avoiding social contact and behaving in distorted ways (Asch, 1984a) and nonverbal cues such as turning away, avoiding eye contact, and ignoring their presence. In addition, certain disabilities prevent disabled people from using expected comunication cues such as articulation, eye contact, or hand movements. Students might consider how such behaviors may affect perceptions of the disabled person and their communications. Davis (1961), Goffman (1963), and Richardson (1976) have written about the rarity of meaningful social interaction between those with disabilities and those without.

6. *Altruism.* People with disabilities are usually perceived as help seekers, rather than givers. The reality is that many people with disabilities need only minimal assistance and provide resources and help for others in their personal and professional lives. Students can be asked to provide examples of helping behavior by disabled persons and to speculate why the misperception persists.

7. *Gender and race issues.* The experiences of disabled women and minorities differ from those of White men. Disability has differential impacts on the status, expectations, and life courses of men and women, including minority men and women (Fine & Asch, 1981). Consideration of these data not only alerts students to the underrepresentation of disabled women and minorities, but also offers perspectives on how discrimination based on disability resembles and differs from gender and race discrimination in its origin and in its consequences (Asch & Fine, in Fine & Asch, 1988). In addition, it is important to learn how disability is viewed by nondisabled people within different racial and ethnic groups, and by women and men, and how these different views affect the life chances of disabled group members.

Personality, Clinical, and Abnormal Psychology

Personality, clinical, and abnormal psychology have suffered from two erroneous assumptions about the disabled: (a) that physical disabilities create psychological disorders—an internal, rather than a sociogenic attribution; and (b) that disabled people are "abnormal." Students should examine both the misperceptions and the actual data (or absence of data) relating to disability and psychopathology. Topics for discussion include the clinical literature, the resemblance between problems of the disabled and those of other minority groups, the etiology of negative responses toward the disabled, and approaches to helpful service delivery.

1. The clinical literature. Disabled people have been viewed in the literature, particularly psychoanalytic literature, as having a variety of problems, including excessive guilt, unmastered and undischarged aggression, and strong primitive defense mechanisms. Some psychoanalysts have argued that a defective body leads to a defective body ego and that a distorted self-image leads to a distorted image of the world. The psychoanalytic treatment literature further reinforces the negative attitude about the mental health of disabled people (Asch & Rousso, 1985; Gliedman & Roth, 1980, Appendix 1).

Students need to be made aware that these beliefs are based on small numbers of distressed patients, without a corresponding examination of disabled individuals who have not sought help. In addition, many authors overlook the impact of parental, familial, and societal treatment on the psychological development of their disabled patients. Providing data on the actual incidence of psychological disorders among the disabled helps dispel the myth that disability causes psychopathology (Anthony & Jansen, 1984).

2. The resemblance between the problems of the disabled in society and those of other minority groups. Hostility and rejection in new social and occupational settings may eventually cause the disabled person to internalize society's deprecating attitudes (Asch & Rousso, 1985), as can occur in members of other minority groups. An emphasis on the effects of such social experiences on mental health promotes a shift in emphasis away from internal psychopathology (Fine & Asch, 1981; Fenderson, 1984).

3. The etiology of negative responses toward the disabled. The frightened and hostile responses many nondisabled people experience toward the disabled are also valid topics in the study of personality and psychopathology. These responses may be rooted in unconscious anxieties regarding wholeness, loss, and weakness (Hahn, 1983). The literature on attitudes toward the disabled stresses intrapsychic factors such as castration anxiety, fears about one's own destructiveness, and fears about one's own body integrity (see Asch & Rousso, 1985, for additional discussions).

4. Approaches to helpful service delivery to the disabled. The APA Task Force on Psychology and the Handicapped (1984) described the need to revise approaches to assessment and treatment to include issues of social discrimination, appreciating the impact such discrimination plays in causing difficulties facing the physically disabled. The Task Force recommended shifting the intervention focus from helping the disabled person "accept" and "adjust to" discrimination, to a more inclusive intervention to change attitudes and behaviors of the nondisabled.

Increasing Awareness and Promoting Change

Many instructors are unnecessarily fearful of disabled students in their classes or as majors. The Rehabilitation Act (96th Congress) spells out the obligations of institutions of higher education to disabled students. In addition, the goals of the APA Task Force (1984) should be adapted to the instructional setting, as personal teaching commitments, for the benefit of disabled and nondisabled students. My personal experiences as a student (Asch, 1984b) may be helpful.

In general, it is reasonable to assume that the disabled student is already able to cope with classroom situations and will tell you if any assistance is needed. If special needs are anticipated, such as for laboratory work, ask the student before making accommodations. In any case, assistance should not diminish expectations for quality or quantity of work. The APA Task Force provides consulting to any disabled person interested in school and career opportunities in psychology and for advisors and department chairs wishing to encourage disabled students to pursue psychology. These resources are available through the APA's Office of Social and Ethical Responsibility in Washington, DC.

A Course on the Disabled Person

This section briefly describes an undergraduate course titled The Disabled Person in American Society offered at Barnard College. This course is an interdisciplinary, multifaceted approach to issues of disability. A deliberate attempt is made to address each topic through the lenses of personal narratives, social science theory, qualitative and quantitative research, law, policy, and ethics. Students use their own experiences with disabilities and disabled persons to critique the readings and use the readings to shed new light on their experiences. Sharing of firsthand experiences with disability, or what it means to know people who have a disability, is done through open discussions, journals, structured interviews, field experiences, or reaction papers to particular topics.

Each section considers common issues, differing in severity, that people with a range of impairments face, while recognizing special problems for specific disabilities (such as epilepsy, arthritis, or visual impairment) in terms of stigma, access, and other issues. Suggested guest speakers include disability rights activists, knowledgeable disabled students, service providers, and family members and friends of disabled people.

Exercises

1. A structured interview with a disabled person helps the student gain understanding of how that person views the social and psychological barriers created by their disability. Students do not have to seek out a severely disabled person in order to achieve insight into the disabled population. Questions ask how the individual's disability has influenced, if at all, her or his life in such areas as education, work, transportation, housing, relationships, and parenting. Answers

are discussed in terms of whether they were surprising to the student, and why or why not.

2.   Students contrast a popularized version of disability as portrayed in a film, play, or novel, with accounts from the social/psychological literature or a personal narrative written by a disabled person. The syllabus that follows offers examples of these narratives.

3.   A debate is held on a current topic, for example, "Should public transit be made accessible to the disabled?" or "Is prenatal diagnosis a boon to society or an attack on people with disabilities?"

"Disabling" exercises, in which instructors provide nondisabled students with ear plugs, occluding glasses, or a wheelchair, are not recommended. Although intended to increase awareness, these exercises equate the experience of a newly disabled person with that of someone who has learned coping skills. Thus, they are likely to arouse fear and pity rather than sensitivity and understanding.

General Resources

Texts for the course are those by Gartner and Joe (1987), Gleidman and Roth (1980), Asch and Fine (1988), and Mappes and Zembaty (1986) and reports by the International Center for the Disabled (1986, 1987) and the National Council on the Handicapped (1986). Two extremely useful journals are *Disability Studies Quarterly* (contact Irving K. Zola, Department of Sociology, Brandeis University, Waltham, MA 02154) and *Disability Rag* (P.O. Box 145, Louisville, KY 40201).

Syllabus

Unit 1: Defining the Problem: Conceptual and Methodological Issues

1.   Defining disability: Facts and values (Benjamin, Muyskens, & Saenger, 1984; Berscheid & Walster, 1972; Federal Register, 1977; Mappes & Zembaty, pp. 243–263; National Council on the Handicapped (NCH), 1986, pp. 3–6; 96th Congress; *School Board of Nassau County v. Arline, 1987*)

2.   Disability cross culturally (Asch & Fine, 1988, article by Scheer & Groce; Groce, 1980)

3.   Data on people with disabilities ("Census study," 1986; *Disability Rag*, June 1984 issue; International Center for the Disabled (ICD), 1986, pp. 1–9; U.S. Census, 1983, pp. 1–8)

4.   Disability as seen in personal narratives and poetry (Asch, 1984b; Baird & Workman, 1986; Brightman, 1984)

5.   Disability as seen in fiction and drama (Gartner & Joe, 1987, Chapters 2 through 4; books such as Greenberg's *In this Sign*, Medoff's *Children of a Lesser God*, or Williams's *The Glass Menagerie*)

6.   How nondisabled social scientists report disabled people's life experiences (Ablon, 1984; Asch & Fine, 1988, article by Frank; Bulman & Wortman, 1977; Evans, 1983; Higgins, 1980; Macgregor, 1979; Schneider & Conrad, 1983; Taylor, Wood, & Lichtman, 1983)

7. Psychology and disability: Attitudes and interactions (Asch, 1984a; Asch & Fine, 1988, article by Makas; Gleidman & Roth, 1980, pp. 67–86 and Appendix 3)

8. From deviance and stigma to minority group theory (Asch & Fine, 1988, articles by Hahn, Mest; Bogdan & Taylor, 1976; Gartner & Joe, 1987, introduction; Goffman, 1963; Katz, 1981; Stroman, 1982)

Unit 2: Disability Over the Life Cycle

9. Growing up disabled (Diamond, 1981; Gleidman & Roth, 1980, Chapters 4 through 7; Lussier, 1980; Rousso, 1984)

10. The disabled child and the family (Asch & Fine, 1988, article by Darling; Darling, 1979, Chapters 1, 2, 7, and 8; Gleidman & Roth, 1980, Appendices 1 & 5, pp. 86–95, 305–363; Massie & Massie, 1984; Turnbull & Turnbull, 1985. Supplemental reading: Jablow, 1982)

11. Education: Elementary through secondary (Asch & Fine, 1988, article by Biklen; *Board of Education of the Hendrick Hudson Central School District v. Rowley*, 1982; Federal Register, 1977, 84.31–.39; Gartner & Joe, 1987, Chapter 6; NCH, 1986, pp. 47–79). Postsecondary (Federal Register, 1977, 84.41–.49; *Southeastern Community College v. Davis*, 1979)

12. Sexuality and disability (Bullard & Knight, 1981, Introduction, pp. 1–2, Chapters 1 through 4, 6, 7, 9, 10, 16, and 21; Fine & Asch, 1988, chapter by Rousso; Kilmartin, 1984)

13. The rehabilitation system, medical and vocational (96th Congress, Title I, 100–103, 112; U.S. Department of Health, Education, and Welfare, 1975; Wright, 1983, Chapter 17)

14. Rehabilitation: Critiques (Caplan, Callahan, & Haas, 1987; Kemp, 1981; Mappes & Zembaty, 1986, pp. 601–626; Scott, 1969, pp. 56–104; Sheed, 1980)

15. Employment (Federal Register, 1977, 84.11–.19; Gartner & Joe, 1987, Chapter 7; ICD, 1986, pp. 22–27, 46–60, 69–81; ICD, 1987; Kent, 1978; *McDermott v. Xerox Corp.*, 1985; *Miller v. Ravitch*, 1983; NCH, 1986, pp. 18–29; *Nelson v. Thornburgh*, 1983; 96th Congress, Title VI, 621–623. Supplemental reading: McCarthy, 1985)

16. Housing, transportation, and social life (*City of Cleburne v. Cleburne Living Center, Inc.*, 1985; Crewe & Zola, 1983, Chapters 9, 12, 13; *Disability Rag*, September 1985 and January 1986 issues; ICD, 1986, pp. 32–34, 62–69; NCH, 1986, pp. 32–46, 50–54)

17. Marriage and parenting (Bullard & Knight, 1981, Chapters 11 and 12; *Carney v. Carney*, 1979; Mappes & Zembaty, 1986, pp. 306–326; Zola, 1982)

18. Disability and gender (Fine & Asch, 1988, chapter by Russo & Jansen; Gartner & Joe, 1987, Chapters 2 and 3)

19. Becoming disabled in midlife (Bonwich, 1985; Brickner, 1976; Burish & Bradley, 1983, chapters by Krantz & Deckel and Gordon & Diller; Fine & Asch, 1988, chapter by Meyerowitz, Chaiken, & Clark)

20. Disability in later life (Asch & Fine, 1988, article by Ainlay; Fine & Asch, 1988, chapter by Simon; Hiatt, 1981, pp. 133–152; Veatch, 1979)

Unit 3: Disability Policy, Politics, and Ethics

21.   Disability rights movement (Asch, 1986a; Asch & Fine, 1988, article by Scotch; Gartner & Joe, 1987, Chapters 1 and 11; ICD, 1986, pp. 109–116. Supplemental readings: Scotch, 1984; Sherman & Robinson, 1982)

22.   Disability policy and resource allocation (Browne, 1985; ICD, 1986, pp. 96–109; Mappes & Zembaty, 1986, pp. 563–585, 601–625; Massie & Massie, 1984, Chapters 18 and 25; Starr, 1982)

23.   Defining the quality of life: Baby Doe (Gartner & Joe, 1987, Chapter 10; Hubbard, 1984; Mappes & Zembaty, 1986, pp. 433–446)

24.   Defining the quality of life: Genetic screening and prenatal diagnosis (Asch, 1986b; Mappes & Zembaty, 1986, pp. 513–527; Rapp, 1984)

25.   Right to die—Should disability matter? (*Disability Rag*, February 1984 issue; Gartner & Joe, 1987, Chapter 5; Mappes & Zembaty, 1986, pp. 359–365)

References

Ablon, J. (1984). *Little people in America.* New York: Praeger.

American Psychological Association Task Force on Psychology and the Handicapped. (1984). Final report of the Task Force on Psychology and the Handicapped. *American Psychologist, 39,* 545–550.

Anderson, C., Lepper, H., & Ross, L. (1980). Perseverance of social theories: The role of explanation in the persistence of discredited information. *Journal of Personality and Social Psychology, 39,* 1037–1050.

Anthony, W. A., & Jansen, M. A. (1984). Predicting the vocational capacity of the chronically mentally ill: Research and policy implications. *American Psychologist, 39,* 537–544.

Asch, A. (1984a). The experience of disability: A challenge for psychology. *American Psychologist, 39,* 529–536.

Asch, A. (1984b). Personal reflections. *American Psychologist, 39,* 551–552.

Asch, A. (1986a). Will populism empower disabled people? In H. C. Boyte & F. Reissman (Eds.), *The new populism: The politics of empowerment* (pp. 213–230). Philadelphia: Temple University Press.

Asch, A. (1986b). Real moral dilemmas. *Christianity & Crisis, 46,* 237–240.

Asch, A., & Fine, M. (Eds.). (1988). Moving disability beyond stigma [Special issue]. *Journal of Social Issues, 44*(1).

Asch, A., & Rousso, H. (1985). Therapists with disabilities: Theoretical and clinical issues. *Psychiatry, 48,* 1–12.

Baird, J. L., & Workman, D. S. (Eds.). (1986). *Toward Solomon's Mountain.* Philadelphia: Temple University Press.

Baker, L., & Reitz, H. (1978). Altruism toward the blind: Effects of sex of helper and dependence of victim. *Journal of Social Psychology, 104,* 19–28.

Bandura, A. (1969). Social learning theory and identification processes. In D. Goslin (Ed.), *Handbook of socialization theory and research* (pp. 213–262). Chicago: Rand-McNally.

Becker, G. (1980). *Growing old in silence.* Berkeley, CA: University of California Press.

Benjamin, M., Muyskens, J., & Saenger, P. (1984). Growth hormones and pressures to treat. *Hastings Center Report, 14,* 5–9.

Berscheid, E., & Walster, E. (1972, March). Beauty and the beast. *Psychology Today,* pp. 32–42.

Biklen, D. (1985). *Achieving the complete school.* New York: Columbia University, Teachers College Press.

Blauner, R. (1964). *Alienation and freedom.* Chicago: University of Chicago Press.

Board of Education of the Hendrick Hudson Central School District v. Rowley. (1982). 458 U.S. 176, 204.

Bogdan, R., & Taylor, S. (1976). The judged not the judges. *American Psychologist, 31*, 47–52.

Bonwich, E. (1985). Sex role attitudes and role reorganization in spinal cord injured women. In M. J. Deegan & N. A. Brooks (Eds.), *Women and disability: The double handicap* (pp. 56–67). New Brunswick, NJ: Transaction Books.

Brickner, R. (1976). *My second twenty years: An unexpected life*. New York: Basic Books.

Brightman, A. J. (Ed.). (1984). *Ordinary moments: The disabled experience*. Baltimore, MD: University Park Press.

Browne, S. E. (1985). Infusing blues. In S. E. Browne, D. Connors, & N. Stern (Eds.), *With the power of each breath* (pp. 15–23). San Francisco, CA: Cleis Press.

Bullard, D. G., & Knight, S. E. (Eds.). (1981). *Sexuality and physical disability*. St. Louis, MO: C. V. Mosby.

Bulman, R., & Wortman, C. (1977). Attribution of blame and coping in the "real world": Severe accident victims react to their lot. *Journal of Personality and Social Psychology, 35*, 351–363.

Burish, T. G., & Bradley, L. A. (Eds.). (1983). *Coping with chronic disease*. New York: Academic Press.

Caplan, A., Callahan, D., & Haas, J. (1987). Ethical and policy issues in rehabilitation medicine [Special supplement]. *Hastings Center Report, 17*(4), 1–20.

Carney v. Carney. (1979). 157 Cal. Rprtr. 383. 598. 24 Cal. 3d, 725. P.2d36 (Sup. Ct.).

Census study reports one in five adults suffers from disability. (1986, December 23). *New York Times*, p. B7.

City of Cleburne v. Cleburne Living Center, Inc. (1985). 87L. Ed. 2d. 313.

Cook, L., & Rossett, A. (1975). The sex role attitudes of deaf adolescent women and their implications for vocational choice. *American Annals of the Deaf, 120*, 341–345.

Crewe, N. M., & Zola, I. K. (Eds.). (1983). *Independent living for physically disabled people*. San Francisco, CA: Jossey-Bass.

Darling, R. B. (1979). *Families against society: A study of reactions to children with birth defects*. Beverly Hills, CA: Sage.

Davis, F. (1961). Deviance disavowal: The management of strained interaction by the visibly handicapped. *Social Problems, 9*, 120–132.

DeJong, G., & Lifchez, R. (1983). Physical disability and public policy. *Scientific American, 48*, 240–249.

Diamond, S. (1981). Growing up with the parents of a handicapped child: A handicapped person's perspective. In J. L. Paul (Ed.), *Understanding and working with parents of children with specific needs* (pp. 223–250). New York: Holt, Rinehart & Winston.

Evans, D. (1983). *The lives of mentally retarded people*. Boulder, CO: Westview Press.

Federal Register. (May 4, 1977). Section 504 Regulations. 45 CFR 84.3J.

Fenderson, D. A. (1984). Opportunities for psychologists in disability research. *American Psychologist, 39*, 524–528.

Fine, M., & Asch, A. (1981). Disabled women: Sexism without the pedestal. *Journal of Sociology and Social Welfare, 8*, 233–248.

Fine, M., & Asch, A. (Eds.). (1988). *Women with disabilities: Essays in psychology, culture and politics*. Philadelphia: Temple University Press.

Gartner, A., & Joe, T. (Eds.). (1987). *Images of the disabled, disabling images*. New York: Praeger.

Gillespie, P., & Fink, A. (1974). The influence of sexism on the education of handicapped children. *Exceptional Children, 5*, 155–162.

Gleidman, J., & Roth, P. (1980). *The unexpected minority: Handicapped children in America*. New York: Harcourt Brace Jovanovich.

Goffman, E. (1963). *Stigma: Notes on the management of spoiled identity*. Englewood Cliffs, NJ: Prentice Hall.

Groce, N. (1980). Everyone here spoke sign-language. *Natural History, 89*(6), 10–16.

Haber, L., & McNeil, J. (1983). *Methodological questions in the examination of disability prevalence*. U.S. Bureau of the Census, Population Division.

Hahn, H. (1983, March–April). Paternalism and public policy. *Society*, pp. 36–46.

Hiatt, L. G. (1981). Aging and disability. In N. S. McClusky & E. F. Borgatta (Eds.), *Aging and retirement* (pp. 133–152). Beverly Hills, CA: Sage.

Higgins, P. (1980). *Outsiders in a hearing world*. Beverly Hills, CA: Sage.

Hubbard, R. (1984, May). Caring for Baby Doe: The moral issue of our time. *Ms.*, pp. 84–88, 165.

International Center for the Disabled. (1986). *The ICD survey of disabled Americans, I*. New York: Louis Harris & Associates.

International Center for the Disabled. (1987). *The ICD survey II: Employing disabled Americans*. New York: Louis Harris & Associates.

Jablow, M. M. (1982). *Cara: Growing with a retarded child*. Philadelphia: Temple University Press.

Kahn, A. S. (1984). Perspectives on persons with disabilities. *American Psychologist, 39*, 516–517.

Katz, I. (1981). *Stigma: A social–psychological analysis*. Hillsdale, NJ: Erlbaum.

Kemp, E. (1981, September 3). Aiding the disabled: No pity please. *New York Times*, p. A19.

Kent, D. (1978). Close encounters of a different kind. *Disabled USA, 1*(5), 10.

Kilmartin, M. (1984, May). Disability doesn't mean no sex. *Ms.*, pp. 114–118, 158-159.

Lerner, M. J. (1980). *The belief in a just world: A fundamental delusion*. New York: Plenum Press.

Lukoff, I. (1960). A sociological appraisal of blindness. In S. Firestone (Ed.), *Social casework and blindness* (pp. 19–44). New York: American Foundation for the Blind.

Lussier, A. (1980). The physical handicap and the body ego. *International Journal of Psychoanalysis, 61*, 179–185.

Mappes, T. A., & Zembaty, J. S. (Eds.). (1986). *Biomedical ethics* (2nd ed.). New York: McGraw-Hill.

Macgregor, F. C. (1979). *After plastic surgery: Adaptation and adjustment*. Brooklyn, NY: J.F. Bergin.

Massie, R., & Massie, S. (1984). *Journey* (2nd ed.). New York: Knopf.

McCarthy, H. (Ed.). (1985). *Complete guide to employing persons with disabilities*. Albertson, NY: Human Resources Center.

McDermott v. Xerox Corp. (1985). 65 NY 2d 213; 480 N.E. 2d 695; 491 N.Y.S. 2d 106.

Merton, R. (1967). *On theoretical sociology*. New York: Free Press.

Miller v. Ravitch. (1983). 60 N.Y. 2d 527; 458 N.E. 2d 1235; 470 N.Y.S. 2d 558.

Miller, A. (1970). Role of physical attractiveness in impression formation. *Psychonomic Science, 19*, 241–243.

National Council on the Handicapped. (1986). *Toward independence: An assessment of federal laws and programs affecting persons with disabilities—legislative recommendations*. Washington, DC: U.S. Government Printing Office.

Nelson v. Thornburgh. (1983). 567 F. Supp. 369.

96th Congress, 1st Session. (1980) *Rehabilitation, comprehensive services, and developmental disabilities legislation*. Washington, DC: U.S. Government Printing Office.

O'Toole, J., & Weeks, C. (1978). *What happens after school? A study of disabled women and education*. San Francisco: Women's Educational Equity Communications Network.

Rapp, R. (1984). XYLO: A true story. In R. Arditti, R. Duelli-Klein, & S. Minden (Eds.), *Test-tube women: What future for motherhood* (pp. 313–328). Boston: Pandora.

Rehabilitation Act of 1973. (1973). Pub. L. No. 93-112, 87 Stat. 357.

Richardson, S. A. (1976). Attitudes and behavior toward the physically handicapped. *Birth defects: Original article series, 12*, 15–34.

Roth, W. (1983, March-April). Handicap as a social construct. *Society*, pp. 56–61.

Rousso, H. (1984, December). Fostering healthy self-esteem. *The Exceptional Parent*, pp. 9–14.

Rubin, A., & Peplau, L. (1975). Who believes in a just world? *Journal of Social Issues, 31*, 65–89.

Schneider, J. W., & Conrad, P. (1983). *Having epilepsy: The experience and control of illness*. Philadelphia: Temple University Press.

School Board of Nassau County v. Arline. (1987). 94L. Ed. 2d. 307.

Schroedel, J. (1978). *Attitudes toward persons with disabilities*. New York: Human Resources Center.

Scotch, R. K. (1984). *From good will to civil rights: Transforming federal disability policy*. Philadelphia: Temple University Press.

Scott, R. A. (1969). *The making of blind men: A study of adult socialization*. New York: Russell Sage Foundation.

Sheed, W. (1980, August 25). On being handicapped. *Newsweek*, p. 13.

Sherman, S. W., & Robinson, N. M. (Eds.). (1982). *Ability testing of handicapped people: Dilemma for government, science, and the public*. Washington, DC: National Academy Press.

Siller, J., Ferguson, L., Vann, D. H., & Holland, B. (1967). *Structure of attitudes toward the physically disabled*. New York: New York University School of Education.

Southeastern Community College v. Davis. (1979). 99 Supreme Ct. 2361.

Starr, R. (1982, January). Wheels of misfortune: Sometimes equality just costs too much. *Harpers*, pp. 7–15.

Strauss, H. (1968). Reference group and social comparison processes among the totally blind. In H. Hyman & E. Singer (Eds.), *Readings in reference group theory and research* (pp. 222–237). New York: Free Press.

Stroman, D. F. (1982). *The awakening minorities*. Washington, DC: University Press of America.

Taylor, S. E., Wood, J. V., & Lichtman, R. R. (1983). It could be worse: Selective evaluation as a response to victimization. *Journal of Social Issues, 39*(2), 19–40.

Titley, R., & Viney, W. (1969). Expression of aggression toward the physically handicapped. *Perceptual and Motor Skills, 329*, 51–56.

Turnbull, H. R., & Turnbull, A. P. (Eds.). (1985). *Parents speak out: Then and now*. Columbus, OH: Charles E. Merrill.

U.S. Bureau of the Census. (1983). *Labor force status and other characteristics of persons with a work disability, 1982* (Current Population reports, Series P-23, 127). Washington, DC: U.S. Government Printing Office.

U.S. Department of Health, Education, & Welfare. (1975). *Report of the Comprehensive Services Needs Study* (Contract No. 100-74-03-09). Washington, DC: U.S. Government Printing Office.

Veatch, R. M. (Ed.). (1979). *Life span: Values and life-extending technology*. New York: Harper & Row.

Weinberg, N. (1976, September). The effect of physical disability on self-perception. *Rehabilitation Counseling Bulletin*, pp. 15–20.

Wright, B. A. (1983). *Physical disability—a psychosocial approach* (2nd ed.). New York: Harper & Row.

Yuker, H. E., Block, J. R., & Young, J. H. (1966). *The measurement of attitudes toward disabled persons*. Albertson, NY: Human Resources Center.

Zola, I. K. (1982). And the children shall lead us. In I. K. Zola (Ed.), *Ordinary lives: Voices of disability and disease*. Cambridge, MA: Applewood Books.

20

Neal King

Teaching About Lesbians and Gays in the Psychology Curriculum

A perusal of psychology texts and curricula, graduate and undergraduate, reveals that the psychology of gays and lesbians is either not considered at all or is still discussed in chapters under the areas of abnormal psychology and psychopathology. When homosexuality is included in a course, there is an initial recognition of the 1973 *Diagnostic and Statistical Manual of Mental Disorders (Second Edition)* reclassification by the American Psychiatric Association of homosexuality as no longer a mental disorder, usually followed by a discussion of theories of "causality" or of the "curative" potential of behavioral therapies.

The officially accepted view within the psychology community today, although still strongly contested within psychoanalytic and behavioral circles, is as follows: Homosexuality is a natural variant of human sexuality and should be presented, studied, and understood as such. Questions of causality or of treatment are no more or less pertinent to the study of gays and lesbians than to the study of their heterosexual counterparts. Further, there is a clear distinction between a homosexual act and a lesbian or gay identity. The entire range of human sexuality from exclusively hetero- to exclusively homosexual is viewed as a continuum along which an individual's identity and sexual activities may move at different stages of life (Kinsey, Pomeroy, & Martin, 1948). Hence, there are gays and lesbians who are biological parents, some having been in heterosexual marriages prior to or concurrently with their lesbian or gay identities, and others in unions with gay-identified partners who have agreed to parent together—as well as lesbians who have decided to rear children as single mothers. Likewise, there are heterosexually identified men and women who include, clandestinely or overtly, same-sex liaisons within their married lives (Humphries, 1970). The gay and lesbian community is seen as microcosmic of the larger community, composed of all ages, both genders, and all socioeconomic groupings. It is also, like the culture it forms a part of, ethnically and religiously diverse, with separate men's and women's issues and concerns as well as common ones.

Homophobia, internal and external, is a core issue and a fundamental part of the gay and lesbian experience. Endemic in the American culture, homophobia is defined as the unreasonable fear of same-sex attractions, attentions, relationships, and persons whose affectional and erotic orientations are toward the same sex. Homophobia is perpetuated and encouraged by major social institutions (churches, courts, educational systems, and psychiatric and psychological professions) and is unavoidably internalized by all of us, regardless of our sexual orientation, who are in this culture (Herek, in de Cecco, 1985; Weinberg, 1972).

An Illustrative Course on Gay and Lesbian Issues

This chapter describes a course specifically designed to explore the psychological issues of being gay or lesbian. The resources presented here can also be incorporated into the general psychology curriculum, in courses on human sexuality, the psychology of social minorities, the psychology of men, the psychology of women, and developmental psychology.[1] The course, titled Sexual Diversity and Social Change: Homosexuality in America, was taught by psychologists in the Sociology Department at the University of California, Berkeley, in 1982 and 1983. One or two faculty members and several graduate students, including this author, served as co-instructors.[2] This co-instruction, necessitated by the more than 300 students enrolled, had the advantage of incorporating a greater variety of individual experience (personal and professional) and resources into the course design and execution.

The first step in teaching such a course is to examine and reevaluate traditional ways of viewing and presenting the subject, beginning most essentially with the personal bias and values of the presenter(s). In addition, an important goal in the course was to counteract the pathologizing and stereotyping of lesbians and gays by revealing their diversity. Hence, we included a wide range of panels and individual presenters, and where possible, presenters and instructors spoke of their own experience and engaged in spirited dialogue with the assembled students.

Course Content

A course on the psychology of lesbians and gays should address the phenomenon of coming out as a part of the developmental experience, theories and beliefs about the development of sexual preference, homophobia and sexism, the historically pathologizing stance toward homosexuality within psychology, the social and historical context of the gay rights movement, the gay and lesbian community as a social minority, and issues and groupings within the community (e.g., religious issues, legal issues, men and women, old and young, ethnic and disabled). The actual topics we covered were also determined by availability of human resources in the greater San Francisco Bay area. Class presentations included a mixture of lectures and didactic materials on the following topics, with accompanying reading:

Deviance and sexual identity (Bell, Weinberg, & Hammersmith, 1981)

---

1. More exact reference to the reader materials, syllabus, and exams for the course described are available from the author, 2127 Channing Way, Berkeley, CA 94704.
2. Thomas Merrifield and Amy Weston were the primary designers and original instructors.

Coming out (Cass, 1979; de Monteflores & Schultz, 1978; Wolfe & Stanley, 1980).

Comparing and contrasting lesbian and gay relationships (chapter by Golden in Boston Lesbian Psychologies Collective, 1987; McWhirter & Mattison, 1984; Peplau, 1982; Tanner, 1978)

Historical perspectives on the gay and lesbian rights movement (Lauritsen & Thorstad, 1974; FitzGerald, 1986)

The Lesbian/Gay History Project (San Francisco)

Gay and lesbian authors

Lesbian mothers and their children (chapters by Crawford and Hill in Boston Lesbian Psychologies Collective, 1987; Hall, 1978)

Parents of gays (Silverstein, 1977; Parents of Gays organizations exist in most large cities—for information contact National Gay Task Force, 80 Fifth Avenue, New York, NY 10011)

Aging gays and lesbians (MacDonald & Rich, 1983; Moses & Hawkins, 1982)

Disabled lesbians and gays (National Gay Task Force, as above, for resources)

Gay and lesbian youth (Hanckel & Cunningham, 1979; Morin & Schultz, 1978; Youth Liberation, 1976)

Racial and ethnic minorities (chapter by Garcia, Kennedy, Pearlman, & Percz in Boston Lesbian Psychologies Collective, 1987; Moses & Hawkins, 1982; Paul, Weinrich, Gonsiorek, & Hotvedt, 1982)

Bisexuality (Klein, 1978; chapter by Schuster in Boston Lesbian Psychologies Collective, 1987)

Lesbian and gay political clubs and elected officials (Shilts, 1982; National Gay Task Force, as above)

Substance abuse (chapter by Brown, Nicolof, & Stiglitz, in Boston Lesbian Psychologies Collective, 1987; contact National Association of Lesbian and Gay Alcoholism Professionals, 1208 E. State Boulevard, Ft. Wayne, IN 46805).

Acquired immune deficiency syndrome (AIDS; Altman, 1982; *American Psychologist*, November 1984).

Mental health issues of lesbian women and gay men (Boston Lesbian Psychologies Collective, 1987; Moses & Hawkins, 1982; Paul et al., 1982; Peplau, 1982).

Religion (Boswell, 1980; Curb & Manahan, 1985; Grahn, 1984; Silverstein, 1977; Task Force on Gay/Lesbian Issues, Archdiocese of San Francisco, 1982; Zannotti, 1986).

Course Assignments

Required readings included several books (both fiction and nonfiction), as well as diverse articles selected by the instructors. The first year's nonfiction books included *The Early Homosexual Rights Movement* (Lauritsen & Thorstad, 1974) and *A Family Matter* (Silverstein, 1977). The second year, the books included *The Homosexualization of America, the Americanization of the Homosexual* (Altman, 1982), *The Lesbian Reader* (Covina & Galana, 1975), and *The Bisexual Option* (Klein, 1978).

Course assignments encouraged the students to address and understand their own individual experience, regardless of their own sexual orientation, and to integrate the presenters' experiences, the readings, and their own life experiences within the context of general psychosexual development. The first assigned paper had as its theme the development of individual identity. Students read and contrasted two novels, *Rubyfruit Jungle* (Brown, 1973) and *The Best Little Boy in the World* (Reid, 1973); in each, the protagonist struggles with and eventually integrates her or his homosexuality into her or his larger identity in two very different styles and cultural and socioeconomic settings. Students were asked to compare these themes with their own experience of sexual awakening, regardless of orientation, and to consider the interplay of such factors as race, class, gender, and geography in this universal process. The assignment facilitated each student's focusing on central issues early in the course, allowing them to investigate and understand them in terms of their own experience. It produced rich personal chronicles that rarely adhered to the length suggested and fueled interest and discussion in subsequent presentations.

Other assignments over the two years included (a) a 4- to 6-page paper on some aspect of gay and lesbian history (e.g., factors leading to the Stonewall rebellion in 1969; passing or cross-dressing women in the 1880s; homosexuality and the Nazis; homosexuality in Ancient Greece; founding of the Daughters of Bilitis; founding of the Mattachine Society; history of lesbian or gay characters in literature, film, and television); (b) a 4- to 6-page paper with an open topic to be chosen by the student as an opportunity to explore more deeply an aspect of the course that he or she found of particular interest (suggested topics included legal issues for lesbian and gay individuals, couples, or families; gays in advertising; cross-cultural issues; or analysis of a poem or a short story; (c) an in-class midterm that required familiarity with and synthesis of many of the readings on such central concerns as sexual identity, homophobia, sexism, and coming out; and (d) a take-home essay final.

Integrating Gay and Lesbian Issues Into General Psychology Courses

In the interest of understanding the rich diversity and complexity of human nature, it is important to integrate issues relating to the lives of lesbians and gays into general psychology courses. The development of sexual preference as an important part of an individual's identity formation should be integral to courses in child psychology, human development, and human sexuality. A number of topic areas in social psychology should also include gay and lesbian issues, for example, homophobia included in a section on prejudice or stereotyping (Herek, in DeCecco, 1985), same-sex coupling included under interpersonal relationships (Chapter 6 by A. Lott in this volume; Blumstein & Schwartz, 1985; Lynch & Reilly, 1985; McWhirter & Mattison, 1984; Peplau, 1982; Tanner, 1978), and gay rights issues included as an illustration of a social movement or as a contemporary social issue (Paul et al., 1982).

Courses in counseling or clinical psychology should include information about homophobia, the effects of oppression on lesbian and gay individuals, and therapists' heterosexist assumptions and negative attitudes toward lesbians and gays (Bayer, 1981; Garfinkle & Morin, 1978; Gonsiorek, 1985; Morin & Charles, 1983; Moses & Hawkins, 1982). Courses in personality and life span development can include biographical illustrations of the lives of lesbians (Birkby, 1973; Krieger, 1983; MacDonald & Rich, 1983) and gays (Ferrara, 1984; Marotta, 1983; Shilts, 1982). In addition, current topical issues such as the AIDS epidemic (see articles in the November 1984 issue of *American Psychologist*), which potentially affect millions of lives, or the 1986 Supreme Court decision upholding the Georgia sodomy statute (Church, 1986; Press, 1986) should be included in social psychology, health, and counseling and clinical courses. These current topics can provide students with responsible education about gays and lesbians, as well as teaching them about the enduring psychological effects of homophobia and oppression on both gay individuals and heterosexuals in this society.

Additional Resources

Resources from the local lesbian and gay community can enhance any course on the psychology of gays and lesbians. In most urban areas in the United States there are gay and lesbian political, historical, social, and professional organizations. The newly created Division 44 of the American Psychological Association is an invaluable resource for the latest research in psychology concerning lesbians and gays. The National Gay Task Force can provide valuable help in locating pertinent community resources in a given region. Films, both in the mainstream media (*Making Love, Desert Hearts, My Beautiful Laundrette,* and *Parting Glances*) and those made for television (*An Early Frost, Consenting Adults,* and *Welcome Home Bobby*) are useful instructional aids and provide foci for discussion. Russo (1981) provided an excellent historical reference for consideration of lesbians and gays in film.

Recommended Readings

Barr, J. (1982). *Quatrefoil.* Boston: Alyson Publications.
Bernard, R. (1982). *A Catholic education.* New York: Holt, Rinehart & Winston.
Berzon, B., & Leighton, R. (Eds.). (1979). *Positively gay.* Millbrae, CA: Celestial Press.
Burch, B. (1982). Psychological merger in lesbian couples: A joint ego and systems approach. *Family Therapy, 9,* 201–208.
Clark, D. (1977). *Loving someone gay.* Millbrae, CA: Celestial Press.
Curry, H., & Clifford, D. (1980). *A legal guide for lesbian and gay couples.* Berkeley, CA: Nolo Press Self-Help Law Books.
Dank, B. (1971). Coming out in a gay world. *Psychiatry, 34,* 180–197.
Freedman, M. (1971). *Homosexuality and psychological functioning.* Belmont, CA: Wadsworth.
Freidman, M. (1984). *Totempole.* San Francisco, CA: Northpoint Press.
Marotta, T. (1981). *The politics of homosexuality.* Boston: Houghton-Mifflin.
McDonald, J. (in press). Individual differences in the coming out process for gay men: Implications for theoretical models. *Journal of Homosexuality.*

Morin, S. F. (1974). Educational programs as a means of changing attitudes toward gay people. *Homosexual Counseling Journal, 1*, 160–165.

Morin, S. F. (1977). Heterosexual bias in psychological research on lesbian and male homosexuality. *American Psychologist, 32*, 629–637.

Silverstein, C. (1981). *Man to man.* New York: William Morrow.

Task Force on the Status of Lesbian and Gay Male Psychologists. (1979). *Removing the stigma* (final report). Washington, DC: American Psychological Association.

References

Altman, D. (1982). *The homosexualization of America, the Americanization of the homosexual.* New York: St. Martin's Press.

Bayer, R. (1981). *Homosexuality and American psychiatry: The politics of diagnosis.* New York: Basic Books.

Bell, A., Weinberg, M. S., & Hammersmith, S. K. (1981). *Sexual preference.* Bloomington: Indiana University Press.

Birkby, P. (Ed.). (1973). *Amazon expedition: A lesbian feminist anthology.* Washington, NJ: Times Change Press.

Blumstein, P., & Schwartz, P. (1985). *American couples.* New York: Pocket Books.

Boston Lesbian Psychologies Collective (Ed.). (1987). *Lesbian psychologies: Explorations and challenges.* Urbana: University of Illinois Press.

Boswell, J. (1980). *Christianity, social tolerance, and homosexuality.* Chicago: University of Chicago Press.

Brown, R. M. (1973). *Rubyfruit jungle.* New York: Bantam Books.

Cass, V. (1979). Homosexual identity formation: A theoretical model. *Journal of Homosexuality, 4*, 219–235.

Church, G. J. (1986, July 14). Knocking on the bedroom door: Supreme Court ruling on privacy and homosexual conduct. *Time, 128*, p. 23.

Covina, G., & Galana, L. (Eds.). (1975). *The lesbian reader.* Berkeley, CA: Amazon Press.

Curb, R., & Manahan, N. (Eds.). (1985). *Lesbian nuns: Breaking the silence.* Tallahassee, FL: Naiad Press.

de Cecco, J. (Ed.). (1985). *Bashers, baiters, and bigots: Homophobia in American society.* New York: Harrington Park Press.

de Monteflores, C., & Schultz, S. (1978). Coming out: Similarities and differences for lesbians and gay men. *Journal of Social Issues, 34*(3), 59–72.

Ferrara, A. (1984). My personal experience with AIDS. *American Psychologist, 39*(11), 1285–1287.

FitzGerald, F. (1986, July 21, 28). A reporter at large (San Francisco). *The New Yorker*, pp. 34 (part 1), 44 (part 2).

Garfinkle, E. M., & Morin, S. F. (1978). Psychologists' attitudes toward homosexual clients. *Journal of Social Issues, 34*(3), 101–112.

Gonsiorek, J. (1985). *A guide to psychotherapy with gay and lesbian clients.* New York: Harrinton Park Press.

Grahn, J. (1984). *Another mother tongue.* Boston: Beacon Press.

Hall, M. (1978). Lesbian families: Cultural and clinical issues. *Social Work, 23*, 380–384.

Hanckel. F., & Cunningham, J. (1979). *A way of love, a way of life: A young person's introduction to what it means to be gay.* New York: Lothrop, Lee & Shepard.

Humphries, L. (1970). *Tearoom trade: Impersonal sex in public places.* Chicago: Aldine Press.

Kinsey, A., Pomeroy, W., & Martin, C. (1948). *Sexual behavior in the human male.* Philadelphia, PA: W. B. Saunders.

Klein, F. (1978). *The bisexual option.* New York: Arbor House.

Krieger, S. (1983). *The mirror dance: Identity in a women's community.* Philadelphia: Temple University Press.

Lauritsen, J., & Thorstad, D. (1974). *The early homosexual rights movement.* New York: Times Change Press.

Lynch, J. M., & Reilly, M. E. (1985/1986). Role relationships: Lesbian perspectives. *Journal of Homosexuality, 12*(2), 53–69.

MacDonald, B., & Rich, C. (1983). *Look me in the eye: Old women, aging, and ageism.* San Francisco: Spinsters, Ink.

Marotta, T. (1983). *Sons of Harvard.* New York: Quill.

McWhirter, D. P., & Mattison, A. M. (1984). *The male couple.* Englewood Cliffs, NJ: Prentice Hall.

Morin, S. F., & Charles, K. (1983). Heterosexual bias in psychotherapy. In J. Murray & P. R. Abramson (Eds.), *Bias in psychotherapy* (pp. 309–338). New York: Praeger.

Morin, S. F., & Schultz, S. J. (1978). The gay movement and the rights of children. *Journal of Social Issues, 34*(2), 137–148.

Moses, A., & Hawkins, R. (1982). *Counseling lesbian women and gay men.* St. Louis, MO: C. V. Mosby.

Paul, W., Weinrich, J. D., Gonsiorek, J. C., & Hotvedt, M. (1982). *Homosexuality: Social, psychological and biological issues.* Beverly Hills, CA: Sage.

Peplau, L. (1982). Research on homosexual couples: An overview. *Journal of Homosexuality, 8*, 3–8.

Press, A. (1986, July 14). A government in the bedroom: In a sodomy case, the high court rules against gays. *Newsweek, 108*, p. 36.

Reid, J. (1973). *The best little boy in the world.* New York: Ballantine.

Russo, V. (1981). *Celluloid closet: Homosexuality in the movies.* New York: Harper & Row.

Shilts, R. (1982). *The mayor of Castro Street.* New York: St. Martin's Press.

Silverstein, C. (1977). *A family matter: A parent's guide to homosexuality.* New York: McGraw Hill.

Tanner, D. (1978). *The lesbian couple.* Lexington, MA: Lexington Books.

Task Force on Gay/Lesbian Issues. (1982). *Homosexuality and social justice* (final report). San Francisco, CA: Archdiocese of San Francisco.

Weinberg, G. (1972). *Society and the healthy homosexual.* New York: Anchor Press.

Wolfe, S. J., & Stanley, J. P. (Ed.). (1980). *The coming out stories.* Watertown, MA: Persephone Press.

Youth Liberation. (1976). *Growing up gay.* Ann Arbor, MI: Youth Liberation Press.

Zannotti, B. (Ed.). (1986). *A faith of one's own: Explorations by Catholic lesbians.* Trumansburg, NY: The Crossing Press.

21

Bernice Lott

Significance of Gender for Social Behavior: Some Topical Courses

Since 1971, a feminist psychology course titled The Female Experience has been part of the Psychology Department curriculum at the University of Rhode Island. The Female Experience course remained for many years the only psychology course in which students were encouraged to examine critically the meaning of gender—its social construction and resulting affective, cognitive, and behavioral consequences. And although some of us in the Psychology Department attempted to make gender issues salient in any course we taught, such issues were not the prime focus. The situation for psychology graduate students was particularly bleak; only an occasional, highly committed graduate student would make room in an already overcrowded schedule for an advanced undergraduate course in feminist psychology.

In oral examinations of graduate students (as part of their comprehensive examination or thesis defense), I often found myself listening to psychologists-in-training (both women and men) respond to questions as though women did not exist, as though men were prototypical humans, or as though gender were not a relevant variable. Stereotyped assumptions about the behavior of women and men were voiced, and traditional psychological theories were accepted uncritically. My efforts to raise gender issues were frequently met with confusion and embarrassment. I could not, of course, blame the students: Their naiveté, conservatism, and downright ignorance were largely related to what they had been reading and studying in their programs. They had learned the psychology they were being taught.

The problem is clearly a critical one. Psychology graduate students leave the university as experts in the field of human behavior—to teach, to further knowledge through research, to practice in mental health settings, and to help others solve problems of human relationships. As far as I could tell, in the training being provided, not only were feminist perspectives on gender rarely if ever presented as relevant to such problems or their solutions, but gender issues in general were seldom made salient.

Feminist Psychology

Many traditional disciplines have been invigorated, expanded, and transformed by feminist scholarship. As I have noted elsewhere (Lott, 1985), this enrichment has taken two interrelated forms:

> (a) self-conscious and critical analyses of the discipline to uncover
> its androcentric bias in both content and method . . . and (b) . . .
> the asking of new questions, and the presentation of new hypotheses
> and theoretical formulations that follow from a focus on the experi-
> ences and conditions of women's lives. (p. 156)

Feminist researchers in psychology, while maintaining a respect for rigor in methodology and adherence to the rules of science, are distinguished by their choice of
problems and ultimate objectives.

In recent assessments of the current and potential impact of feminist scholarship on psychology in general, and social and personality psychology in particular
(Deauz, 1985; Henley, 1985; Lott, 1985; Wallston, 1987), significant positive contributions that have been mentioned include asking new questions; making explicit the role of personal experience and values in science; treating gender as a
stimulus to which persons respond; questioning earlier research that ignored or
accepted unproved assumptions about women; and studying issues of particular
relevance to women's lives. Feminist scholarship has focused primarily on
women; however, an understanding of the personal and social functions of gender
inevitably leads to a consideration of the special experiences of both women
and men.

Where could the students in my university learn about the contributions being
made by feminist scholarship to psychology and come to appreciate the possibilities this research holds to inform and enrich their present and future work? One
undergraduate course on the female experience was not enough.

Topical Courses

Some colleagues and I responded to this problem and challenge by introducing
two gender-focused, open-content, topical courses at both the graduate and the
undergraduate levels. On the graduate level, a Seminar in Social Psychology is
now the vehicle for teaching gender-focused topics. It is offered as an elective
to graduate students in our three programs—clinical, experimental, and school
psychology—and is also open to qualified students from other departments. On
the undergraduate level, the umbrella course for gender-focused topics is Topics
in Social Psychology, which is open to juniors and seniors who are psychology
majors or who have a general psychology background. Each independent topics
course (graduate or undergraduate) has a separate identifying letter so that a student may enroll in, and receive credit for, more than one.

Thus far, five gender-focused topical courses have been developed and taught
at least once—two on the graduate and three on the undergraduate level. The
general format, objectives, requirements, and material or issues covered for each
shall be described in this chapter. Readings and additional course materials for
each class are listed at the end of the chapter.

Hostility and Violence in the Lives of Women

I first co-taught this graduate seminar in 1978[1] and since then have offered it approximately every 2 years. In this class, two major issues are examined in depth: (a) hostility toward women, and women's victimization and survival; and (b) women's aggression against others. The students read and discuss primary and secondary sources and relate empirical data to theoretical formulations.

Specific issues discussed are sexism and misogyny, sexual harassment, pornography, sexual assault (including incest, date rape, and wife rape), physical abuse of women, and aggressive behavior by women toward women, children, and men. A major objective of the course is to understand the antecedents and consequences of hostile behavior as it is related to gender and as it impacts on women's lives. A second objective is to consider possibilities and requisites for positive change. Each student is required to take one or two written examinations, review a body of research on a specific issue, and design a relevant research proposal.

Femininity, Androgyny, and Mental Health

The graduate seminar on femininity, androgyny, and mental health is one I try to offer every other year. In it, we dissect, examine, evaluate, and discuss the concept of femininity (a) as a set of stable traits versus behavior correlates of situational demands; (b) as it has been nominally and operationally defined and measured; and (c) as a cultural stereotype having impact on women's mental health. The significance of gender differences in adult behavior and the assumptions, findings, and problems in the literature on sex role orientation and androgyny are examined. In addition, the facts and fictions of femininity are considered in relation to women's mental health, and women's mental health is then considered in relation to the situations of women's lives and to the goals, practices, and assumptions that characterize traditional, "gender-fair" (Worell & Remer, 1982), and feminist psychotherapy. Finally, issues of personality and mental health are considered from a social–psychological perspective, in relation to attitudes and beliefs about women.

Students take one or two examinations and prepare a research proposal focusing on a specific issue, including a thorough review of the relevant literature. The topics covered during the semester are femininity (childhood socialization, cultural assumptions, stereotypes, measures, and behavior of women); androgyny (concepts and measures, selected research findings, and issues and problems); and mental health (concepts, gender-related findings and issues, correlates of mental health in women, and psychotherapy).

The Psychology of Poverty

I developed the undergraduate course on the psychology of poverty to examine the significance of gender for poverty in the United States today. Its primary focus

---

1. Co-teachers referred to in this chapter are Kathryn Quina of the Psychology Department ("Hostility and Violence") and Wilford Dvorak of the English Department ("Adolescence").

is the experience of poor people, the majority of whom are women and their children. Students consider the circumstances of poverty and its consequences for behavior, aspirations, family functioning, relationships, and mental health. Using a social–psychological perspective, we focus on relations between situational variables and behavior and interactions between status and role. In sum, we examine the personal, social, and cultural correlates of poverty with special emphasis on motivation and learning and apply psychological principles to the experiences of the poor in both urban and rural settings.

A major objective of the course is to reduce the psychological distance between middle-class students and poor people, who are typically perceived as being far removed both physically and psychologically from the majority culture (e.g., as living mainly in isolated areas or in ghettoes, on the streets, or in rural shacks). To this end, the readings are largely first-person accounts or second-person observations of life among this country's poor from the rural poor on farms, in mills, and on reservations to urban welfare mothers and street-corner men. Guests with personal experience dealing with poverty are invited to present information and to lead discussions. These guests have included community organizers working with poor people and American Indians from the local area.

The specific issues covered in this class include the economics of poverty, living in rural poverty (migrant workers, residents of Appalachia, American Indians, subsistence farmers), living in urban poverty, behavioral consequences of poverty, and solutions.

Adolescence of Women in Fiction and Autobiography

The undergraduate course on the adolescence of women in fiction and in autobiographies, which I developed and co-taught with a member of the English Department, offers students two different approaches to learning about adolescent female development. We compare the perspective and methods of social science with those of literature and relate each to the objectives of feminist scholarship. Beginning with a presentation of psychological theories and findings on adolescence, we move to a discussion of methods of analysis through literature.

Students then read fictional and autobiographical works by women, as sources of rich information on growing up female in the 20th century. The readings permit comparisons of experiences, aspirations, and social contexts in which women from a variety of cultures and ethnic backgrounds move from childhood to adult status. Students read about the lives, dreams, and struggles of adolescent women from other cultures and countries (e.g., Simone de Beauvoir in pre-World War II France) and about American adolescents from different ethnic backgrounds (e.g., Chinese American, African American, Eastern European). Each woman's life as she has presented it is read not for accuracy, but for its reflection of an individual's development within the context of a particular time, place, and culture. The experiences of each adolescent woman described in fiction or autobiography are examined for personal elements and for elements common to other adolescent women of her generation and of other time periods, in other societies or ethnic groups.

Each student takes two examinations and writes a paper—a fictional story, an autobiographical essay, or a library research paper. Discussions focus on in-depth analyses of each of eight books, concerning adolescent women across modern cultures prior to 1950 (Simone de Beauvoir, Anne Frank, and Hannah Senesh) and across ethnic groups in the United States (Anzia Yezierska, Sylvia Plath, Harper Lee, Maxine Hong Kingston, and Maya Angelou). Discussions in this class are especially intense because college students are immediately able to relate their own "growing up" years to those they read about and to appreciate how gender has influenced the experiences of those years.

Men and Masculinity

Developed and taught by Albert Lott, the course titled Men and Masculinity examines the role of contemporary men in the United States in a historical and ethnic context. Students explore the meanings of masculinity and analyze the relevance of those meanings for men's attitudes, beliefs, and behavior. They focus especially on contemporary social issues that have affected men's expectations and aspirations—particularly in their relationships with women and with other men and their roles as sons, fathers, lovers, husbands, providers, and achievers. Topics covered are what it means to be a man today, perspectives on men (historical, biological, anthropological, sociological, and psychological), elements of the male role (antifemininity, success, aggression, sexuality, and self-reliance), homosexuality and homophobia, unequal power with women, nurturance by and for men, and men's liberation. Students are required to write two essay examinations and complete a term project. The latter may include research proposals, video studies, attitude surveys, or library research.

Conclusions

The special topics courses outlined were developed to enrich the curriculum in psychology for graduate and undergraduate students. The success with which they have done so may be inferred from the high quality of student projects, the intensity and sophistication of class discussions, and the continued involvement of the students in applied activities, internships, and community programs. Student evaluations of these classes are invariably positive and enthusiastic. When graduate students in the Psychology Department's Clinical Program were surveyed several years ago about their training, they selected the topical seminars as among the most valuable courses they had taken. A number of research proposals written by the graduate students to satisfy the course requirements in the seminars have been used later as the bases for master's theses, dissertations, conference presentations, or journal articles that focus on the significance of gender for social behavior.

Although the courses described in this chapter are enriching, valuable, and in my view essential to a contemporary psychology program, readers must not be misled into believing that large numbers of students have flocked to them. None of the courses are required. They must compete with the standard courses that undergraduates majoring in psychology are urged to take and with courses necessary for graduate students preparing for licensure as psychotherapists or a career in experimental research or school psychology. A sentence I have heard often is "Oh, how I wanted to take your course this semester, but I just couldn't!"

The courses described here are not generally viewed as high-priority courses by most colleagues in my department, some of whom are probably only vaguely aware that they are offered or view the courses as fringe offerings. Students who take these topical courses have heard about them typically from other students, and the recommendation to enroll is more likely to come from a peer than from a faculty advisor, unless the latter is involved in the Women's Studies Program. Thus, only a small number of psychology students are learning to evaluate gender critically and appreciate its significance in human relationships and about the contributions being made to psychology by feminist scholarship. Perhaps the readers of this book will join with others to make the necessary additions and changes to their own curricula so that the objective of this volume—a psychology of people— will be enhanced and made real.

Recommended Resources

Listed below are books and films that have been used in each of the courses described in this chapter. They are presented only as illustrative materials, since new materials continue to become available.

Hostility and Violence in the Lives of Women

Readings. In addition to material from some of the following books, relevant up-to-date journal articles are assigned and required for each week's discussion. The journal articles serve as the focus for discussion of feminist scholarship and empirical fact finding; the books provide background and information and contribute to an experiential perspective.

Armstrong, L. (1978). *Kiss Daddy goodnight.* New York: Hawthorn.

Barry, K. (1979). *Female sexual slavery.* Englewood Cliffs, NJ: Prentice-Hall.

Bart, P., & O'Brien, P. H. (1985). *Stopping rape.* New York: Pergamon Press.

Brady, K. (1979). *Father's days.* New York: Dell.

Brownmiller, S. (1975). *Against our will: Men, women and rape.* New York: Simon & Schuster.

Butler, S. (1978). *Conspiracy of silence: The trauma of incest.* San Francisco: Volcano Press.

Chapman, J. R., & Gates, M. (Eds.). (1978). *The victimization of women.* Beverly Hills, CA: Sage.

Dinnerstein, D. (1977). *The mermaid and the minotaur: Sexual arrangement and human malaise* (Chapter 6). New York: Harper & Row.

Dworkin, A. (1981). *Pornography: Men possessing women.* New York: Putnam.

Farley, L. (1978). *Sexual shakedown.* New York: McGraw-Hill.

Giles-Sims, J. (1983). *Wife battering.* New York: Guilford Press.

Griffin, S. (1981). *Pornography and silence.* New York: Harper & Row.

Groth, A. N. (1979). *Men who rape: The psychology of the offender*. New York: Plenum Press.

Jones, A. (1980). *Women who kill*. New York: Fawcett.

Lederer, L. (1980). *Take back the night*. New York: Morrow.

Lott, B. (1987). *Women's lives: Themes and variations in gender learning*. Monterey, CA: Brooks/Cole.

MacKinnon, C. A. (1979). *Sexual harassment of working women*. New Haven, CT: Yale University Press.

McNulty, F. (1981). *The burning bed*. New York: Bantam.

Russ, J. (1985). *Magic mommas, trembling sisters, puritans and perverts*. Trumansburg, NY: The Crossing Press.

Russell, D. E. H. (1982). *Rape in marriage*. New York: Macmillan.

Stanko, E. A. (1985). *Intimate intrusions*. Boston: Routledge & Kegan Paul.

Films.

Not a love story. (1983). New York: National Film Board of Canada.

Rape culture. (1975). Cambridge, MA: Cambridge Documentary Films.

Killing us softly. (1979). Cambridge, MA: Cambridge Documentary Films.

Incest: The victim nobody believes. (1978). Northbrook, IL: MTI Teleprograms.

We will not be beaten. (1979). New York: Women Make Movies.

Rethinking rape. (1985). Seattle, WA: Film Distribution Center.

Abortion: Stories from North & South. (1984). New York: Cinema Guild.

We Dig Coal. (1982). New York: Cinema Guild.

Femininity, Androgyny, and Mental Health

Readings. Relevant journal articles are assigned for each week's class meeting in addition to readings from the books listed below. Empirical and theoretical articles from the contemporary psychological literature are the focus of each class meeting.

Brodsky, A. M., & Hare-Mustin, R. T. (1980). *Women and psychotherapy: An assessment of research and practice*. New York: Guilford Press.

Chodorow, N. (1978). *The reproduction of mothering*. Berkeley: University of California Press.

Deutsch, H. (1944). *The psychology of women (Vol. 1)*. New York: Grune & Stratton.

Freud, S. (1964). Femininity. In *New introductory lectures on psychoanalysis* (pp. 112–135). New York: Norton. (Original work published in 1933)

Gilligan, C. (1982). *In a different voice*. Cambridge, MA: Harvard University Press.

Gomberg, S., & Franks, V. (Eds.). (1979). *Gender and disordered behavior*. New York: Brunner/Mazel.

Kaplan, A. G., & Sedney, M. A. (1980). *Psychology and sex roles: An androgynous perspective*. Boston: Little, Brown.

Kelman, N. (Ed.). (1967). *Feminine psychology*. New York: Norton.

Lott, B. (1981). *Becoming a woman*. Springfield, IL: Charles C. Thomas.

Mayo, C., & Henley, N. (Eds.). (1981). *Gender and nonverbal behavior.* New York: Springer-Verlag.

Miller, J. B. (1976). *Toward a new psychology of women.* Boston: Beacon.

The Psychology of Poverty

Readings. Some of the older books listed below are now difficult to obtain but again are presented here as illustrative.

Allen, P. G. (1983). *The woman who owned the shadows.* San Francisco: Spinsters, Ink.

Brand, J. (1978). *The life and death of Anna Mae Aquash.* Toronto: Lorimer.

Byerly, V. (1986). *Hard times cotton mill girls.* Ithaca, NY: ILR Press.

Chute, C. (1985). *The Beans of Egypt, Maine.* New York: Ticknor & Fields.

Coles, R. (1970). *Uprooted children: The early life of migrant workers.* Pittsburgh: University of Pittsburgh Press.

Coles, R., & Coles, J. H. (1978). *Women of crisis: I.* New York: Delacorte.

Erdrich, L. (1984). *Love medicine.* New York: Holt, Rinehart & Winston.

Kahn, K. (1974). *Hillbilly women.* New York: Avon.

Liebow, E. (1967). *Tally's corner.* Boston: Little, Brown.

Naylor, G. (1983). *The women of Brewster Place.* New York: Penguin.

Sheehan, S. (1977). *A welfare mother.* New York: Mentor.

Sheehan, S. (1984). *Kate Quinton's days.* New York: Mentor.

Stack, B. (1974). *All our kin: Strategies for survival in a Black community.* New York: Harper & Row.

Williams, M. D. (1981). *On the street where I lived.* New York: Holt, Rinehart & Winston.

Adolescence of Women in Fiction and Autobiography

Readings. In addition to the books listed below, a list of supplementary books written by women and highlighting adolescent experiences is distributed to the students in this class for background reading.

Angelou, M. (1971). *I know why the caged bird sings.* New York: Bantam.

De Beauvoir, S. (1974). *Memoirs of a dutiful daughter.* New York: Harper Colophon. (Original work published in 1958)

Frank, A. (1953). *The diary of a young girl.* New York: Pocket Books.

Kingston, M. H. (1977). *The woman warrior.* New York: Vintage.

Lee, H. (1961). *To kill a mockingbird.* New York: Harper & Row.

Plath, S. (1972). *The bell jar.* New York: Bantam.

Senesh, H. (1973). *Her life and diary.* New York: Schocken.

Yezierska, A. (1975). *Bread givers.* New York: Persea. (Original work published in 1925)

Films.

Legacy of Anne Frank. (1968). Del Mar, CA: CRM/McGraw-Hill Films.

To kill a mockingbird. (1962). Hauppage, NY: Swank Motion Pictures.

I know why the caged bird sings. (1978). Deerfield, IL: Learning Corporation of America.

Men and Masculinity

Readings. Most of the assigned reading is from Doyle, listed below, but supplemental assignments are made from each of the others.

David, D., & Brannon, R. (Eds.). (1982). *The forty-nine percent majority: The male sex role.* Reading, MA: Addison-Wesley.

Doyle, J. (1983). *The male experience.* Dubuque, IA: William Brown.

Gary, L. (Ed.). (1981). *Black men.* Beverly Hills, CA: Sage.

Lewis, R. (Ed.). (1981). *Men in difficult times.* Englewood Cliffs, NJ: Prentice-Hall.

Pleck, J., & Sawyer, J. (Eds.). (1974). *Men and masculinity.* Englewood Cliffs, NJ: Prentice-Hall.

Films.

Men's lives. (1974). New York: New Day Films.

To have and to hold. (1982). New York: New Day Films.

The male couple. (1985). Los Angeles: Humanus Home Video.

New relations. (1980). Boston: Fanlight Productions.

References

Deaux, K. (1985). Sex and gender. In L. Porter & M. Rosenzweig (Eds.), *Annual review of psychology 1985* (Vol. 36, pp. 49–81). Palo Alto, CA: Annual Reviews.

Henley, N. M. (1985). Psychology and gender. *Signs, 11,* 101–119.

Lott, B. (1985). The potential enrichment of social/personality psychology through feminist research, and vice versa. *American Psychologist, 40,* 155–164.

Wallston, B. S. (1987). Social psychology of women and gender. *Journal of Applied Social Psychology, 17,* 1025–1050.

Worell, J., & Remer, P. (1982, July). Sex fair guidelines for state association ethics committees. *Division 35 Newsletter,* pp. 9–10.

22 ───

Rhoda Kessler Unger

The Psychology of Social Issues: Commonalities From Specifics

In the past 20 years, psychology departments have begun offering courses about special populations such as women, Blacks, or the elderly. Although such courses can provide students with detailed knowledge of a particular group, they can also create new problems. In particular, the focus on a specific population may obscure many similarities in the way psychology has historically dealt with marginal groups. Given the large amount of new data about women, gays and lesbians, people of color, the poor, the disabled, and the elderly that have been generated in recent years, the attempt to cover a number of groups in depth within one course can be overwhelming.

Furthermore, in order to address adequately the questions raised by the study of these groups, it is important to go beyond psychology's traditional empirical base and draw on material from philosophy, the history of science, and the sociology of knowledge. My solution is to emphasize important issues and commonalities across groups and integrate information from diverse sources in a course on the psychology of social issues.

There are other reasons for developing a course on social issues with attention to many different populations rather than a focus upon any particular one. A more varied group of students appear to be attracted to the course, and discussion among them can be lively and illuminating. Some of these students may later take more specialized courses that they otherwise might have ignored, believing that because they did not belong to the group under scrutiny, the issues raised were not relevant to them.

In addition, a social issues course is particularly useful for developing cognitive skills as well as sociopolitical awareness. Students can develop critical thinking skills and learn to recognize recurring patterns of bias in psychology by analyzing similar arguments that have been used to support, for example, claims of deficiencies in different groups. They can also acquire a critical view of the accumulation of knowledge from seeing how different scholars, using many different theories, can explain the same "fact" (cf. Bruffee, 1982) and by generating alternative explanations of their own.

The Social Issues Course

For the past 4 years, I have taught a social issues course to upper level undergraduates majoring in a social science who have had one or two courses in psychology

The assistance of Roland Siiter in the writing of this article is greatly appreciated.

or sociology. The general goals are for students to (a) learn the connection between scientific research and sociopolitical values; (b) examine causal explanations offered by psychology for individual and group differences; (c) analyze social policies developed to deal with individuals and groups who differ from the norm; and (d) understand the connection between the causal explanations and the social policies offered as solutions. The materials used include both general theoretical and methodological critiques of social science and specific data-based articles about particular groups. Because there is no single suitable text available, a syllabus of readings is provided at the end of this chapter. One text (Rubinstein & Slife, 1984) attempted to provide multiple views of controversial issues, but I have found it to be too elementary and too general for the purposes of this course.

The course is divided into five parts (see Syllabus). The first part focuses on the nature–nurture controversy in its various forms, as it has been applied to different groups in the past and present. Questions include "What form do nature–nurture arguments take in relation to sex, race, and social class?"; "Do such arguments share common features independent of the content area in which they are applied?"; "Have theories about the nature of group differences changed over time?"; and "What are the similarities between theories that are no longer accepted and those in current use in social science and society?" Specific content areas include the nature of human instincts (particularly those involving nurturance and aggression), the uses of mental testing, and current theories about group differences in biological function—particularly brain laterality and sociobiology—and their evidential base.

Part 2 considers how social problems are defined and on whom they are blamed. One issue that is examined is the language of psychology and society in general (see Rich, 1980, on "compulsive heterosexuality" and Blumenthal, 1972, on the social consequences of differential definitions of violence). Other important issues concern the nature of social roles and how they may be used to both describe and prescribe behaviors for the role occupant (see Pleck, 1981, on masculinity), and the relation between problem explanation and solution (see Ryan, 1971, on "blaming the victim"). Instructors can choose from many content areas to illustrate these issues. Race- and sex-related differences in achievement and aggression are areas that evoke a great deal of interest and discussion. The final portion of this section of the course deals with the status and power differences between researchers and members of the socially marginal groups they study, and the implications for psychological knowledge. Fine (1983–1984) and Caplan and Nelson (1973) are particularly rich resources on these issues.

The third part of the course deals with the impact of individual and societal ideology on the creation of social knowledge. We examine the connection between the personal ideology of scientists and the questions they ask, as well as the conclusions they reach (much of the recent work in the sociology of knowledge is useful here; see Unger, 1983, 1986); methodological problems produced by researcher bias; and how societal expectations and practices may generate problematic behavior. The concept of the self-fulfilling prophecy is a very useful one, and there are a number of empirical demonstrations of the phenomenon that students find compelling (see Henley, 1977).

Section 4 focuses on some of the conceptual issues that may have already emerged in discussions of the previous material. Important concepts include the issue of the self versus one's social role, situational consistency and specificity, observer bias, and the question of reversibility of problematic behavior. Some instructors may be interested in exploring the conceptual framework of developmental psychology (e.g., Scarr, 1984) or social psychology (O'Leary, Unger, & Wallston, 1985).

The final section of the course is devoted to solutions to social problems as they change over time. The most important issue is the extent to which problems are defined as individual or private as opposed to being viewed as a matter for public concern. Some remedies such as psychosurgery or psychotherapy may be discussed here in terms of the demographics of client populations (see Chapter 4 by Landrine in this volume), the ethics of who makes decisions about which solutions to try, and the extent to which individuals defined as being in a problematic relationship with society are free to choose their own solutions (e.g., Chorover, 1981).

I emphasize a cost–benefit analysis in this area and have students generate and criticize all possible solutions. A major goal is student realization that no single solution is optimal for everyone involved and that social problems as well as psychological thinking about them change constantly. Free-will versus societal control provides an excellent debate with which to close the course, provided that students recognize that some of us are freer than others.

Specific illustrations of the concepts examined in the course may be drawn from many different areas involving race, sex, age, or sexual orientation. The syllabus offers a range of possible alternatives that can, of course, be altered or supplemented according to an individual instructor's inclinations. Unfortunately, it is easier to criticize research than to generate meaningful questions (Wallston, 1981). It is important, therefore, to find a positive way to end the course. The goal is to teach students to think critically about psychology, not to discourage them about the ultimate value of the field.

Instructional Techniques

It is clear that a social issues course cannot be taught by means of a lecture format. Many of these ideas are new to students, and a considerable amount of explication is required. However, both critical thinking skills and motivation are enhanced by active collaboration in the classroom process (Bouton & Garth, 1983). I have found several techniques to be useful in this regard. First, all students are required to participate in a panel discussion in which several different positions must be presented and to write a term paper presenting more than one side of an issue (students' tendencies to offer only one side can be minimized by requiring an outline early in the semester). Second, members of marginal groups with whom students have little likelihood of contact are invited to present their views in class. Third, participation in simulation games offers students the opportunity to view the world from a different position than one's own. Role-playing games involving gender ("The Academic Game") or race ("Ghetto") are good vehicles for generating alternative world views. Bredemeier and Greenblat (1981) have provided an excellent review of the educational effectiveness of various simulation games.

Exam questions should stress conceptualization rather than informational content. Consistent with a collaborative model, students may be asked to provide questions (and answers) for exams. I have found a number of short-answer questions to be more useful than a few global essays. These questions stress the similarities and differences between concepts, request evidence for or against a particular position, or require analysis of a point made in one of the readings. I offer students study outlines before exams with the information that some of the questions will appear on the exam.

Evaluation of the Course

Postcourse questionnaires indicate that students are stimulated by the course. More than half who responded mentioned spontaneously that learning about multiple perspectives was the most valuable aspect of the course. In order to determine whether students' attitudes were influenced by the course, the Attitudes About Reality Scale (Unger, Draper, & Pendergrass, 1986) was administered at the beginning and at the end of the semester. This scale is designed to measure views about the nature of the relation between the person and reality on a continuum from a logical positivist world view (the perception that there is a fixed, universal, objective reality) to a belief in social constructionism (a view that reality is subjective, relativistic, and situationally bound).

It has been found that students who enrolled in a course with a social issues focus, Psychology of Women, were initially more socially constructionist than students enrolled in other comparable level courses, such as Social Psychology (Unger et al., 1986). Average scores of students enrolling in Psychology of Women approached levels of social constructionism found among feminist scholars (Unger, 1984–1985). Such students changed still further in the direction of social constructionism after completion of Psychology of Women (Howe, 1985; Unger et al., 1986).

Students enrolled in Social Issues, however, had initial scores that were not significantly different from those enrolled in Social Psychology. Although students may select courses based upon preexistent ideology, the newness of a course in social issues and lack of information about its content appear to have minimized self-selection. Nevertheless, students enrolled in Social Issues changed significantly in the direction of social constructionism, compared with students in Social Psychology who had initially comparable scores. Changes in the students were most marked in those aspects of the scale that measure beliefs in biological determinism and the influence of values on how science works.

Implications

In sum, a course focused on common issues generated from the study of special populations by psychology appears to be an effective means to introduce students to both psychology and intellectual criticism. It appears to make them more aware that values and science are inextricably intertwined (Sherif, 1979). Of course, students can then bring their critical skills to more objective courses within mainstream psychology.

Social Issues Course Syllabus

Part 1: The Nature–Nurture Controversy

1. Historical and philosophical context of social problem definition (Buss, 1978; Eacker, 1972; Koch, 1981; Sampson, 1978)
2. Explanations for differences between groups—the nature–nurture controversy in race, sex, class (Fausto-Sterling, 1985, Chapter 2; Gould, 1981, Chapters 1 through 4; Herrnstein, 1971)
3. History of biological explanations for group differences (Gould, 1981, Chapter 5; Buss, 1979, chapter by Samelson; Shields, 1975)
4. Biological theories of human behavior, and critiques (Buss, 1979, chapter by Lubek; Paul, Weinrich, Gonsiorek, & Hotvedt, 1982, chapters by Kirsch & Rodman, Weinrich; Shields, 1984)

Part 2: How Social Problems and Social Roles are Defined

5. The power to name in social science and society (Burnham, 1983; Epstein, Krupat, & Obudho, 1976; Karr, 1978; Spender, 1980, Chapters 5 through 7)
6. Consequences of the power to define (Apfelbaum, 1979; Cook, 1979; Samelson, 1978; Satariano, 1979)
7. Individual differences in problem definitions and its consequences (Fine, 1983–1984; Buss, 1979, chapter by Furby; Lykes, 1983; Rich, 1980)
8. Conceptual flaws in the analysis of marginal groups (Caplan & Nelson, 1973; Gadlin & Ingle, 1975; Sampson, 1981; Unger, 1983)

Part 3: The Impact of Ideology on the Creation of Social Knowledge

9. Impact of personal values on research (Buss, 1976; Kimble, 1984; Sherwood & Nataupsky, 1968)
10. Impact of ideology on methodology; some suggested remedies (Montero & Levin, 1977, chapters by Kahana & Felton, Maykovich, and Weiss; Parlee, 1981; Sherif, 1979)
11. Role of society in creating social problems: social categorization and the self-fulfilling prophecy (Dion, 1975; Hacker, 1951; Paul et al., 1982, chapter by Paul; Watson, 1973, chapters by Proshansky & Newton, Tajfel; Word, Zanna, & Cooper, 1974)
12. Role of society in producing individual "pathology" (Janoff-Bulman & Frieze, 1983, chapter by Scheppelle & Bart; Malamuth, 1981; Riger & Gordon, 1981; Thomas & Drabman, 1978)

Part 4: Stable versus Situational Factors in Explanations

13. Problems in attributing causality—confusion between self and role and between person and situation (Blumenthal, 1972; Brickman, 1977; Eagly & Wood, 1985; Unger, 1981)
14. Stability of social problems—issues in reversibility and consistency of effects (Kagan, 1976; Newcombe, 1980; Scarr, 1984; Unger, 1979; Watson, 1973, chapter by Katz)

Part 5: Solutions to Social Problems: Changes Over Time

15. Individual solutions for social change (Janoff-Bulman & Frieze, 1983, chapters by Kidder, Boell, & Moyer and Miller & Porter; Paul et al., 1982, chapters by Coleman, Davison; Watson, 1973, chapter by Kiev)
16. Societal solutions for social change (Kahn, 1972; McGrath, 1983, chapters by Bruner, McGrath, and Zimring & Hawkins)

Additional Resources: Allport (1954), Guthrie (1976), Jones (1972), Katz (1976), Riegel (1979), Rosenberg (1982), and Sarason (1981).

References

Allport, G. W. (1954). *The nature of prejudice.* Reading, MA: Addison-Wesley.
Apfelbaum, E. (1979). Relations of domination and movements for liberation: An analysis of power between groups. In W. Austin & S. Worchel (Eds.), *The social psychology of intergroup relations* (pp. 188–204). Monterey, CA: Brooks/Cole.
Blumenthal, M. D. (1972). Predicting attitudes towards violence. *Science, 176,* 1296–1303.
Bouton, C., & Garth, R. Y. (1983). *Learning in groups.* San Francisco: Jossey-Bass.
Bredemeier, M. E., & Greenblat, C. S. (1981). The educational effectiveness of simulation gaming. *Simulation and Gaming, 12,* 307–332.
Brickman, P. (1977). Crime and punishment in sports and society. *Journal of Social Issues, 33,* 140–164.
Bruffee, K. (1982). Liberal education and the social justification of belief. *Liberal Education, 68,* 95–114.
Burnham, D. (1983). Black women as producers and reproducers for profit. In M. Lowe & R. Hubbard (Eds.), *Women's nature: Rationalizations of inequality* (pp. 29–38). New York: Pergamon Press.
Buss, A. R. (1976). Galton and sex differences: An historical note. *Journal of the History of the Behavioral Sciences, 12,* 283–285.
Buss, A. R. (1978). The structure of psychological revolutions. *Journal of the History of the Behavioral Sciences, 13,* 57–64.
Buss, A. R. (Ed.). (1979). *Psychology in social context.* New York: Irvington.
Caplan, N., & Nelson, S. D. (1973). On being useful: The nature and consequences of psychological research on social problems. *American Psychologist, 28,* 199–211.
Chorover, S. L. (1981). *From genesis to genocide.* Cambridge, MA: MIT Press.
Cook, S. W. (1979). Social science and school desegregation: Did we mislead the Supreme Court? *Personality and Social Psychology Bulletin, 5,* 420–437.
Dion, K. L. (1975). Women's reactions to discrimination from members of the same or opposite sex. *Journal of Research in Personality, 9,* 294–306.

Eacker, J. N. (1972). On some elementary philosophical problems of psychology. *American Psychologist, 27*, 553–565.

Eagly, A. H., & Wood, W. (1985). Gender and influencibility: Stereotype vs. behavior. In V. O'Leary, R. Unger, & B. Wallston (Eds.), *Women, gender, and social psychology* (pp. 225–256). Hillsdale, NJ: Erlbaum.

Epstein, Y. M., Krupat, E., & Obudho, C. (1976). Clean is beautiful: Identification and preference as a function of race and cleanliness. *Journal of Social Issues, 32*, 109–118.

Fausto-Sterling, A. (1985). *Myths of gender.* New York: Basic Books.

Fine, M. (1983–1984). Coping with rape: Critical perspectives on consciousness. *Imagination, Cognition, and Personality, 3*, 249–267.

Gadlin, H., & Ingle, G. (1975). Through the one-way mirror: The limits of experimental self-reflection. *American Psychologist, 30*, 1003–1009.

Gould, S. J. (1981). *The mismeasure of man.* New York: Norton.

Guthrie, R. V. (1976). *Even the rat was white: A historical view of psychology.* New York: Harper & Row.

Hacker, H. (1951). Women as a minority group. *Social Forces, 30*, 60–69.

Henley, N. M. (1977). *Body politics: Power, sex and nonverbal communication.* Englewood Cliffs, NJ: Prentice-Hall.

Herrnstein, R. (1971, September). IQ. *The Atlantic Monthly*, pp. 43–64.

Howe, K. G. (1985). The psychological impact of a women's studies course. *Women's Studies Quarterly, 13*, 23–24.

Janoff-Bulman, R., & Frieze, I. H. (Eds.). (1983). Reactions to victimization [Special issue]. *Journal of Social Issues, 39*(2).

Jones, J. M. (1972). *Prejudice and racism.* Reading, MA: Addison-Wesley.

Kagan, J. (1976). Emergent themes in human development. *American Scientist, 64*, 186–196.

Kahn, R. L. (1972). The justification of violence: Social problems and social resolutions. *Journal of Social Issues, 28*, 155–175.

Karr, R. G. (1978). Homosexual labeling and the male role. *Journal of Social Issues, 34*, 73–83.

Katz, P. A. (Ed.). (1976). *Towards the elimination of racism.* New York: Pergamon Press.

Kimble, G. A. (1984). Psychology's two cultures. *American Psychologist, 39*, 833–839.

Koch, S. (1981). The nature and limits of psychological knowledge: Lessons from a century qua "Science." *American Psychologist, 36*, 257–269.

Lykes, M. B. (1983). Discrimination and coping in the lives of Black women. *Journal of Social Issues, 39*(3), 79–100.

Malamuth, N. M. (1981). Rape proclivity among males. *Journal of Social Issues, 37*(4), 138–157.

McGrath, J. E. (Ed.). (1983). Social issues and social change: Some views from the past [Special issue]. *Journal of Social Issues, 39*(4).

Montero, D., & Levin, G. N. (Eds.). (1977). Research among racial and cultural minorities: Problems, prospects, and pitfalls [Special issue]. *Journal of Social Issues, 33*(4).

Newcombe, N. (1980). Beyond nature and nurture. *Contemporary Psychology, 25*, 807–808.

O'Leary, V. E., Unger, R. K., & Wallston, B. S. (Eds.). (1985). *Women, gender, and social psychology.* Hillsdale, NJ: Erlbaum.

Parlee, M. B. (1981). Appropriate control groups in feminist research. *Psychology of Women Quarterly, 5*, 637–644.

Paul, W., Weinrich, J. D., Gonsiorek, J. C., & Hotvedt, M. E. (Eds.). (1982). *Homosexuality: Social, psychological, and biological issues.* Beverly Hills, CA: Sage.

Pleck, J. H. (1981). *The myth of masculinity.* Cambridge, MA: MIT Press.

Rich, A. (1980). Compulsory heterosexuality and lesbian existence. *Signs, 5*, 631–660.

Riegel, K. (1979). *Foundations of dialectical psychology.* New York: Academic Press.

Riger, S., & Gordon, M. T. (1981). The fear of rape: A study in social control. *Journal of Social Issues, 37*, 71–92.

Rosenberg, R. (1982). *Beyond separate spheres: Intellectual roots of modern feminism.* New Haven, CT: Yale University Press.

Rubinstein, J., & Slife, B. D. (Eds.). (1984). *Taking sides: Clashing views on controversial psychological issues* (3rd ed.). Guilford, CT: Dushkin Publishing Group.

Ryan, W. (1971). *Blaming the victim.* New York: Vintage Press.

Samelson, F. (1978). From "race psychology" to "studies in prejudice": Some observations on thematic reversals in social psychology. *Journal of the History of the Behavioral Sciences, 14,* 265–278.

Sampson, E. E. (1978). Scientific paradigms and social values: Wanted, a scientific revolution. *Journal of Personality and Social Psychology, 36,* 1332–1343.

Sampson, E. E. (1981). Cognitive psychology as ideology. *American Psychologist, 36,* 730–743.

Sarason, S. (1981). *Psychology misdirected.* New York: Free Press.

Satariano, W. W. (1979). Immigration and the popularization of social science, 1920 to 1930. *Journal of the History of the Behavioral Sciences, 15,* 310–320.

Scarr, S. (1984,). The danger of having pet variables. *Newsletter of the APA Division on Developmental Psychology,* pp. 24–34.

Sherif, C. W. (1979). Bias in psychology. In J. Sherman & E. Beck (Eds.), *The prism of sex* (pp. 93–133). Madison, WI: University of Wisconsin Press.

Sherwood, J. J., & Nataupsky, M. (1968). Predicting the conclusions of Negro–White intelligence research from biographical characteristics of the investigator. *Journal of Personality and Social Psychology, 8,* 53–58.

Shields, S. A. (1975). Functionalism, Darwinism, and the psychology of women: A study in social myth. *American Psychologist, 30,* 739–754.

Shields, S. A. (1984). "To pet, coddle, and do for": Caretaking and the concept of maternal instinct. In M. Lewin (Ed.), *In the shadow of the past: Psychology portrays the sexes* (pp. 256–273). New York: Columbia University Press.

Spender, D. (1980). *Man made language.* London: Routledge & Kegan Paul.

Thomas, M. E., & Drabman, R. S. (1978). Effects of television violence on expectations of others' aggression. *Personality and Social Psychology Bulletin, 4,* 73–76.

Unger, R. K. (1979). Toward a redefinition of sex and gender. *American Psychologist, 34,* 1085–1094.

Unger, R. K. (1981). Sex as a social reality: Field and laboratory research. *Psychology of Women Quarterly, 5,* 645–653.

Unger, R. K. (1983). Through the looking glass: No Wonderland yet! (The reciprocal relationship between methodology and models of reality). *Psychology of Women Quarterly, 8,* 9–32.

Unger, R. K. (1984–1985). Explorations in feminist ideology: Surprising consistencies and unexamined conflicts. *Imagination, Cognition, and Personality, 4,* 397–405.

Unger, R. K. (1986). Looking toward the future by looking at the past: Social activism and social history. *Journal of Social Issues, 42,* 215–227.

Unger, R. K., Draper, R. D., & Pendergrass, M. L. (1986). Personal epistemology and personal experience. *Journal of Social Issues, 42,* 67–79.

Wallston, B. S. (1981). What are the questions in psychology of women? A feminist approach to research. *Psychology of Women Quarterly, 5,* 597–617.

Watson, P. (Ed.). (1973). *Psychology and race.* Chicago: Aldine.

Word, C. O., Zanna, M. P., & Cooper, J. (1974). The non-verbal mediation of self-fulfilling prophecies in interracial interaction. *Journal of Experimental Social Psychology, 10,* 109–120.

Section IV

Programmatic Models
for Change

23

Marylyn Rands

Gender Balance in the Introductory Psychology Course: A Departmental Approach

The Psychology Department at Wheaton College, a 4-year liberal arts college for women, has carried out an extensive project to integrate the new scholarship on women into its introductory courses. This project was part of a college-wide program, supported by the Fund for the Improvement of Postsecondary Education, to achieve gender balance in undergraduate education (Spanier, Bloom, & Boroviak, 1984). The goal was to integrate the new scholarship on women across the entire curriculum, rather than isolate it in separate women's studies courses.

To achieve this aim, the Psychology Department decided to revise the introductory course, with the expectation that the new material would filter into upper-level courses as a result of this effort. Six sections of introductory psychology were offered at Wheaton, four in the fall and two in the spring, each taught by a different faculty member. The entire department of nine members cooperated in planning the revised course, although individuals differed in their ideological positions regarding the goals of the project.

Planning for Curriculum Revision

Development of our project was facilitated by my serving as a part-time coordinator for three semesters during the planning stage and the initial year of implementation (1981–1982). The project has not had a coordinator since that time and thus has proceeded less systematically, although many course changes have persisted.

Our first step was to assess the degree to which students were already exposed to scholarship on women in the present introductory courses. We started out by closely examining the content of several current textbooks and discovered that all were biased in that they ignored gender differences, tended to discuss women only as examples of negative behavior (e.g., depression or phobias), or failed to show positive female role models. Other shortcomings we identified were women's role in the history of psychology, bias in the sex of research samples and the generalizability of findings from those samples, the origins of sex differences, and the overlapping nature of distributions of most sex differences. When we surveyed the faculty, we found that all six professors currently teaching introductory psychology did attempt to compensate for textbook weaknesses by emphasizing neglected topics such as gender differences in achievement motivation, gender role socialization, and fear of success; however, a large number of potential topics were not being included, and the biases were not addressed.

Our second step was to hold a series of discussions to plan the content and structure of the revised course. Some of this discussion occurred during regular department meetings, but an important feature was a 5-day workshop at the end of the first semester when we brought in Janet Spence, a social psychologist known for her work on concepts of masculinity and femininity (e.g., Spence & Helmreich, 1978). The goals of that workshop were to discuss issues and aims in changing the introductory course, to review relevant research and theory, to design a new course, and to design an evaluation procedure.

Issues and Aims in Changing the Introductory Course

The general goals of the existing introductory course were summarized as follows:
1. Introduce psychological topics,
2. Provide experience with methods of inquiry,
3. Teach psychology as intellectual history,
4. Teach scientific reasoning and critical thinking, and
5. Illustrate the development of psychological knowledge as an ongoing process.

For the new course, three additional goals were identified:
6. Include new scholarship on women,
7. Explore psychology's effect on women's roles, and
8. Examine biases in psychological research and theory, particularly in regard to gender.

Review of Relevant Research and Theory

In our workshop, we discussed three major topics that could be included in the gender-balanced course. Research on achievement motivation could be used to illustrate how theories based on studies of men often fail to apply when generalized to women (Spence & Helmreich, 1978). This research also illustrates how psychologists can use failure to obtain generalizability as an impetus for the development of more complex theories and constructs. Gilligan's (1982) work on women's cognitive development is another example which can provide students with an awareness of new theories and how they are generated and tested.

A second topic was the difference between traits and roles as they pertain to gender (Spence & Helmreich, 1978), a distinction that is not always clear even in published studies. Because some psychological traits tend to be associated more strongly with one sex than another within cultures, there is a tendency when describing individuals in terms of traits to make an illogical connection between trait and role (e.g., females are nurturant; babies need nurturance; therefore, females should take care of the babies). By making clearer distinctions between roles and traits, students can better understand some of the links among gender, self-concept, and gender-role acquisition.

A third area of discussion was psychobiology. Topics that would be important to include in a balanced curriculum are (a) hormones and behavior (To what extent do hormones influence behavior?); (b) sociobiology (To what extent should we interpret animal behavior as precise models for human behavior, and to what extent should we consider them merely as metaphors?); and (c) sexual dimorphisms in the brain (What are the conceptual and methodological difficulties in interpreting research in this area?). (For a more extensive discussion of these questions, see Chapter 9 by Villars in this volume.) It is especially important for students to have a grounding in psychobiology, so that they may evaluate theories and research on the biological bases of behavior with a critical eye and come to understand the difficulty in sorting out genetic and social determinants of behavior.

There is much more information available on the psychology of women than could be incorporated into an introductory course. Several good resources that suggest a range of topics and projects are provided by Denmark (1983), Golub and Freedman (1987), and Russo and Malovich (1980, 1981); also see Chapter 3 by Bronstein and Paludi in this volume. It is especially helpful when colleagues share ideas and articles; a high point of our workshop and of our entire project was the sharing by faculty members of their expertise on topics in their own fields.

Design for the New Course

In order to establish a uniform base across the six sections of introductory psychology, we selected a common text and a common book of readings. No textbook totally met our requirements, and we eventually tried three in three different semesters. In the absence of a gender-balanced textbook, it is important to choose one that satisfies other criteria such as breadth of coverage or methodological rigor; we learned that it is easier to add scholarship on women, or even to elaborate on a text's biases, than to make up for overall weaknesses in content or presentation.

The supplementary reader we chose was *The Longest War: Sex Differences in Perspective* (Tavris & Offir, 1977; revised by Tavris & Wade, 1984), which provides chapters on the biological and psychological bases of behavior, as well as sociological and anthropological views. Although there are weaknesses in the book (particularly in regard to overgeneralization), we found that students enjoyed it, and it gave us a common basis for testing factual knowledge.

Individual professors were free to decide on the specific content of their course and the method of teaching. A large file of articles on many topics was made available to faculty along with a bibliography of those articles. Some faculty members also offered to lecture in one another's classes on topics in their area of expertise. The coordinator and two student assistants developed the file of articles and the bibliography, organized evaluation materials, tabulated and analyzed data, and facilitated communication among department members throughout the project.

Project Evaluation

Two of the participating faculty members designed the evaluation of the revised curriculum, which focused on four areas. It was designed to assess students' reactions to the method and content of the course, test their factual knowledge about women, and measure changes in their attitudes toward women and in their own personalities over the semester (using instruments taken from Spence & Helmreich, 1978). In addition, a form was designed for professors to rate their experiences and impressions of the course.

Project Outcomes

Since the outcomes of this project are reported more fully elsewhere (Rands, 1984), only a brief summary is presented here. Students' attitudes toward women did not change across the semester; however, ratings of their own personality traits showed them to be higher on traits traditionally considered to be masculine, but not on traits traditionally considered to be feminine, at the end of the semester than at its beginning. Compared with other introductory courses at Wheaton, ours was perceived by students to be more enjoyable, better at teaching them to question biases in data and theory, better at showing differences between women and men, and better at informing about the contributions of women in the field.

On the basis of professors' self-ratings, students were divided into groups based on how much their professor emphasized scholarship on women: There was a strong-emphasis group (3 female professors) and a moderate-emphasis group (1 female and 2 male professors). It is important to note that there were no differences in factual knowledge between these two groups of students. However, strong-emphasis classes were perceived as more valuable, with students reporting a greater understanding of human nature, interpersonal relationships, self, and career goals.

Strong-emphasis professors were perceived as more competent, fair, and sensitive than moderate-emphasis professors, and their students were more willing to recommend the course to others. They were rated higher on favorability toward and interest in women, and students in these classes reported more freedom to generate ideas or to disagree with issues pertaining to women. However, results regarding professors' effectiveness must be interpreted with caution because of the partial confounding of sex of professor with emphasis (all in the strong-emphasis group were female).

Professors also reported positive experiences in teaching the new course. It was intellectually stimulating to encounter new ideas and research which in some cases changed our own thinking about psychology and about women. It was also gratifying to work together as a department; several of our faculty were new at the time, and this project provided an opportunity to get to know one another. All of us were satisfied with our course changes and planned to continue with these changes; we enjoyed our role in helping to raise the consciousness of our young female students. Our negative experiences were not having enough time to assimilate new material, too much administrative discussion, concern about politicizing our students, and concern over trying to do too much.

Conclusion

In examining the content of our traditional course, we identified a number of important areas in which gender needed to be integrated into introductory psychology. As expected, we now incorporate more of this material into upper-level courses as well. Perhaps the most important outcomes of our efforts to revise the course are the benefits for students. Our students reported a better self-image, and we believe the project encouraged the development of critical thinking and better understanding of social issues. In order to succeed, the project required the following resources: a coordinator with release time for the project, a readily accessible collection of useful resource materials, a department-wide commitment to the project, and time for individual faculty members to incorporate the new materials into their individual courses. Designing and implementing the project was unexpectedly demanding, but it proved to be a worthwhile way of vitalizing our courses and of providing more equitable treatment of women in the curriculum.

References

Denmark, F. (1983). Integrating the psychology of women into introductory psychology. In C. J. Scheirer & A. Rogers (Eds.), *The G. Stanley Hall Lecture Series* (Vol. 3, pp. 33–75). Washington, DC: American Psychological Association.

Gilligan, C. (1982). *In a different voice: Psychological theory and women's development.* Cambridge, MA: Harvard University Press.

Golub, S., & Freedman, R. J. (Eds.). (1987). *Psychology of women: Resources for a core curriculum.* New York: Garland Press.

Rands, M. (1984, April). *Gender balance in the introductory psychology curriculum.* Presented at a meeting of the Eastern Psychological Association, Baltimore, MD.

Russo, N. F., & Malovich, N. J. (1980). Content on sex and gender: Introductory psychology. In J. M. Gappa & J. Pearce (Eds.), *Sex and gender in the social sciences: Reassessing the introductory course.* Washington, DC: U.S. Department of Education, Women's Educational Equity Act Program.

Russo, N. F., & Malovich, N. J. (1981). *Assessing the introductory psychology course.* Washington, DC: American Psychological Association.

Spanier, B., Bloom, A., & Boroviak, D. (1984). *Toward a balanced curriculum: A sourcebook for initiating gender integration projects.* Cambridge, MA: Schenkman.

Spence, J. T., & Helmreich, R. L. (1978). *Masculinity & femininity: Their psychological dimensions, correlates, and antecedents.* Austin: University of Texas Press.

Tavris, C., & Offir, C. (1977). *The longest war: Sex differences in perspective.* San Diego: Harcourt Brace Jovanovich.

Tavris, C., & Wade, C. (1984). *The longest war: Sex differences in perspective* (2nd ed.). San Diego: Harcourt Brace Jovanovich.

24

Kathryn Quina and Mary A. Kanarian

Continuing Education

According to the National Center for Education Statistics, 43% of the college students in the United States are age 25 or older, and 45% attend college part time (Hruby, 1985). Among women age 25 to 34, enrollment leaped 187% across all levels of higher education in the 1970s (Fisher-Thompson, 1980). Variously called "reentry," "resumed ed," or "continuing education" students, such adults are no longer an oddity but a fact of life in most college classrooms.

Continuing education constitutes a vital force in the future of higher education. One reason is economic: Schools have largely counteracted the population decline in the younger generation by attracting nontraditional students (Magarrell, 1983). At the same time, social changes, including rapid technological growth and increased leisure, have brought many adults into higher education (Entwistle, 1983). Yet, a surprising number of educators have failed to appreciate this trend (Hruby, 1985). Hodgkinson (1983) writes,

> In many cases instruction is carried on as if the [students] were normal postpubescent adolescents, while the average in the class may be 40, and the level of sophistication very high. (p. 11)

Compared with younger counterparts, older students are more diverse (Chickering, 1981): They are more likely to be women (Prahl & Hall, 1980), to be disabled (Asch, 1984), and in some programs to be members of a minority group. Their reasons for entering college are varied. Some people already in the work force seek retraining for different careers or new roles in current careers; for others, college is a dream delayed until children have entered school or preparation for a new or different self-sufficiency necessitated by divorce, disability, or death of a spouse. Whatever their motives, older students are especially attracted to course work in psychology because of their rich experience in human relationships (Entwistle, 1983). Thus, it is especially important for teachers of psychology classes to attend to the special needs and issues raised by the adult student population.

The number of programs geared to adult student populations has also increased dramatically; for example, programs targeting adult women increased from only 20 in the early 1960s to more than 500 by 1980 (Scott, 1980). The College of Continuing Education of the University of Rhode Island (URI), whose programs are described in this chapter,[1] was one of the earliest specialized degree programs

---

1. Information on programs described in this chapter is available from Kathryn Quina, Department of Psychology, University of Rhode Island, Kingston, RI 02881.

in the United States, starting with night courses for returning veterans in the 1940s and moving into programming for women in the early 1960s. Compared with traditional academic structures, the administrative environment of continuing education programs offers a particularly effective route to achieving awareness and appreciation of diversity. Flexible hours, locations, and budgets, along with a willingness to risk new types of programs, allow us to bring education to the community, and thus to new groups of people, and to adapt offerings to diverse student populations. We have offered psychology courses in seven locations, including onsite courses in a mental health facility. Special courses and workshops made possible by the continuing education format are also successful draws.

Instructional Considerations With Older Students

Special Problems and Constraints

Time and geographic mobility. Adult students usually have significant demands on their time beyond those of their courses. Most attend school part time, hold part- or full-time jobs, and have families in addition to attending school.[2] Arranging schedules can be a serious problem, particularly when child care is involved (Smallwood, 1980). In spite of these demands, most adult students manage time for their studies quite effectively. However, these constraints on their time mean that adults have to schedule their precious study hours carefully, often well in advance. A well-thought-out syllabus, with assignments and exam dates clearly indicated, is essential, and any changes should be negotiated with class members in advance. Reserve readings should be available early in the course, where they can be easily copied, because many students cannot spend long hours in the library. If extraclass activities such as attending a talk on a different evening are assigned, options must be provided for those whose schedules are not flexible.

Second, adult students do not have time for unfruitful work. In our experience, supplementary readings and homework assignments are pursued enthusiastically when they increase understanding of the material. However, tedious busywork, such as multiple homework problems on the same skill or extra reading that is not discussed or tied into the course goals or evaluation, is viewed dimly, as is the instructor who assigns it. Adult students also resent ambiguous goals or unguided tasks and appreciate knowing the kind of information on which to concentrate. Helpful techniques for defining goals and objectives and ways to present and evaluate learning without creating undue time burdens are available in teaching handbooks such as McKeachie (1986).

Lack of mobility is often a serious problem, especially for adults who are interested in graduate school but who because of family commitments cannot easily travel more than 50 miles. Advising these students requires empathy, a good set of strategies to maximize their chances for admission to a local program, and alternatives if they are unsuccessful. We have had great success placing students in

---

2. Based on data collected by the University of Rhode Island and by Quina et al. (1982).

local graduate programs, because they develop personal contacts through internships and research and achieve recognition and reputations for excellence among graduate admissions committee members (also see Halgin, 1986). More problems await adults in graduate school (Fisher-Thompson, 1980). The December 1986 American Psychological Association (APA) *Monitor* ("Parenting and part-time internships," p. 3) offered a discussion of the issues for adult women in graduate training and a description of one successful part-time clinical predoctoral internship program.

Rusty academic skills. Among our students, some hold advanced degrees, while others earned equivalency diplomas after dropping out of high school years ago. Many reentry students did not take college preparatory courses in high school, especially women who were routinely advised to enter business (i.e., secretarial) tracks. Performance-based admissions procedures have allowed continuing education to represent a fresh start for everyone. However, instructors must be conscious of the fact that study skills, particularly "test-wisdom," decline with the elapsed time since formal education, so that continuing education students often have deficiencies in academic skills (Taylor, Morgan, & Gibbs, 1981). Although well-developed verbal skills, general knowledge, and writing ability usually balance out adults' academic deficiencies, specific areas may be problematic. Timed exams and multiple-choice questions are not good measures of adult learning, in part because of age-related declines in speed of processing (Thompson, 1982) and in part because adults are simply not test-wise to the format. Reentry courses, such as the Pro-Seminar offered at URI, are very effective in rebuilding both skills and confidence (see also Prahl & Hall, 1980).

Math avoidance is another serious problem for many adult students. Unlike contemporary high school mathematics curricula that include calculus, algebra and trigonometry were the limit for even the brightest students over 30 years of age when they were teens. However, the major difficulty may not be lack of experience. Buerk (1985) has suggested that some of the anxiety expressed over mathematics arises from the effort to "make meaning" out of abstract material, which indicates high, not low, cognitive ability. Statistics and methodology instructors can relieve some problems by using thinking skills techniques (Halonen, 1987; Chapter 8 by Quina and Kulberg in this volume) and by taking time to answer student questions fully. Advisors should evaluate a student's math history and suggest ways to correct deficiencies before statistics courses are undertaken.

Minority and low-income access. In spite of their potential, one problem not effectively addressed by most continuing education programs is their failure to attract minority adults, particularly from low-income groups. Some excellent programs exist (Project on the Status and Education of Women, 1974); however, the vast majority of adult students nationally are White and of middle income (Greenberg, 1980). Unless financial aid for part-time, adult students becomes more widely available (Moran, 1986) and universities extend their commitments to include greater access both physically through locations in minority and low-income residential areas and psychologically through minority faculty, the educational and income gaps between members of the middle-class and the poor and between minorities and nonminorities will increase.

Joys and Challenges of Teaching Adult Students

Personal histories. Adults bring to the college classroom an extraordinary collection of life experiences. Using the Holmes–Rahe Life Stress Scale (Holmes & Rahe, 1967) expanded to include experiences such as rape, our sample of 50 female students collectively had experienced every single event except a jail sentence (Quina et al., 1982). Adult students' histories also include a rich array of careers and accomplishments. Among our students over the past 10 years are retired and current state legislators, engineers, scientists, and teachers. Many have lived and worked in other countries. Their volunteer work includes accomplishments such as coaching a national championship skating team, running a drug and alcohol treatment program, and founding a community action group.

The first implication is that for this group, a professor does not have a traditional authority role. Rather, the teaching role is one of an expert in her or his field of study—a role respected and valued by the adult student but restricted in its scope (see Chickering, 1981). One way to conceptualize this role is as a paid consultant to the learning process. As a consultant, the teacher respects and appreciates the client, listens to her or his needs, and provides the services of promoting knowledge and understanding and helping students develop skills.

A second implication is that classroom interaction can be expanded to incorporate learning from students' experiences. Discussions can be stimulated without the grueling efforts often needed to get younger students to talk. We present formal definitions of a concept and elicit examples from students' own lives. Journals and newspaper searches for applied examples also work well. However, we must offer two warnings from our experience: (a) Some students, particularly one of a kind in the class, do not like to be singled out to give the minority view; and (b) younger students may not appreciate favoritism to an older student's perceived wisdom and need to enter their own active discovery process. Therefore, discussions need to be balanced in such a way that all views and all students are respected, and students of different cohorts can learn from one another.

The third implication is that content that interests older students may differ from content that interests younger students. For example, in the developmental psychology class, we have found that younger students are often fascinated by prenatal and postnatal development, whereas most parents do not want to hear about how entertaining babies' development can be, but rather are very concerned about their maddening teens and their aging parents. The popular movie *Back to School* humorously illustrates the real problems for successful entrepreneurs in some theoretical business classes. The challenge of providing equivalent content to traditional courses—the same theories, data, and methods—in a context appropriate for the lives of these students is compounded by the fact that textbooks are seldomly addressed to older readers (Quina, Kanarian, & Rorbaugh, 1981). Paludi (1986) has offered an excellent comprehensive developmentally based package for the psychology of women course with different resources for each topic that appeal differentially to older and younger students. In fact, our adult students virtually take over the instruction of the psychology of women course by midsemester, because they start from a life-stage in which the gender issues raised by textbooks are personal realities.

In any course, students should be encouraged to examine the validity of the theories and examples presented. If they do not apply to students' life experiences, the instructor can use this opportunity to discuss the material's shortcomings. We have found that such discussions have led to research ideas and student projects.

Adult students are also likely to have widely varying interests within a course. Allowing independent work on a topic of the students' choice can greatly enhance interest and learning. For example, in introductory or developmental psychology, students read a popular psychology book of their choice (e.g., Sheehy, 1979) and critique it according to theoretical and empirical guidelines discussed in class. In social and organizational psychology, students apply concepts to situations in their daily or work lives in essays and class discussions. Such individualized assignments also allow for personal meaning in the student's relationship with the material, a concept described further in the next sections.

Motivating factors. We tend to regard younger students, perhaps inappropriately, as if they are in school to grow up, including developing their identities and seeking marriage partners (Erikson, 1963), preparing to enter society (Bennett, in Hruby, 1985), and obtaining job skills in order to earn money. Older students enter school for the more varied reasons we have described. Whatever their specific reason, however, adults seem to share an important common thread of personal development as a primary motivation for returning to school (Entwistle, 1983).

The presence of highly motivated students in the classroom is a joy as well as a challenge. Eagerness to learn means attentive, active listening; but the demanding learner also requires that the instructor be prepared to respond to questions and provide new information. Performance in school is often tied to issues of self-esteem, especially for women (Geisler & Thrush, 1975). Eagerness to achieve drives these students to excellence in performance, but also brings out a high need for feedback and encouragement. Greenberg (1980) suggested ways to address these needs directly.

Courses can also be used to attract and retain students from underrepresented groups. For example, among our successful graduates are several persons with alcohol-troubled histories, who were initially attracted to our campus by a special certificate program in alcohol counseling. Our interdisciplinary Summer Institute in Women's Studies, "Strategies for Sexual Equality" (Quina & Paxson, 1987), has demonstrated the importance of a course addressing relevant issues and offering competent role models to adult women students who are unsure about school and about themselves.

Motivational factors also affect extraclassroom interactions. Although older students are more self-directed, they also often take up more time asking questions and reviewing plans and frequently need more anxiety management than do younger students. Awards and honors, as external recognitions of achievement, carry special significance for adult students. Yet many schools fail to recognize good performance among part-time students; for example, our Dean's List, Honors Program, and other awards were not available to part-time students until a group of us worked to change university policies.

Cognitive processes. In the past 20 years, an exciting literature on adult cognitive processes has emerged (e.g., Belenky, Clinchy, Goldberger, & Tarule, 1986;

Chickering, 1975; Knefelcamp & Slepitza, 1978; Weathersby, 1977), based largely on Perry's (1970) work on intellectual development during the college years. These researchers suggest that adult students are often more intellectually sophisticated, in terms of Perry's (1970) schema, than traditionally aged students. Specifically, older students are more capable of dealing with relativism and unresolved dilemmas than their younger counterparts, who are more likely to think in dualistic terms of right versus wrong. Other related measures, such as ego development (Loevinger, 1976), reveal similar maturity in adult students, more of whom are capable of postconventional thinking (Chickering, 1975; Weathersby, 1981). Our research suggested that coping with major life events (e.g., death of a child or spouse, divorce, disability) is related to adult students' greater complexity of thinking (Quina, Kanarian, & Stang, 1981).

The increased range of intellectual styles in the classroom requires more flexibility in teaching. The disadvantages of teaching a relativistic thinker from dualistic right-or-wrong material and vice-versa are well documented (Buerk, 1985; Perry, 1970). Knefelcamp (1974) described developmental assignments that optimize each student's own level of cognitive sophistication. Another interesting approach uses these developmental theories for classroom reading and discussion (with special focus on learning styles), helping students learn both about themselves and developmental psychology while acquiring good academic skills (Chickering, 1975).

At the same time, research summarized by Entwistle (1983) suggested that adult students who have not had previous experience with higher education may have a misconception of what the advanced learning process involves. Although they may possess more sophisticated abilities, some enter school expecting the rote memorization of factual details because of their educational histories and adopt a surface approach of studying material with the intention of identifying potential examination questions. In contrast, a deep approach attempts to extract personal meaning from the material, utilizing conceptual skills beyond memorization. The deep approach fosters better understanding, greater factual recall, and higher test scores (Marton & Saljo, 1976). This personal link to material also is more satisfying, making deep learning especially beneficial for adult learners (Entwistle, 1983).

Exercises and discussion can help students practice deep learning skills, especially when students expect to be evaluated on higher conceptual levels of learning. We have found that adult students quickly learn to extract general principles with practice in class discussions. For example, in an exercise in the Psychology of Women class, students list stereotypes of battered women, mothers of incest victims, and wives of adulterous men, and then identify the common themes—they are viewed as nagging, unattractive or unkempt, and nonsexual and are blamed for the men's actions. We then use class readings to list actual data countering these stereotypes and discuss the role of stereotypes in perpetuating the phenomenon of blaming the victim. Preparation for examinations includes handouts on the types of items to expect based on Bloom's taxonomy (Bloom, Englehart, Furst, Hill, & Krathwohl, 1956) and practice questions. Where appropriate, we use take-home essay exams that demand integration of ideas from several sources of information. Other specific assignments and class exercises that increase the personal meaning of material are located throughout this volume.

On a larger scale, some continuing education programs have redesigned the entire curriculum to meet adult students' special intellectual needs and demands. Mentkowski and Doherty (1984) described an exciting program for adult women students built on such active learning experiences that target communication, analysis, problem solving, values, and personal responsibility.

Professional Continuing Education

Continuing education offers another important mechanism for increasing sensitivity to women and minorities. Through advanced professional development workshops and courses, we can reach out, retrain, and revise the perspectives and practices of teachers, clinicians, and other service providers who completed their training before contemporary scholarship on women and minorities was widely available. Surveys on continuing education programming have shown that a substantial number of professionals will attend a program that offers an opportunity to gain knowledge or skills that will enrich them personally or professionally (Quina & Crowley, 1984). At URI, we offer summer Alternate Therapies Workshops on topics such as child sexual abuse to professionals and advanced graduate students at convenient hours and locations. Weekend formats are particularly appealing to working participants.

Many states require advanced-level continuing education for maintaining professional licensure in fields such as psychology, nursing, and social work. Workshops on issues of importance to women and minority clients can be used to meet those requirements. The process of obtaining endorsement by the responsible professional state or national association is time consuming and requires planning, but it is usually worth the investment.[3]

References

Asch, A. (1984). The experience of disability: A challenge for psychology. *American Psychologist, 39,* 529–536.

Belenky, M. F., Clinchy, B. M., Goldberger, N. R., & Tarule, J. M. (1986). *Women's ways of knowing.* New York: Basic Books.

Buerk, D. (1985). The voices of women making meaning in mathematics. *Journal of Education, 167*(3), 59–70.

Bloom, B. S., Englehart, N. D., Furst, E. J., Hill, W. H., & Krathwohl, D. R. (1956). *Taxonomy of educational objectives. Handbook I: Cognitive domain.* New York: McKay.

---

3. Division 35 of the American Psychological Association (APA) presents workshops on issues related to women and minorities. Current programs for psychologists offered by endorsed sponsors are listed each month in the APA *Monitor.* Information on becoming an endorsed continuing education sponsor in psychology, as well as a list of current sponsors, is available from the Continuing Education Programs Office, American Psychological Association, 1200 Seventeenth Street, N.W., Washington, DC 20036.

Chickering, A. (1975). Adult development—implications for higher education. In C. E. Cavert (Ed.), *Conference proceedings: Designing Diversity '75* (2nd National Conference on Open Learning and Nontraditional Study, pp. 203–219). Lincoln, NE: University of Mid-America.

Chickering, A. (Ed.). (1981). *The modern American college.* San Francisco: Jossey Bass.

Entwistle, N. (1983). Learning and teaching in universities: The challenge of the part-time adult student. In R. Bourne (Ed.), *Part-time first degrees in universities.* London: Goldsmiths' College. (Available from ISEM, 10429 Barnes Way, St. Paul, MN 55075)

Erikson, E. (1963). *Childhood and society* (2nd ed.). New York: Norton.

Fisher-Thompson, J. (1980). *Re-entry women and graduate school.* Washington, DC: Association of American Colleges, Project on the Status and Education of Women.

Geisler, M. P., & Thrush, R. S. (1975). Counseling experiences and needs of older women students. *Journal of the National Association of Women Deans, Administrators, and Counselors, 39*(1), 3–7.

Greenberg, E. (1980). Designing programs for learners of all ages. *New Directions for Higher Education, 29,* 103–106.

Halgin, R. P. (1986). Advising undergraduates who wish to become clinicians. *Teaching of Psychology, 13*(1), 7–12.

Halonen, J. S. (Ed.). (1986). *Teaching critical thinking in psychology.* Milwaukee, WI: Alverno Institute.

Hodgkinson, H. (1983). *Guess who's coming to college: Your students in 1990.* Washington, DC: National Institute of Independent Colleges and Universities.

Holmes, T. H., & Rahe, R. H. (1967). The Social Readjustment Rating Scale. *Journal of Psychosomatic Research, 11,* 213–218.

Hruby, N. J. (1985). MIA: The nontraditional student. *Academe, 71*(5), 26–27.

Knefelcamp, L. L. (1974). Developmental instruction: Fostering intellectual and personal growth of college students. *Dissertation Abstracts International, 36*(3): 1271A.

Knefelcamp, L. L., & Slepitza, R. (1978). A cognitive–developmental model of career development: An adaptation of the Perry scheme. *The Counseling Psychologist, 6*(3), 53–58.

Loevinger, J. (1976). *Ego development: Conceptions and theories.* San Francisco: Jossey-Bass.

Magarrell, J. (1983). Early surveys find enrollment holding steady. *Chronicle of Higher Education, 28*(11), 1, 18–19.

Marton, F., & Saljo, R. (1976). On qualitative differences in learning: I. Outcome and process. *British Journal of Educational Psychology, 46,* 4–11.

McKeachie, W. J. (1986). *Teaching tips: A guidebook for the beginning college teacher* (8th ed.). Lexington, MA: Heath.

Mentkowski, M., & Doherty, A. (1984). Abilities that last a lifetime: Outcomes of the Alverno experience. *AAHE Bulletin, 36*(6), 5–24.

Moran, M. (1986). *Student financial aid and women: Equity dilemma* (Report 5). Washington, DC: Association for the Study of Higher Education.

Paludi, M. (1986). Teaching the psychology of gender roles: Some life-stage considerations. *Teaching of Psychology, 13,* 133–138.

Perry, W. G. (1970). *Intellectual and ethical development in the college years.* New York: Holt, Rinehart & Winston.

Prahl, E., & Hall, R. M. (1980). *Confidence and competence: Basic skills programs and refresher courses for re-entry women.* Washington, DC: Association of American Colleges, Project on the Status and Education of Women.

Project on the Status and Education of Women. (1974). *Recruiting minority women, No. 2.* Washington, DC: Association of American Colleges.

Quina, K., & Crowley, J. (1983). *Continuing education survey.* Report submitted to American Psychological Association Division 35.

Quina, K., Kanarian, M., & Rorbaugh, J. B. (1981, August). *Value of gender-related balance in continuing education instruction.* Presented at the annual meeting of the American Psychological Association, Los Angeles.

Quina, K., Kanarian, M., & Stang, D. (1982, March). *Stress and role conflict in the BMOC (Busy Mom on Campus)*. Presented at the annual meeting of the Association for Women in Psychology, Seattle.

Quina, K., Kanarian, M., Stang, D., Buttenbaum, M., Marceau, M., & Angell, J. (1982, March). *The older woman in school: Research and intervention models*. Presented at the New England Association for Women in Psychology Conference on the Psychology of Women, Boston.

Quina, K., & Paxson, M. A. (1987). *The Women's Studies Summer Institute: A feminist awareness experience*. Presented at the annual meeting of the Association for Women in Psychology, Denver.

Scott, N. A. (1980). *Returning women students: A review of research and descriptive studies*. Washington, DC: National Association for Women Deans, Administrators, and Counselors.

Sheehy, G. (1979). *Passages*. New York: Bantam.

Smallwood, K. B. (1980). What do adult women college students really need? *Journal of College Student Personnel, 21*, 65–73.

Taylor, E., Morgan, A. R., & Gibbs, C. (1981). The orientations of Open University students to their studies. *Teaching at a Distance, 20*, 3–12.

Thompson, D. (1982). Adult development. In Mitzel, H. E. (Ed.), *Encyclopedia of educational research*, Vol. 1 (5th ed.) (pp. 76–83). London: Collier Macmillan.

Weathersby, R. P. (1977). *A developmental perspective on adults' uses of formal education*. Doctoral dissertation, Harvard University, Graduate School of Education.

Weathersby, R. P. (1981). Ego development. In A. W. Chickering (Ed.), *The modern American college* (pp. 51–75). San Francisco: Jossey-Bass.

25

Vickie M. Mays

The Integration of Ethnicity and Gender Into Clinical Training: The UCLA Model

In the last decade, there has been an increasing awareness of clinical psychology's need to prepare its members for effective practice and culturally sensitive research with racially and culturally diverse populations (Bernal & Padilla, 1982; Green, 1981; Ridley, 1985; Sarf, 1980; Wyatt & Parham, 1985). This chapter presents a discussion of issues and methods for integrating gender and ethnicity into clinical psychology training programs.

Conceptualization of a Training Model

One major philosophical question regarding the inclusion of gender and ethnic content in clinical training is whether to incorporate these issues into existing courses or to develop specific courses (Bernal & Padilla, 1982). I believe that a comprehensive approach works best. In a training model of this type, ethnic and gender issues are taught within the preexisting core clinical courses and then balanced with specialty courses at an advanced level. Using this approach, the core clinical courses, which cover areas such as psychopathology, personality organization, and assessment, provide students with an awareness of the ubiquitous effects of ethnicity and gender at the very heart of clinical psychology (Korchin, 1980). Specialty courses on ethnic or gender concerns are then used to provide in-depth coverage of specific clinical topics (e.g., Black women's mental health, African American family).

Several models have been designed to provide ethnic and cultural training in mental health, including the Mental Health Project at Brandeis University, the University of Hawaii, and the University of Miami School of Medicine. Lefley (1984) described the Miami model, which is based on four types of training modalities: didactic, cultural immersion, practicum experiences, and goal-oriented planning. Each of these modalities is designed to increase participants' awareness, skills, and knowledge of the mental health concerns of ethnic minorities.

The author would like to thank Dr. Evalina Bestman for comments on an earlier draft. All statements in this manuscript represent solely the view of the author and not the policies or views of the clinical training program at the University of California at Los Angeles.

Training in the Miami model begins with didactic sessions that include historical overviews of mental health factors among diverse ethnic groups. Lectures provide information on religion, value systems, sex roles, world views, cultural beliefs, supernatural belief systems (including Haitian voodoo, Bahamian obeah, Black American root healing, and African Cuban santeria), and alternative healing methods. In particular, didactic sessions attempt to provide information on normative behaviors, life-styles, stressors, patterns of coping, and sources of informal support for each of the ethnic groups.

Then, cultural immersion is used to involve trainees: participant-observation of street and church experiences, visits to ethnic community clinics, and occasionally client home visits. Observations from these visits are used by trainees in follow-up classroom discussions. Classroom experiences using videotapes, role-plays, and simulations of therapist–client interactions provide practicum opportunities. The University of Miami School of Medicine training ends with the development of specific plans by the participants for incorporating this training into their clinical work.

Experiences at the University of Miami indicate that this excellent model is best used with advanced trainees. Its adaptation might work well within a psychology training clinic or in conjunction with a local community mental health center, where preestablished working relationships with the ethnic community exist.

The University of California at Los Angeles (UCLA) model of minority mental health training is best suited to a scientist and practitioner program. The model is designed to address two training goals: (a) training competent and culturally knowledgeable minority scientists and practitioners, and (b) training multiculturally effective nonminority scientists and practitioners (Myers & Baker, 1986). In addressing the first concern, the aim is not merely to increase the number of minority clinicians, but also to provide them with a training experience that addresses the issues they will encounter in their professional lives while teaching, conducting research, administering and delivering clinical or consulting services, and participating in professional activities.

Following from these two goals are several program objectives (Myers & Baker, 1986, pp. 7–8):

1. Increasing the number of ethnic minority students in existing graduate training.

2. Changing the narrow, ethnocentric biases prevalent in existing clinical models of assessment, diagnosis, treatment, and research.

3. Incorporating culturally varied clientele into supervised clinical practicum training and addressing the basic problems and issues at the core of cross-ethnic, cross-class, and cross-gender psychotherapy and supervision encounters.

4. Attending to the issues of acculturation as an important factor in mental health of upwardly mobile ethnic minorities, for both clients and clinicians.

5. Training culturally diverse nonminority clinicians.

In sum, the goals of the UCLA Minority Mental Health Training Program are not merely to increase the number of minority students, but also, through ongoing efforts of the Program's faculty and students, to work toward changing the cultural and gender biases that exist in current models of treatment, assessment, research, and clinical practica (Myers & Baker, 1986).

Implementation of Training

Changes in training programs usually originate from demands outside the training program itself. For example, clinical psychology broadened its scope of training when psychologists were called on to supply their expertise in schools, community settings, and family psychotherapy, in addition to working in hospitals in traditional areas of diagnosis and treatment (Clark, 1973). Changes in clinical psychology relevant to ethnic and gender issues have often been the result of political and educational efforts in psychology or society at large (Sue, 1983). Enforcement of culturally relevant training comes through various American Psychological Association (APA) mechanisms such as program accreditation, which require sensitivity to ethnic and gender issues or through APA's human resource monitoring (Howard, et al., 1986). At the state level, legislation is being enacted that would require candidates for licensure to demonstrate knowledge of specific psychological issues for ethnic groups (Wyatt & Parham, 1985). In addition to these long-term methods of implementation, there are other short-term remedies that may result in increased ethnic and gender awareness in clinical training.

Faculty

Ideally, every clinical training program should have a multiethnic and gender-balanced faculty who would offer coverage of ethnic and gender issues in core, as well as specialty, courses. Current human resource projections, however, indicate this is not possible (Howard et al., 1986). For example, although the number of Blacks receiving degrees in clinical psychology is increasing, they tend to find employment in the health services sector. In addition, Asian Americans and American Indians continue not to be attracted to psychology in significant numbers. Therefore, department chairs and clinical training directors must seek innovative ways to offer courses and experiences that help students to understand racial, ethnic, and gender issues.

One method may be through role swapping (Romero & Pickney, 1980). In many university settings, ethnic minorities, although not in tenure-track psychology slots, can be found in service-provider roles or staff positions in the university's counseling center, health or medical school, placement center, or special programs as academic counselors. Role swapping, as advocated by Romero and Pickney, encourages these individuals to provide course offerings in the psychology department in exchange for a reduced service or administrative load. This idea could be extended to include mutual exchanges between psychology departments or psychology training programs and the person's administrative unit in a manner beneficial to each participant. For example, psychology department faculty or clinical training staff could provide supervision time, evaluation services, research consultation, or long-term therapy services in exchange for an ethnic staff member from another university administrative unit teaching, providing supervision, or conducting workshops for clinical psychology trainees.

For psychology departments not in urban areas, it may be particularly advantageous to work out a system of mutual exchange if their trainees are not getting exposure to racially and culturally diverse populations (Halgin, 1986). Many universities have special programs for counseling and tutoring ethnic minority and low-income students. Staff in these programs are often ethnic minority mental health professionals. These programs could serve as practicum sites or research settings. Psychology departments teaching courses on intervention techniques, evaluation methods, community psychology, or social systems may find these programs as ideal potential sites for student projects.

Departments that maintain a psychology training clinic may find that ethnic minority practitioners, in exchange for university affiliation, would provide clinical supervision or research opportunities for trainees working with ethnic clients. In psychology clinics with a paucity of ethnic clients, ethnic minority practitioners from private practice or local community mental health settings may be willing to develop videotapes of diagnostic interviews, clinical interventions, or therapy sessions with ethnic clients with necessary assistance or resources provided by the university. If the university is unable to provide the expertise and equipment necessary to produce videotapes, then audiotapes illustrating ethnic and cultural issues in the management of core clinical issues such as the handling of missed appointments, dealing with clients' reactions to racism, or racial or cultural bias in assessment and diagnosis can be very useful to university faculty and students. Video- or audiotapes archived from presentations by guest lecturers, focusing on ethnic and gender issues, can also serve as training resources. This latter approach can help compensate for the dearth of published research on ethnic issues. The Psychology Training Clinic at UCLA maintains a collection of audiotapes of its weekly guest lecturer presentations for student and faculty use.

Where ethnic minority or female psychologists are unavailable, department chairs or directors of clinical training may find it useful to contact the APA's Distinguished Lecturers Program for a resource person. Other strategies include seeking funds for ethnic and women visiting scholars through pre- and postdoctoral training grants. For example, funds were obtained through UCLA's postdoctoral minority training grant for week-long in-residence visits by senior ethnic scholars to present colloquia and luncheon talks and meet informally with students, faculty, and practicum supervisors (Myers & Baker, 1986).

Courses

Sue (1981) has underscored the need for courses that increase awareness of the history, strengths, and needs of ethnic and racial groups. He advocated that these courses must go beyond a cognitive focus on racial and ethnic issues to incorporate both affective and skill (i.e., practicum) components for working with members of these groups. In the UCLA clinical training program, one required practicum experience consists of a series of advanced psychological methods courses that begins in the second year of the curriculum. For example, students take a two-quarter advanced sequence in psychological assessment, including lectures by ethnic faculty, case material, videotapes, and guest lecturers on the intricacies of assessment with various ethnic groups. They are also required to take a third course in this series, which involves a clinical placement. This course can include marital therapy, behavior modification, family therapy, clinical interventions with children, interpersonal processes, or a course that I teach called Political,

Social, and Economic Issues in the Delivery of Services to Ethnic Minorities. Students with a particular interest in working with ethnic minorities are assisted in finding appropriate placements for this practicum component. Sites for these practica have included Veterans Administration hospitals, UCLA's Psychology Training Clinic, community mental health centers, community groups, and legislative offices.

Some Final Thoughts

Graduate clinical programs need to consider the resources they are willing to commit to achieve ethnic and racial diversity in their training. Suggested program goals are given in Fortune (1979). Assistance in developing ethnic and racial diversity and awareness is available in the form of consultation with ethnic scholars from either APA's Distinguished Lecturers Program or the appropriate Board of Ethnic Minority Affairs committee (e.g., the Committee on Ethnic Minority Human Resource Development). However, the development of a comprehensive and diverse training program also requires mobilization of local resources, as well as creative approaches to implementing programmatic changes at a local level.

For psychology departments with limited resources, it may be useful to identify resources that exist in other programs and departments, for example, counseling, education, public health, nursing, sociology, personnel and guidance, urban planning, African American studies, Chicano studies, and women's studies. Courses in these departments on ethnic or gender issues in mental health may provide an excellent balance to the clinical student's training experience.

Priority should be placed on the recruitment and retention of a critical mass of ethnic faculty and students. In the long run, this is what makes an ethnically diverse training program viable. At a faculty level, it may also be necessary to monitor the gender balance of the faculty to ensure that sufficient numbers of women are present to act as role models for students. A critical mass of minority and women faculty will also help ensure stability and prevent overload on any one individual in representing the minority and female perspectives. However, although it is important to have ethnic minority and women faculty members, it is deleterious to the underlying purpose of these programs if they alone carry the responsibility for bringing ethnicity and gender into the training program. To truly integrate these issues within the discipline of psychology, all members of the clinical faculty must take it upon themselves to develop and monitor their awareness and knowledge of, and skills for dealing with, gender and ethnic issues in clinical practice and research.

This integrative goal is an important element of the success of the UCLA clinical training program. The UCLA program provides an atmosphere in which all students take seriously the importance of ethnic and gender issues in their clinical training, because these issues may be raised by nonethnic faculty. As an example, concern with how ethnicity and gender influence clinical practice is an area of assessment in the second-year oral exams that clinical students are required to pass in order to advance in the program. Students are aware in preparing their clinical case presentations for a two-faculty examiner team that they must be able to discuss the research and practice issues of ethnic and gender issues. Each faculty member, regardless of ethnic background or gender, assesses the students' competency in this area. Hence, both the faculty and the students are reminded of the program's commitment and perspective on the scholarly importance of these issues. Our experience demonstrates that the integration of gender and ethnicity in clinical training may best be accomplished as a program philosophy, rather than as mere curriculum inclusions.

References

Bernal, M., & Padilla, A. (1982). Status of minority curricula and training in clinical psychology. *American Psychologist, 37*, 780–787.

Clark, R. R. (1973). The socialization of clinical psychologists. *Professional Psychology, 4*(3), 329–340.

Fortune, R. C. (1979). Multicultural education: A part of basic education? *Multicultural Education: Theory into Practice, 2*(2), 118–124.

Green, L. (1981). Training psychologists to work with minority clients: A prototypic model with Black clients. *Professional Psychology, 12*(6), 732–739.

Halgin, R. P. (1986). Problems of service and research in psychology department clinics. *Professional Psychology: Research and Practice, 17*(2), 131–135.

Howard, A., Pion, G. M., Gottfredson, G. D., Flattau, P. E., Oskamp, S., Pfafflin, S. M., Bray, D. W., & Burstein, A. G. (1986). The changing face of American psychology: A report from the Committee on Employment and Human Resources. *American Psychologist, 41*(12), 1311–1327.

Korchin, S. J. (1980). Clinical psychology and minority problems. *American Psychologist, 35*(3), 262–269.

Lefley, H. P. (1984). Cross-cultural training for mental health professionals: Effects on the delivery of services. *Hospital and Community Psychiatry, 35*(12), 1227–1229.

Myers, H., & Baker, B. L. (1986). National Institute of Mental Health clinical training grant proposal submitted to National Institute of Mental Health, Rockville, MD. Unpublished manuscript, University of California at Los Angeles.

Ridley, C. (1985). Imperatives for ethnic and cultural relevance in psychology training programs. *Professional Psychology: Research and Practice, 16*(5), 611–622.

Romero, D., & Pickney, J. (1980). Role swapping: An antidote to professional burnout. *Counselor Education and Supervision, 20*, 6–14.

Sarf, H. (1980). Psychologists need integrated education in political–social and psychological theory. *Political Psychology, 2*(2), 118–126.

Sue, D. W. (1981). *Counseling the culturally different: Theory and practice.* New York: Wiley.

Sue, S. (1983). Ethnic minority issues in psychology: A reexamination. *American Psychologist, 38*, 583–592.

Wyatt, G. E., & Parham, W. (1985). The inclusion of culturally sensitive course materials in graduate school and training programs. *Psychotherapy: Theory, Research, Practice and Training, 22*(2S), 461–468.

26

Kathryn Quina and Phyllis Bronstein

Epilogue

The scholars contributing to this volume are committed in their personal and professional lives to creating and teaching a psychology that is representative and equitable. Some have performed extensive literature searches and created extremely useful bibliographies; several have authored or presented scholarly papers on their subjects; all have developed exemplary ways to incorporate that scholarship into their teaching. This commitment has not been without its professional costs, but it has also brought personal rewards. For this closing chapter, we asked the authors to describe, in personal terms, the costs, the challenges, and the joys they experienced in their own paths toward curriculum reform. We share some of their experiences, in an effort to provide models of personal courage and to make it easier for others who step forward as agents of change.

The Costs

The most common negative experience was a feeling of isolation. Some of the authors were (or had been at one time) the only woman or the only minority in their home departments. The problem of being the token has been discussed by Yoder and Sinnett (1985), and the scholar who finds herself or himself in such a situation is urged to read the personal accounts and suggestions in Rose (1986) and Ruddick and Daniels (1977).

Another negative experience reported by the contributors was being treated as a marginal scholar because their research subject was minorities or women. One author wrote:

> The prevailing attitude among the _____ administration is one of contempt for ethnic studies . . . reflected, for example, in the derogation of work published in ethnic minority journals. If the journal is new, or embedded within a Third World matrix, the response [has been] stinging, vitriolic, and defamatory.

In fact, professional acceptance was not a typical experience. Several of the authors were not granted tenure, had serious problems during the tenure process, or had left a position because they anticipated or experienced such problems. Devaluation of work by women and minorities is well documented in the research literature (Kahn & Robbins, 1985; Levinger, 1987; Sandler & Hall, 1986). One of the more senior authors adopted a proactive stand on this issue, sending copies of a research article from Kahn and Robbins (1985) to several administrators as a timely reminder during a merit review of more junior women colleagues. Perhaps we can all learn from her courageous example.

Regardless of gender or race, efforts to improve teaching were not always received warmly. One contributor was warned against putting time into an instructional development program because it would "look bad"—if she had time for teaching, she must not have enough research ideas!

If teaching is not valued, teaching about minorities or women is even more risky for the faculty member. A few of the authors experienced direct hostility about their classes in ethnic, minority, or women's studies:

> [I felt] administrative reluctance to require or even offer courses of diversity on a regular basis. The tendency is to do so when students request it or a site visit is expected.

Another wrote:

> Although students who have taken these courses have given unanimously positive evaluations, enrollments remain low. Some students have told me that their advisors have told them not to take such a "fluff" course, but rather to concentrate on "more serious" courses. One semester the course was left out of the departmental listing.

The general problem of devaluation of teaching by women, which undoubtedly applies to minority or ethnic professors, is discussed by Unger (1977). This devaluation may come in the form of a sneak attack: vicious attacks from students on teacher evaluations, especially frustrating because the teachers were not able to work on the issues in the classroom.

> The thing that really hurts is when you get back your teacher evaluations and realize that some students are harboring hostility about your inclusion of nontraditional research that wasn't expressed during the class, even though I tried to run a very open class.

The Challenges

Several authors warned about particular challenges that revising the curriculum can create. For those integrating gender or minority issues into a mainstream course, there is always the potential for charges of bias (discussed in Hyde, 1985, Chapter 1). This dynamic may arise when a nonminority or a male student hears discussion about racist or sexist behaviors and reacts defensively (e.g., "my instructor hates men"). An experienced instructor suggested that defensive student reactions should be anticipated early. She articulates an assumption—over and over—that we are all basically racist and sexist and that the goal is not to target individuals but to explore the issues.

A related challenge is the problem student: the hostile student, often a male or not a member of a minority group, who feels threatened by the material or by the reversal of classroom power.

> I had an older man who just wouldn't stop making sexist jokes and disagreeing with me (arguing that I must have misunderstood the data, for example, although he had never read the text). He insulted other students (including men) regularly by denying their experiences. I tried to be nice, but it didn't help. Class energy was going into anger at him, which of course gave him attention (which he wanted). Finally one day I confronted him, politely but firmly describing what was happening in the classroom process, and asked him to be quiet unless he had something positive to contribute. After class, the other students thanked me, and he apologized—he admitted he had really been out of line. I also found out he made a habit of taking classes from young women and harassing them.

As a solution, one experienced instructor suggested:

> Whenever possible, I try to let the other students handle a disruptive student—it's amazing what a little peer pressure can do to an obnoxious class member, especially if one person is holding others back.

Another challenge is raised by the students who take a course on women or ethnic minorities and who are not members of that particular group themselves. Many students who could benefit from such a course do not enroll if the course is not a requirement; but if it is required, they may express hostility. This is always a delicate issue, and one that many of the authors have discussed in this volume.

Walsh (1986) discussed another problem regarding courses that draw minority and women students such as those on the Psychology of Women. The class discussions and readings raise consciousness—and anger— about discrimination. Younger students in particular do not want to hear that they may face hardships or barriers to success in their future and may react with rejection. Understanding the source of students' reactions is a first step. Helping students channel their anger into useful, positive goals becomes an additional task for the instructor.

> I always spend the last class (in Psychology of Women) in a group discussion with a positive, problem-solving focus—listing small goals that seem more attainable, things they can do to be a part of the solution. I also describe internship sites such as the rape crisis center or women's shelter and encourage them to take advantage of our volunteer-for-credit program. Many of them do and report that being able to act on their concerns is one of the most important outcomes of the course.

A more general problem arises with younger students. Students may not have gained much historical or wider social perspective from prior learning; thus, the instructor of a course that utilizes those perspectives may find it necessary to teach some basic material as well as the intended subject matter. For example, one instructor reported:

> I was really surprised to realize that most of my students didn't know anything about the Holocaust or Vietnam. Thus I had to give them a history lesson along with my psychology lesson. They were equally surprised about this new in-depth psychological perspective on what had previously been only names and dates. It spurred me to develop my presentation more fully, and I believe my students have come to appreciate the psychological meaningfulness of those events.

Finally, there is the problem of the instructor who, having students' trust, becomes the "ear" for many students who share the isolation and frustration of being a minority or who have experienced various forms of discrimination. The prevalence of these experiences and the seriousness of some students' problems can seem overwhelming. The instructors who mentioned this problem to us felt that it was important not to ignore these students' issues, but warned that new faculty would need to locate other resources for referral (such as the student counseling center) and to set limits early in their relationships with students.

> One of the toughest situations I experience is when students come to me and confide about instructors who have been racist or sexist, and I can't do anything about it. Years ago, as a powerless assistant professor, I heard sexual harassment complaints, but at the time there was no campus policy, and nobody I talked to would listen. All I could do was commiserate with students. Now I have more power to help, but it is still risky to confront or get involved in a student complaint against a colleague.

Another wrote:

> It seems like every minority student on campus has come to see me at one time or another, and most of them have taken my course—my enrollments are higher than others', but of course I don't get an assistant. I appreciate students' support of me, but I also can't get my work done unless I stay away from campus. Then my colleagues think I'm not contributing. It's been a real dilemma.

The role of academic mentor is an important one, as the testimony of Walter Massey (1987), a Black theoretical physicist, revealed:

> In my fourth year, when it seemed to me that I would never complete my dissertation or be able to compete in the world of theoretical physics, I went to my thesis advisor and told him I wanted to quit. In fact, I sat in his office and cried. But he had a confidence in my ability to succeed that I did not have myself. . . . Unfortunately, not everyone is so fortunate. Minority students . . . often find it unavailable.

Massey, President-Elect of the American Association for the Advancement of Science, attributed his survival and subsequent success to the "support, advice, assistance, and guidance" of his professors—three mentors in particular. His challenge to each of us must not be ignored.

The Rewards

There was also a joyous side to our contributors' reactions. When asked if they would pursue their academic course again, we heard mostly *yes*. Several of the authors had data to demonstrate that their classes were very well received, with generally high teacher evaluations and other feedback. The kinds of reinforcement described were often personal and usually came from students. Some examples follow.

On the discipline:

> I've come to realize that these new disciplines offer a great deal of promise in American higher education. They challenge traditional assumptions and methodologies, and they reverse a long string of published work that has castigated ethnic minority Americans.

On the students:

> By my second semester, several minority students had enrolled in my class, through word of mouth. When I applied for a permanent position, it was the minority students who organized a class letter in support of my candidacy [from a White female professor].

On the classroom experience:

> When I look at a classroom bustling with discovery, filled with caring and concern of students for one another, I know I am doing the right thing. I would do this even if they didn't pay me. I just wish I could have learned this material when I was in school; I think it would have made a big difference in my life path, or at least it would have been easier.
>
> It's wonderful to see the excitement generated by the students—ethnic or not—at having this course. In this time of racial harassment, the students felt they were genuinely provided with alternatives and opportunities to talk.

On the future:

> Ethnic minority students become empowered with knowledge and inoculated with a thirst for research so that they may make a contribution. My faith in people and their potential for change, growth, and understanding is renewed when individuals allow themselves to be committed to change. Recently, a White male student from an

upper-class background acknowledged how shocked he was to discover the impact of poverty on young Hispanic children. He was committed to eventually becoming a Ph.D. psychologist, with the intent of making a difference. In the meantime, he planned to support social policy, contribute money, and convince his family and friends to take notice of such social problems as poverty.

Two years ago, a former student called me. He was now teaching his own classes, and he had just had an experience he wanted to share. One of his students from an earlier semester had stopped by his office to ask for more information about gender bias (which he had described in a lecture), because she was designing her senior thesis and wanted it to be unbiased. He just wanted me to know how important that lesson had been to him and that it was being learned by others. It made me think—I teach 100, some of them teach 100 more, and so on, multiplying the effect!

Conclusions

A volume like this is hard to conclude. In fact, we hope that this is merely one of the beginnings of the process of curriculum change and that no conclusion will suffice. Many of the authors in this volume have offered further information through personal communication on their topics of interest, so the process can be pursued individually as well as collectively. Perhaps it is more fitting to end with a request, then, that instructors using the ideas in this book share their own ideas as well as their problems, challenges, and rewards with us or with individual authors for future editions.

References

Hyde, J. S. (1985). *Half the human experience.* Lexington, MA: Heath.

Kahn, E. D., & Robbins, L. (Eds.). (1985). Sex discrimination in academe [Whole Issue]. *Journal of Social Issues, 41*(4).

Levinger, G. (Ed.). (1987). Black employment opportunities: Macro and micro perspectives [Whole Issue]. *Journal of Social Issues, 43*(1).

Massey, W. E. (1987, July 15). If we want racially tolerant students, we must have more minority professors. *The Chronicle of Higher Education, 76.*

Rose, S. (Ed.). (1986). *Advice for women scholars.* New York: Springer.

Ruddick, S., & Daniels, P. (Eds.). (1977). *Working it out: 23 women writers, artists, scientists, and scholars talk about their lives and work.* New York: Pantheon Books.

Sandler, B. R., & Hall, R. M. (1986). *The campus climate revisited: Chilly for women faculty, administrators, and graduate students.* Washington, DC: Project on the Status and Education of Women, Association of American Colleges.

Unger, R. K. (1977, September). *The teacher evaluation form as an instrument of sexism.* Paper presented at the annual convention of the American Psychological Association, San Francisco.

Walsh, M. R. (1986). The psychology of women course as a continuing catalyst for change. *Teaching of Psychology, 12*(4), 198–203.

Yoder, J. D., & Sinnett, L. M. (1985). Is it all in the numbers? A case study of tokenism. *Psychology of Women Quarterly, 9*(3), 413–418.